Great Battles of the Ancient World
Part I

Professor Garrett G. Fagan

THE TEACHING COMPANY ®

PUBLISHED BY:

THE TEACHING COMPANY
4151 Lafayette Center Drive, Suite 100
Chantilly, Virginia 20151-1232
1-800-TEACH-12
Fax—703-378-3819
www.teach12.com

ISBN 1-59803-051-5

Garrett G. Fagan, Ph.D.

Associate Professor of Classics and Ancient Mediterranean Studies and History, The Pennsylvania State University

Garrett G. Fagan has taught at The Pennsylvania State University since 1996. He was born in Dublin, Ireland, and educated at Trinity College, Dublin. He received his Ph.D. from McMaster University, Hamilton, Ontario, and has held teaching positions at McMaster University, York University (Canada), the University of North Carolina at Chapel Hill, Davidson College, and The Pennsylvania State University. In all of these institutions, students have given very high ratings to his courses on the Classical world. He has also given numerous public lectures to audiences of all ages.

Professor Fagan has an extensive research record in Roman history and has held a prestigious Killam Postdoctoral Fellowship at the University of British Columbia in Vancouver and an Alexander von Humboldt Research Fellowship at the University of Cologne, Germany. He has published numerous articles in international journals, and his first monograph, *Bathing in Public in the Roman World*, was published by the University of Michigan Press in 1999. He has also edited a volume from Routledge on the phenomenon of pseudoarchaeology (2005). His current research project is on spectatorship at the Roman arena, and he is also working on a book on ancient warfare.

Table of Contents

Great Battles of the Ancient World
Part I

Great Battles of the Ancient World

Scope:

It is strange to think that the fates of states, nations, and even far-flung empires could be decided by men armed with sharp implements clashing over the course of a few hours on a few square miles of land or sea. The ancient battle, in all its fury and violence, is the focus of this course. We study many great military engagements of the ancient Mediterranean world and address various historical issues raised by those engagements. We also consider wider issues pertaining to warfare in the ancient world, such as its origins and evolution in the prehistoric era, technological and tactical developments in early states, and the nature of battle as a cultural phenomenon and a human experience. Our focus is primarily on the military side of things, with somewhat less attention paid to the sociological, economic, or ideological aspects of warfare, though these topics do not go entirely ignored.

The course divides into three roughly equal parts. The first eight lectures chart the development of warfare from prehistoric times down to the glory days of the great states of the ancient Near East and Egypt. After seeking to define what warfare is exactly, we survey different models for the origins of warfare in the Upper Paleolithic (c. 37,000–12,000 years ago) and Neolithic (c. 10,000–5,000 years ago) and test them against the archaeological evidence, so far as interpretive limitations will allow. When written records first become available with the Early Dynastic city-states of Sumer (c. 3000–2350 B.C.), we already find warfare well developed and a staple of interstate relations. Armies of infantry and rudimentary chariotry clash over honor, irrigation rights, and boundary lands. We then travel to Egypt and survey the changing and evolving nature of warfare in the Old to New Kingdoms (c. 2700–1070 B.C.) and survey our first true engagements at Megiddo (c. 1479/68 B.C.) and Kadesh (1285/75 B.C.). The problem of the tactical use of chariotry is discussed. Finally, we examine the fearsome Assyrian war machine as it developed c. 900–612 B.C. and the sophisticated army that allowed the Assyrians to forge the largest empire yet seen in the region. The siege capabilities of the Assyrians come under particular scrutiny. In this section, we also briefly address the disputed matters of the Trojan War and Homeric warfare.

The next eight lectures focus on warfare among the Greeks. The prior consideration of Homeric matters sets the stage for contemplating hoplite battle in mainland Greece as it emerged in the period c. 700–600 B.C. The hoplite was a particular type of armored infantryman who fought in a close formation called the phalanx. The nature of hoplite battle and its supposed oddities are examined, and various scholarly camps on these difficult questions are outlined. Then, we turn to the Persian Wars (490–479 B.C.) and examine the Battles of Marathon, Thermopylae, Salamis, and Plataea that decided this titanic clash. Naturally enough, Persian arms are reviewed here as well. The Athenian expedition to Sicily (415–413 B.C.) is the next matter for analysis, set against an appreciation of the limitations inherent in Classical Greek siege warfare. The military "revolution" in 4th-century Greece—which saw many attempts to modify traditional hoplite tactics and equipment—provides the backdrop for consideration of Philip II of Macedon (359–336 B.C.) and his creation of a new and formidable military machine, spearheaded by the cavalry and a reformed phalanx, in the early years of his reign. This new, integrated, and flexible army was then led by Philip's son Alexander against the Persians. We survey the three great battles that made Alexander the king of Persia: the Granicus River, Issus, and Gaugamela.

The third and final part of the course addresses the legions of Rome. We first survey the origins and early development of the legion, down to its description (from personal observation) by Polybius, writing c. 150 B.C. Strangely, Polybius omits discussion of the legions' tactical system, so some uncertainty accrues to the question of *how* exactly the Romans won the battles that gave them dominion over the whole Mediterranean basin. We discuss various models and scenarios to fill this gap in our knowledge, both ancient and modern. Rome's colossal struggle with Hannibal precedes the great clashes of the legion and the Macedonian phalanx as they took place in Italy in the 3rd century B.C. and in the Balkans and Asia Minor in the 2nd. Polybius's analysis of the strengths and weaknesses of each formation is assessed against the facts of these engagements. Jumping ahead, we consider Roman skill in siege warfare as exemplified by Caesar's siege of Alesia (52 B.C.) and the siege of Masada in Judea (A.D. 72–73).

Our last two battles are Roman defeats and introduce us to the German tribal warrior. We examine the Battle of the Teutoburg

Forest in A.D. 9, which many consider one of the most important battles in European history. Here, three Roman legions under P. Quinctilius Varus perished in an ambush set by Arminius, a Cheruscan war leader. This defeat stopped Roman expansion east of the Rhine and established a lasting cultural boundary at the heart of Europe. Then at Adrianople in A.D. 378, another Germanic people, the Goths, inflicted a crushing defeat on the eastern emperor Valens, who lost his life on the field. Adrianople is widely considered the single most important battle in the "fall" of the Roman Empire, as it crippled the empire's military resources beyond repair.

The course ends with a final lecture on the place of warfare in the ancient Mediterranean world and consideration of the proposal that the Greeks invented a peculiarly "Western way of war" that has been with us ever since the 7th century B.C.

Lecture One
Why Study Battles? What Is War?

Scope:

Why study battles? Does the study of battles promote militarism? Battles represent crucibles of intense change, where competing lines of historical development confront each other under the most intense circumstances. The point is made forcefully by positing counterfactual results for battles generally viewed as particularly decisive: What would have happened if Lee had won at Gettysburg or Hitler at Stalingrad? Whether we approve of it or not, the societies of the ancient Mediterranean placed a high value on war and warfare. Participation in battles was, in most cases, the defining feature of a man's worth, courage, and virtue. In this lecture, we address these basic issues and chart some of the different approaches thus far taken in the study of battles, from the orderly events depicted in E. Creasy's *The Fifteen Decisive Battles of the World* (first published in 1851) to the recent, influential, and very different approach of John Keegan in his seminal *The Face of Battle* (1976). The lecture ends with an attempt to define what exactly warfare is, because that question bears directly on the problem of war's origins, which is addressed in the next lecture. Two views are seen to dominate the discussion: the *operational* and the *social-constructivist* models of warfare.

Outline

I. There are several reasons why the study of battles is a useful, even essential historical exercise.

    A. Battles represent intense nodes of historical change, where the fortunes of a people or a nation can be decided in a few hours and on a few square miles of land.

        1. Battles are, in many ways, the condensed essence of historical change.

        2. Counterfactual speculation about alternative outcomes to major battles in history illustrates the point well.

    B. The objection that the study of battles and warfare promotes an unhealthy militarism, which is something we ought to be getting away from, is specious.

C. Whether we approve of it or not, the societies of the ancient Mediterranean placed a premium on warfare in the religious, political, social, and ideological spheres. Ignoring or downplaying that fact risks serious distortion in the study of antiquity.

D. War can be studied from various angles, but considering warfare without considering battles is like a theology that does not mention God. Combat is the core of war, the point of the whole endeavor.

E. In this course, we will focus on the ancient Mediterranean basin because this is my particular area of expertise and because this region stands at the root of the Western experience.

    1. The chronological limits of the course stretch from the later Old Stone Age (c. 12,000 years ago) to the Later Roman Empire.

    2. Its geographic focus is on the ancient Mediterranean basin.

    3. In the course, we first cover the origins of warfare and the earliest evidence of warfare in the ancient Mediterranean.

    4. We then move on to consider in a general diachronic order many of the greatest battles of the ancient world and the political, historical, and military background and consequences of each. Along the way, we will study how military tactics, techniques, organization, weaponry, and other aspects of warfare evolved over the ages.

    5. Points of contention between scholars or competing camps of scholarly opinion will be discussed.

    6. We will conclude with reflections on the importance of warfare in the ancient Mediterranean world.

II. The battle narrative, as we understand it, first appears with the Greeks, thus leaving much room for scholarly disagreement in considering battles among the people of the ancient Near East, as we shall soon see.

A. The "great battle" format has a long pedigree, but historical approaches have changed significantly over the last century or more, transforming how battles are studied.

B. The format was born in the 19th century, where it was used largely in a sort of "triumph of the West/victory of civilization" cheerleading exercise.

    1. Sir Edward Creasy's 1851 classic *Fifteen Decisive Battles of the World* is emblematic of the style.

    2. Creasy introduced the notion of the "decisive battle," which stressed the outcome and the results of the battle as its most important features.

    3. There is a certain ambiguity about the concept of decisiveness: it can be either strategic or tactical.

C. Studies such as Creasy's and their descendants impose an order on battles, as if they are great chess games played with human pieces.

    1. The focus is on the command decisions, and troops behave like pawns, enacting the wishes of their commanders.

    2. To a degree, this format is unavoidable; otherwise, the chaos of the battlefield would be unrepresentable.

    3. This "unit-focused" format has continued after Creasy down to our own day, but it always risks overschematization.

D. John Keegan's *The Face of Battle* (1976) transformed how battles were studied.

    1. Keegan was critical of previous studies, especially those of the Creasy variety.

    2. He emphasized the human face of the battle experience. Thus, we might dub this approach *experiential*.

    3. The success of this approach is reflected in excellent recent works, such as Anthony Beevor's *Stalingrad* (1998).

E. Recently, Victor Davis Hanson has revitalized the genre partly by advocating a controversial thesis, which we will examine in detail as the course progresses.

F. It must be remembered, however, that Keegan's approach is just that: an approach, not a method.

    1. For ancient battles, where the sources are so sketchy, it is often very difficult to reconstruct the human "face of battle."

    2. We are unlikely to get more than a composite impression of the ancient experience.

    3. Whether such a composite picture ever accurately reflects ancient reality in a specific instance of battle is beyond establishing.

    4. The composite picture risks being seriously misleading, as we shall see.

III. Central to this course is the problem of defining what warfare is.

A. We all recognize that warfare is something different from other forms of human communal violence (such as rioting or capital punishment). But what is distinctive about it?

    1. Human aggression is insufficient as an explanation, as it underlies all forms of violence, most of which are manifestly not war.

    2. Multiple combatants alone do not secure the definition of some violence as war.

    3. Nor does the consent of the community or prior planning.

    4. Warfare combines all of the above, and something else as well.

B. One approach is to define war in *operational* terms. Warfare is what warfare does.

    1. This approach was championed by anthropologist Harry Holbert Turney-High in 1949 and is favored by many military historians today.

    2. Warfare is a social institution that adheres to universal principles, which are only partially applied (if at all) in "primitive" war.

3. The most salient principle is that of tactical formations (which imply a command and control structure); thus, warfare occurs only when such formations can be demonstrated.

4. The line separating a society that uses formations from one that does not constitutes a *military horizon*, below which falls most "primitive war" documented by anthropology.

5. A good example of primitive war is that of the Yanomamo people of the Amazon forests.

C. Another approach is to view war primarily in terms of social organization and identity.

1. Anthropologist Raymond C. Kelly identifies a handful of warless societies.

2. He notes that these societies can be very violent internally (wife-beating and revenge murders), so that peacefulness and warlessness are not synonyms.

3. This observation emphasizes the socially constructed nature of warfare among other forms of human violence.

4. The key to war is the "calculus of social substitutability," whereby any member of a rival community, not a particular malefactor or his relatives, becomes a legitimate target.

D. As we shall see in the next lecture, which option you prefer greatly affects where in the past you locate the origins of warfare.

Essential Reading:

Ferrill, *The Origins of War*, pp. 9–31.

Keegan, *The Face of Battle*, especially pp.14–78.

Supplemental Reading:

Cowley, *What If?*, especially pp. 1–91.

Hanson, *Carnage and Culture*, pp. 1–24.

Kelly, *Warless Societies and the Origins of War*, pp. 1–73.

Turney-High, *Primitive War*, pp. 5–137.

Questions to Consider:

1. Is the study of battles retrograde, even reactionary? What justifications can you offer for studying warfare?

2. How can war be defined? What are the consequences of how warfare is defined?

Lecture One—Transcript
Why Study Battles? What Is War?

Hello, my name is Garrett Fagan from Penn State University, and this is The Teaching Company's course on *Great Battles of the Ancient World*. This is my second course with the company, and I am delighted to be back.

When considered dispassionately, the ancient battle, perhaps even more so than its modern counterpart, has the distinct miasma of derangement about it. Think about it for a minute. Many thousands of men, aged from their mid-teens to their mid-sixties, would gather on a patch of ground. They would bring with them the instruments of butchery. And I mean that quite literally: knives, swords, axes, and metal-tipped poles. Horses, elephants, carts or chariots could also be present.

Everyone lined up opposite each other. Rituals were performed, deities invoked, words of encouragement spoken. Then, on a given signal, the opposing lines converged, and the work of the slaughterhouse got underway. The details of what happened in these ghastly moments we will postpone for later contemplation, but they truly defy the modern imagination—Hollywood attempts at recreation not withstanding.

When it was all over, the contested field would be awash with corpses, blood, intestines, body parts, as well as writhing and wailing wounded people, animals, and discarded, broken weapons. The victors pillaged the bodies of the vanquished. The survivors then went home, most likely to fight another day, if not against the same foe, then surely against someone else.

These raw facts are enough to appreciate how strange the whole business of battle was and remains still, *mutatis mutandis*. It's a deeply irrational, even perverse, procedure. And yet on the outcomes of such encounters, often fought over the course of a few hours, on a few square miles of land or sea, can rest the fate of entire nations, people, or far-flung empires. So here is a primary reason to study battles; they represent intense nodes of historical change. A good way to appreciate this is by speculating counterfactually about alternative outcomes to major battles, ancient or modern.

In 334 B.C. for instance, a young Macedonian king named Alexander the Great crossed into Asia and invaded the Old Persian Empire. There was an undertaking of simply mind-boggling ambition, given that the Persian realm was several orders of magnitude vaster than Alexander's modest holdings in the northern Balkans.

Persian resistance was first encountered at the Granicus River in northwest Asia Minor, modern day Turkey. There, while charging into the midst of Persian cavalry, Alexander found himself isolated from his companions and surrounded by the enemy. A Persian rider shattered Alexander's helmet with an axe or a sword, in some accounts with a blow so strong that the blade actually grazed the Macedonian's scalp. The Persian rider then prepared to deliver his killing blow.

At just this moment, Alexander's friend Cleitus the Black rode in and either transfixed the Persian with his lance or sliced off his striking arm at the shoulder with a sword. Again, the ancient accounts differ on this detail. Had Cleitus' intervention come a split second too late, Alexander's great adventure in Asia would have come to a very abrupt end, right there at the Granicus, in its very first challenge. He himself, today one of the giants of history, would have been relegated to the small print, a young and inexperienced king who ruled only two years and perished while entertaining the monumental folly of conquering an empire so much larger than his own.

Counterfactual contemplation like this serves, in my view, to demonstrate how dynamic battles are as agents of historical change, whether we like that fact or not. What would have happened if Napoleon had won at Waterloo, Lee at Gettysburg, or Hitler at Stalingrad? Or if William of Normandy had been defeated at Hastings while invading England in 1066; or Eisenhower, going in the opposite direction, trying to breach Fortress Europe in 1944? How would our lives be different today?

Battles, for all their madness, are worthy of study if for no other reason than that they are the crucibles of history. I have sometimes encountered the following moral objection to the study of military matters; the study of battles and warfare promotes an unhealthy militarism, which is something that we ought to be getting away from with this line of thinking.

I first encountered this argument some years ago, when I used to subscribe to a professional e-list. The list was a very useful clearinghouse of information on any number of topics relating to the classics and ancient history. You would post a query or a comment to the list, and other professionals or graduate students would reply. It was a great way to collect all manner of material rapidly and handily.

One day a subscriber asked a question of a military nature about the great Persian invasions of Greece in 480-479 B.C., the main battles of which we discuss in Lectures Ten, Eleven, and Twelve of this course. Members offered helpful responses. Then, one subscriber, a relatively eminent professor in Canada, entered the fray to chastise the discussants for their military knowledge. Teaching students about warfare, he asserted, glorified a horrible process, militarized their thinking, and made them more likely to support or even engage in war when they were all grown up.

He then revealed something extraordinary: he boasted that in his courses he covered the Persian wars in about five minutes of one class, in order to move onto the important matters about classical Greece, the ones that really deserved study, in his opinion: the art and architecture, the civic-mindedness, the glorious cultural achievements in drama, history, rhetoric, and philosophy. By teaching students about invasions and battles, we were doing them a grave disservice, he asserted.

I was flabbergasted then, and, thinking about it now, I'm still flabbergasted. While much could be said about this professor's position on warfare, I really felt that he was not doing his job honestly. He was presenting his students with a skewed and distorted picture of who the ancient Greeks were and what they valued. The Greek victory in the Persian wars marked the defining moment of their ancient history, initiated the Classical Age, and generated the self-confidence that stood at the root of their subsequent triumphs in the cultural arenas, the things that the professor wanted to focus on. To look at the results without appreciating the causes, it seems to me, is to do history some considerable violence.

Whether we like it or not, the plain fact is that war and warfare have been constant companions of European civilization since we first have written records to read. In all probability, the relationship between humans and organized intra-species killing is a lot older than that. We do our commitments to historical truth no favors if, in the name of misguided moralism, we close our eyes to this essential feature of the record. So let us dispense at the outset with the specious argument that the study of war promotes militarism and killing.

To reiterate, whether we approve of it or not, the societies of the ancient Mediterranean basin placed a premium on warfare in practically all areas of endeavor: in the religious, political, social, and ideological spheres. Ignoring or downplaying that fact risks serious distortion in the study of antiquity.

Let us stay with the Greeks as an example. While they weren't militaristic in a modern totalitarian sense, like the Nazis or red Russia, they were certainly very warlike. The men of Greece, in no small measure, calibrated a man's worth against his performance in battle. So much of their mythology, their art, or their literature is focused on warfare and explored its consequences and morality. Athletics, a defining feature of Greek culture, was primarily seen as a good way to train for war. Among the Greeks themselves, the most admired Greek city-state was Sparta, which was also the most warlike of the lot. The Athenians, for all of their cultural achievements, were almost constantly engaged in wars for most of the fifth and fourth centuries B.C. They projected their military power across the Aegean south to Egypt and east to Asia Minor, modern day Turkey. As we shall see in Lecture Thirteen, they even made an attempt on Sicily to the west. This was democratic Athens, home of Euripides, Sophocles, Thucydides, and Socrates. And it was all war, all the time.

The same is true, even more so, for Pharaonic Egypt, the Assyrian Empire in the Near East, or for ancient Rome. Warfare was central to the ideology of all these states, central to the lives of their elites, and central to the experience of the commons. Warfare, indeed, was central to the historical experience and the development of the entire ancient Mediterranean world.

Now, war as a phenomenon can be studied from a variety angles, but considering warfare without considering battles is like doing theology without mentioning God. Combat is the core of war, the point of the whole endeavor.

As we shall examine in more detail in the next lecture, warfare has been with us for a very long time. In my opinion, we turn a blind eye to the study of it at our own peril. Rather, it is a process that demands understanding and, of all the aspects of war that are most pressing, battle is Exhibit A.

For whatever about the ideological, social, religious, or cultural aspects of war, which are all subjects eminently worthy of study, warfare ultimately boils down to people killing other people. Without that organized lethality, there is no war to speak of. And the battle, of course, is where the killing gets done.

Battle, therefore, is the essence of war reduced to its purest form, the heart and soul of war, the *raison d'être* for all those other things that accrue to war, those things which facilitate battle: the logistics, the ideology, the value system, the propaganda, and the economic preparations whatever they may be. All of these aspects of war, I repeat, each worthy of research, are really secondary to the brutal business of battle. As such, battles offer the most direct avenue into the dark heart of human warfare.

So much then for justification, now I will discuss the parameters of this course. Our chronological limits stretch from prehistory down to the later Roman Empire. We shall begin with a period before there were humans at all. After considering the issue of what war is, we initially examine the prehistoric roots of warfare, and discuss the various scholarly and methodological problems of investigating them. Then we proceed, in more or less diachronic order, through the warfare of ancient Sumer and Egypt, the Assyrians, and onto the Greeks and Romans. The last battle that concerns us took place in the 4th century A.D., and we conclude with reflections on the prominence of warfare in the ancient Mediterranean world, as well as some discussion about its nature and, perhaps, the inheritance that it offers us in the modern world. Throughout, our primary focus is on land warfare, as we survey both battles in the open field and sieges, but we do not ignore or overlook naval warfare entirely.

The focus of the course is firmly on the ancient Mediterranean world. For those wishing to learn about Chinese or Mayan or Aztec warfare, there is not much to offer in what follows. The reason for this is simple. My expertise lies in the ancient Mediterranean, and I am not in a position to speak with any authority about military developments outside that cultural sphere. A teacher, like a good general, ought to know his limitations, and I freely acknowledge mine.

In the course of our journey we survey numerous accounts of individual battles. But we do much more than that as well. Along the way, we will study how military tactics, techniques, organization, weaponry, and other aspects of warfare evolved over the ages. Points of contention between scholars are often; competing camps of scholarly opinion are outlined and discussed as we proceed. It needs to be stated at the outset that the study of war is so multifaceted that it is impossible to give every aspect of each topic its full due. But it is my modest hope that the audience will at least gain an acquaintance, not just with the details of specific engagements, but also with the wider debates that those engagements elicit.

The battle narrative first appears with the Greeks. By "battle narrative" I mean an account of proceedings that includes some indication of what actually transpired while the issue was still in doubt. Ideally, we would hear about initial troop deployments, unit movements and maneuvers, and the course of the fighting itself. Prior to the Greeks, as we shall be seeing, battles are eluded to more than they are described. In Mesopotamian, Egyptian, or Assyrian accounts, for instance, the focus tends to be on the butchery of the defeated enemy as they flee for their lives. The actual fighting is often glossed over in a single sentence or in very vague phrases. So, although the oldest records of battles go back to the third millennium B.C. five thousand years ago, it is often very difficult to reconstruct what we might term the "mechanics of combat" for these very early eras. This leaves plenty of scope for scholarly interpretation, and so for disagreement, scholarly battles if you will, as we shall see soon enough.

The genre of the "Great Battle" has a long and august pedigree, but historical approaches have changed significantly over the last century or more, transforming how battles are studied.

The Great Battle genre was born in the 19th century, where it was manifested largely as a sort of cheerleading exercise for "The Triumph of the West" or "The Victory of Civilization." Sir Edward

Creasy's 1851 classic *Fifteen Decisive Battles of the World* is emblematic of this style.

Creasy introduced the concept of the "decisive battle," which stressed the outcome of an engagement as its most important feature. But there is a certain ambiguity about the concept of decisiveness. Decision can be reached at the tactical or on the strategic plane; most battles have been tactically decisive insofar as someone wins or loses on the day, but not all engagements settle matters at the strategic level. We shall see examples of battles later in the course that were spectacularly decisive on the tactical level but wholly indecisive strategically.

The Great Battle narrative in the Creasy vein also imposes an order on battles, as if they were great chess games played with human pieces. The focus is on the command decisions, and the troops behave like pawns enacting the wishes of the planners. The tendency is exemplified in the traditional battle map, where units are arrayed in neat columns and lines, and the so-called phases of the engagement are charted on distinct plans.

Now, to a degree this format is unavoidable, otherwise the chaos of the battlefield would be wholly unrepresentable; so the "unit-focused" format has continued right down to our own day. But in all such works, there is a danger of overly schematizing the battle experience, of imposing order from above where little or none existed on the ground.

John Keegan's *The Face of Battle*, first published in 1976, transformed how battles were studied. Keegan was critical of previous studies along the lines I have just outlined, especially those of the Creasy variety. He emphasized the individual soldier as the human face of battle and shifted the focus from the movement of the unit to the experience of the individual combatant on the argument that thousands of individual decisions beyond the commander's often decided a battle's outcome.

We might dub this approach "experiential." Its focus was on what being in a battle was actually like, and what made soldiers stay and fight rather than just run away and go home.

The unit-focused and experiential approaches can be combined very effectively, as illustrated in such excellent recent works as Anthony Beevor's *Stalingrad,* published in 1998. Here, the gyrations of the armies taking part in the largest land operation in history, Hitler's invasion of Russia in 1941, are skillfully analyzed in conjunction with the personal experiences of the combatants, as recovered from letters home from the front. And it makes for compelling stuff.

Building on these bases, the work of Victor Davis Hanson has re-energized the Great Battle genre for the ancient world, but in part by using it to advocate a controversial thesis.

In *The Western Way of War*, published in 1989, and *Carnage and Culture*, published in 2001, and in some other books, Hanson follows Keegan's lead and focuses on the "experiential" dimension of battles. However, he ties this approach to much more sweeping claims about warfare, culture, and the Western experience as a whole. It is sufficient here to outline the main thrust of the argument, which we'll be returning to at various stages over the course of these series of lectures. According to Hanson, decisive battles originated with the Greeks in the period around 700-650 B.C. and are not found earlier or elsewhere.

The Greeks bequeathed to the West an approach to war that emphasized the direct confrontation, the bringing to bear of maximum force in a concentrated and frightful engagement. Deception, ambushes, hit-and-run fights, and other forms of deceit were to be eschewed. Hanson believes that this insistence on seeking a decisive, frontal engagement is a uniquely western trait and marks all of western warfare right down to the present. It helps explain also why the western way of war has proven so much more lethal than the combat techniques of other cultures.

Such, at least, is Hanson's broad argument, in a very distilled form. We shall return to consider it in more detail at the appropriate places in the lectures that follow. For the moment, it is sufficient to bear it in mind as we proceed.

It must be remembered, however, that Keegan's or Hanson's approach have some severe limitations. For ancient battles, where the sources are so sketchy, it is often very difficult to reconstruct the human "face of battle." Most of Keegan's engagements are relatively well documented—Waterloo and the Somme for instance. His earliest battle was Agincourt, which was fought on 15th of October 1415. And for that he relies less on direct testimony from the combatants, as there is none, and more on the probabilities drawn from analysis of armor and weapons, conditions on the ground, and the clash of different types of troops. This method is appropriate for ancient battles, but the sources are even sketchier for antiquity than they are for the 15th century.

Our scattered ancient sources will necessarily draw on evidence from different battles fought at different times and places. Our best hope can therefore be for little more than a generalized impression of what transpired. Whether a composite picture arrived at in this way accurately reflects ancient reality in a specific instance of battle is a matter open to question. Indeed, such a composite picture risks being seriously misleading. This requires us to be very careful with the evidence and not to rush too quickly from the specific to the general. These comments pertain less to specific battles than to arguments that try to draw broad generalizations from bits and pieces of evidence taken from different battles fought in different times and places.

To close out this introductory lecture, let us now turn to the issue of what warfare actually is. People recognize war when they see it, but it has proven difficult to formulate a convincing general definition. There is something about warfare that marks it off as distinct from other forms of human communal violence, such as rioting or gang fights, and we know this almost instinctively. But can we put a finger on what that something is?

Some scholars have seen human aggression as the key to war. But aggression, while certainly a requisite for war, is insufficient as an explanation for it, all unto itself, since it underlies all forms of violence, most of which are not manifestly war. Wife-beating, child abuse, individual murder, mugging, all stem from aggression but are not forms of war, despite glib metaphors about "wars against women" or "wars on crime" and so on. Aggression isn't enough.

Perhaps the presence of multiple combatants characterizes war. But gang fights, bar fights, clan vendettas, riots, these all have multiple combatants, but they do not constitute warfare either.

War clearly requires the consent of the community and prior planning. So, are communal sanctions and advanced planning diagnostic of war? Well, capital punishment requires both, and it's not warfare either.

Clearly warfare requires all of the above elements: multiple combatants, aggression, planning, and communal consent. But in and of themselves, warfare does not make these things, even when found in combination. Something more is needed. Identifying that missing element is the issue around which the scholarly debate about defining war circles.

To gain some appreciation of the character of this debate, we shall examine two definitions of warfare. The first is what I term "operational." This view, favored by many military historians, sees warfare above all as a particular set of procedures.

This approach was championed by anthropologist Harry Holbert Turney-High in his 1949 book *Primitive War: Its Practice and Concepts*. Turney-High, who had himself served in uniform, argued that warfare is a social institution that adheres to certain near-universal principles. The most important of these principles is that of correct formations, mainly the column for approach and the line for engagement. The use of tactical formations implies much about a society's complexity. It requires command and control, high levels of planning and specialization, and logistical support. Turney-High regarded the use of formations as so central to warfare, that he thought societies lacking them fell below what he termed the "Military Horizon." True warfare exists only above this line; conflicts conducted below the Military Horizon do not meet the basic criteria for true warfare.

Such conflict Turney-High termed "primitive war", and I use that term with inverted commas, "primitive war", and it is marked by disorganized fighting, a high degree of ritualization, reduced lethality, and a lack of clear objectives. It also has distinctly game-like qualities. Distinguishing primitive war from sport or social ritual is often very difficult. This is because, of course, in Turney-High's view, it wasn't war at all.

As an example of primitive war, scholars often point to the Yanomamo people of the Amazon basin, who were observed for several decades by anthropologist Napoleon Chagnon in the 1960s and onwards. The Yanomamo number about 10,000 in all and they live in scattered villages. They fight mostly over women. Conflicts take four main forms, in ascending order of lethality. First are chest-pounding duels, one on one, between disputing parties. Each strikes the chest of the other with alternate blows until one party cannot continue. Then come club fights. Here, aggrieved parties hit each other on the head with 10-foot poles until one cannot continue. I can't imagine those fights go on for terribly long. To be hit in the head with a 10-foot pole is not something that a person is going to endure for long. Now, there is a potential during the club fights for partisans to get involved in the fight, in which case, the combat escalates, but fatalities tend to be very rare, even if that happens.

If satisfaction has not been gained by club fights, spear fighting becomes a possibility. These encounters involve groups of aggrieved parties chasing each other with spears, and people now get killed. Finally, there are out-and-out raids and ambushes, where the killing can be intense. Reciprocal raids take place between villages, and any member of an opposing village is considered a legitimate target. The ultimate type of raid is termed the "dastardly trick," whereby a complicit third party invites one side of the dispute to a feast, only to have them ambushed and slaughtered at the table by their enemies who are concealed nearby.

Now, the ritualized and game-like features of these conflicts well illustrate the characterizing features of Turney-High's concept of "primitive war." Turney-High was adamant that such forms of fighting ought not to be dignified with the label "warfare." Warriors are not soldiers, chiefs are not generals, and raids or ambushes are not battles. To his mind, none of these things crossed the Military Horizon into the realm of genuine warfare, which requires tactical formations, command and control, logistical planning, and clear objectives.

For Turney-High and those who follow him, warfare is therefore a matter of how people actually conduct fighting. In a nutshell, warfare is as warfare does. This is the essence of the operational definition of warfare.

A very different approach is to view war also as primarily a matter of social organization but to place a greater emphasis on issues of identity rather than practice. Anthropologist Raymond C. Kelly catalogues a handful of warless societies. He notes that these societies can be very violent internally with endemic wife-beating and revenge murders being rampant for instance, so that peacefulness and warlessness are not synonymous. This observation emphasizes the socially constructed nature of warfare among the various forms of human violence.

In Kelly's view, warfare has several characteristics, some of which we have reviewed already: the collective application of violence, communal sanction, or advanced planning. But the truly key element, in his view, is what he calls—this is a bit of a mouthful— "the calculus of social substitutability." This a mindset in which any member of a rival community, not just a particular malefactor or his relatives, is seen as a legitimate target.

The calculus is facilitated by a "segmental" social organization that is, a society whose members enjoy a variety of nested identities beyond their immediate families, so they are members of families, clans, tribes, villages, regions, states, nations, and so on. This situation provides a wider menu of options for the calculus of social substitutability to choose from, and so it facilitates war. There are more options for categorizing people, and therefore more reasons to attack them. More choices are available.

In contrast, warless societies are nearly always unsegmented in organization. That is, their members have little or no identity beyond the family or the clan. Unsegmented societies are small-scale, where most people know everyone else. There is little or no scope for the calculus to operate, and so most conflicts are resolved non-violently. Even if violence is employed, it will be targeted at a particular malefactor rather than at an opposing collective. Warfare is unlikely to arise in such a social context.

Like Turney-High, Kelly cites primitive wars and warriors as examples, but he considers these conflicts to be genuine wars, since the calculus of social substitutability is in effect. Among the Yanomamo, for instance, once matters escalate to the raid or the dastardly trick, all members of an offending collective are targeted. In Kelly's model, once that line has been crossed, we are in the province of war.

On this view, then, warfare is ultimately a social attitude rooted in identity, rather than a particular set of procedures. It should be noted that on Kelly's model, the shooting of a Crip gang member by a Blood gang member in Los Angeles, would constitute a form of warfare because the Crip has been targeted merely for being a Crip, not because he has done anything specifically wrong to his murderer.

So these are two ways of defining war: as a set of procedures or as a state of mind. As we shall examine in more detail in the next lecture, which definition one adopts greatly affects where in the past the origins of warfare can be located.

We end with a look at the Maring people of New Guinea, who were observed in the 1960s. Similarly to the Yanomamo, the Maring had a hierarchy of conflicts. First came the "nothing fight," so called, where both sides, numbering in the 100s or even 1000s, showed up at an agreed-upon spot on the boundaries between two territories and shot arrows at each other from a distance. There were very few casualties, since huge shields protected the combatants. Nothing fights could go on for weeks until one side got bored and no longer turned out. Under certain conditions, nothing fights could escalate into "true fights," so called. These took place at much closer proximity, using stone spears and axes. The bashing went on until everyone got tired and went home. But it then resumed the following day and continued until one side failed to show up. The final level of fighting was raiding and routing which saw serious invasions of enemy territory and involved the slaughter of men, women, and children and the widespread destruction of property.

Are Maring wars primitive or true wars? Kelly would say they are true wars, since the calculus of social substitutability is in effect from the get-go. Turney would answer in the negative, since formations are rudimentary, and command-and-control, logistical support, and clear objectives are absent.

A problem raised by such ethnographic evidence is whether the Maring, or any other traditional society, display military characteristics that were also displayed by prehistoric peoples. To investigate that point, we next turn our attention to the problem of warfare's origins.

Lecture Two
The Problem of Warfare's Origins

Scope:

The definitional problem discussed at the end of the last lecture in no small measure shapes the possible responses to the issue of warfare's origins. Adoption, on the one hand, of an operational definition suggests that warfare is a late arrival on the stage of human history, a product of state organizations or their immediate predecessors, going back perhaps 8,000 years into the Neolithic period. On the other hand, if one subscribes to the social-substitution view of warfare, its origins can be pushed back tens of thousands of years into the Paleolithic period. Yet another possibility is the sociobiological proposition that warfare is a genetic inheritance. The archaeological evidence for warfare against which these propositions may be tested falls into three classes: human remains bearing evidence of trauma, artifacts that function solely or primarily as weapons (such as maces), or monuments (such as fortifications or iconographic depictions of warriors painted on cave walls). The interpretation of each class of evidence, however, is far from straightforward. We explore these difficulties through consideration of examples. Finally, the value of ethnographic comparanda to the interpretation of prehistoric evidence is addressed.

Outline

I. Locating the origins of war depends on how war is defined.

    A. The operational definition favors the conclusion that warfare, as such, originated with state or immediately prestate organizations.

        1. The population level, command-and-control system, specialization, and social organization necessary for tactical formations require state organization.

        2. Large chiefdoms may reach this level of organization.

        3. This view would suggest an appearance of warfare within the last 8,000 years.

    B. The social-constructivist definition allows for warfare far earlier in human history.

1. Warfare so defined can be identified among simple preagricultural peoples, such as the Andaman Islanders of the Indian Ocean.
2. This view would suggest a far earlier appearance of warfare in the Paleolithic, perhaps tens of thousands of years ago.

C. It might seem that these propositions can be tested against the prehistoric evidence, which by definition is entirely archaeological.
1. If no convincing evidence for warfare can be found prior to state formation (c. 3000 B.C.), the operational definition gains strength.
2. If good archaeological evidence for prehistoric warfare can be found, the social-constructivist definition looks the more convincing.
3. But how one defines war guides the identification of the evidence in the first place; there is a risk of circularity in reasoning.

II. The archaeological evidence for prehistoric warfare falls into three classes, but each presents serious difficulties of interpretation.

A. First, we have the discovery of human remains with evidence of trauma.
1. Very ancient bones are known with evidence of trauma on them (breaks, fractures, cuts, and so on).
2. It is unclear how this trauma was caused: warfare, animal attacks, accidents?
3. Group finds seem more promising, such as Ofnet in Germany, where 37 severed human skulls were found carefully arranged in a cave; or Jebel Sahaba in the Sudan, where the remains of 57 individuals from infants to elders were found, some of them having suffered violent deaths.
4. Problems of interpretation plague even these initially promising finds.

B. Second, finds of weapons offer evidence for early war.
1. Prehistoric deposits routinely yield potential weapons, including axes, javelins, and arrowheads.
2. Such objects can also serve nonmilitary functions.

3. Tools with exclusively military functions, such as maces and daggers, appear relatively late.
4. Such weapons may have served as symbols of power and status.

C. Finally, monuments and iconography reflect the practice of early war.
1. Defensive walls and fortifications are known from prehistoric sites, such as Jericho in Israel, Çatal Hüyük in Turkey, or ring forts in Europe.
2. Walls and fortifications have been interpreted in social, symbolic, and religious terms by some.
3. Even if such structures were defensive, what threat were they warding off (human, animal, natural)?
4. Cave paintings appear to show "warriors" en route to battle or on parade. One depicts a "battle" with a flanking movement in progress; another, an "execution" or gloating over a fallen enemy.
5. How do we differentiate parading warriors from a hunting party? What were the conventions of depiction in prehistoric art?

D. To an extent, these problems of interpretation stem from the mute nature of archaeological evidence, which gains meaning only through interpretation.

III. In the absence of written evidence for prehistory, one approach has been to use ethnographic accounts of "primitive" people as a lens through which to view the archaeological evidence.

A. Anthropology offers a treasure trove of data on the prosecution of conflict among numerous less complex societies.
1. Perhaps the conventions of modern so-called primitive people can enlighten us as to prehistoric behavior.
2. Turney-High, for instance, moves seamlessly between modern ethnographic records of Plains Indian, African, or Papua New Guinean war to historical records of war among the ancient Scythians, Gauls, or Germans.
3. In this perspective, "primitive war" is essentially all of a kind, wherever or whenever it was practiced.

B. A more thoroughgoing application of this method is found in Raymond Kelly's *Warless Societies and the Origins of War*.

    1. Kelly first establishes what is truly distinctive about warfare (the social-substitution model).

    2. He charts warfare among the Andaman Islanders.

    3. From this, he formulates a model for conditions generating early war.

    4. He applies this model to the archaeological evidence and locates the emergence of warfare in the Upper Paleolithic (35,000–10,000 years ago).

C. Critics condemn this whole approach as condescending to modern "traditional" societies; modern ethnography throws little or no light on ancient conditions.

    1. An extreme version condemns all ethnography to the dust heap by appealing to a sort of Heisenberg Uncertainty Principle, whereby the social behavior of a particular people is altered by the very presence of anthropologists among them.

    2. Less extreme concerns are that modern traditional cultures have not been frozen in time; they, too, have evolved over the past 35,000 years.

    3. Influences from settled, more warlike societies may have corrupted the "purity" of the supposedly prehistoric behavior of modern traditional cultures.

    4. The response is that the comparison is between types of social organization, not precise patterns of combat.

IV. The generality of warfare demands convincing explanation.

A. The vast majority of known human societies, ancient and modern, simple or complex, practice some sort of identifiable warfare.

    1. On all continents, in nearly every time period, evidence of intercommunity violence can be found.

    2. Peaceful and nonwarlike societies are the exception, not the rule, whether they are ancient or modern.

B. The universality of warfare points to deep-seated roots, and culture-specific arguments begin to weaken in the face of the great diversity of communities practicing warfare.

1. One approach has been ethological: The study of animals, particularly our primate relatives, implies an evolutionary origin for coalitional male violence.
2. The sociobiological approach has met with stiff resistance from those, like Kelly, who insist that warfare is a cultural construct.
3. It is important to be clear on the evidence and the issues it generates, however. Overt emotions or politics ought not to shape conclusions.

Essential Reading:

Guilaine and Zammit, *Origins of War*.

Keeley, *War Before Civilization*.

Kelly, *Warless Societies and the Origins of War*, pp. 75–161.

Supplemental Reading:

Dawson, *The First Armies*, pp. 22–73.

Keegan, *A History of Warfare*, pp. 76–126.

LeBlanc, *Constant Battles*, especially pp. 77–198.

Wrangham and Peterson, *Demonic Males*.

Questions to Consider:

1. How does the definitional issue affect the interpretation of archaeological evidence? Can the physical evidence be interpreted unambiguously?
2. Is modern ethnography applicable to prehistoric evidence for warfare? Are criticisms of such a procedure justified?

Lecture Two—Transcript
The Problem of Warfare's Origins

We ended the last lecture by attempting to define what warfare is and saw two different approaches to defining the problem. In this lecture, we focus more closely on the issue of war's origins. But the problems of definition and origins are inherently linked.

As a rule, anthropologists distinguish a hierarchy of social orders that runs from families, to clans, to tribes, to chiefdoms, and finally to states. Each has its own defining characteristics. But even a casual glance reveals the essential feature of the sequence, each level includes more and more people: a clan embraces more people than a family, a tribe more than a clan, a chiefdom more than a tribe, and so on.

If we favor the "operational" definition of warfare, the conclusion has to be that war, so defined, originated with the state, or with immediately pre-state organizations, since the use of tactical formations requires a certain level of population density, specialization, and social organization that is unlikely be found below these levels. If so, warfare cannot have been a regular feature of human life much before the Neolithic era, C. 8-10,000 years ago. Remember, this definition of war does not rule out earlier forms of intra-species organized violence; it just refuses to consider such violence warfare.

Alternatively, the "social substitution" definition of warfare allows us to consider many types of conflict not conducted with formations as war. Warfare defined in this way can be identified among very simple, pre-agricultural peoples, certainly among tribes and possibly even clans if we include the "vendetta." This would suggest a far earlier appearance of warfare sometime in the Paleolithic, perhaps tens of thousands of years ago. Do note, however, that low population densities probably meant that conflicts were rare. In most cases, simple bands of hunter-gatherers, having an unsegmented social order of clans or small tribes and with lots of open space around them, could move easily away from potential threats rather than stand and fight it out. So, while warfare may have existed in these very early years, it was probably rather infrequent.

It might seem that either of these propositions could be tested against the prehistoric evidence, which, by definition, will be entirely archaeological. If, on one hand, no convincing evidence for warfare can be found prior to state formation in C. 3,000 B.C., then the "operational" definition gains strength. But if, on the other, good archaeological evidence for prehistoric warfare can be found early on, then the "social substitution" definition looks the more convincing.

The quest for evidence, however, proves to be a very difficult, since there is no easy way to determine from physical remains alone how particular acts of violence were carried out, and modality is the core of the "operational" definition. Even more difficult is that one's definition of war guides the very identification of the types of evidence to be considered in the first place, so there is a risk of circularity in reasoning. That is, one can use a particular definition of war to identify pertinent evidence, and then use that same evidence to justify the definition. So, in effect, the definition confirms itself.

With these caveats in mind, let's survey the archaeological evidence. Taken as a whole, archaeological evidence for prehistoric warfare falls into three classes, but each presents its own interpretive difficulties.

The first class is human remains that display evidence of trauma. Very ancient bones are known featuring injuries: breaks, fractures, punctures, cut marks, and so forth. But it is usually unclear how this trauma was caused. Was an arm or a head broken in warfare, in an attack by a wild animal, or in a clumsy accident? There is often no way to tell; there is just the damaged bone, mute and inscrutable. In some cases, puncture wounds in skulls are clearly the result of human action, since the holes correspond in shape and size to known stone tools. But, again, who did the killing, and why? Was it a sacrifice? Maybe an execution? An isolated murder? Was the killer in formation? There is usually no way of telling.

For warfare, the very minimal requirement would be violent death attested in groups, and such finds have indeed been made. A Mesolithic Era cave at Ofnet in Germany from about 7,000 years ago yielded 37 skulls that had been deliberately severed from their owners' trunks, painted in ochre, and then carefully arranged in two circular nests. The skulls came from men, women, and children. And they bore clear evidence of massive violence in the form of axe holes and bludgeon injuries. To some scholars, this is hard evidence of

Stone Age warfare, at least in Germany. That most of the skulls come from women and children suggests again, to some scholars, a massacre during a raid. A parallel is found in the documented procedure among some so-called primitive peoples of taking trophy heads from fallen enemies. This explains the unusual configuration of this particular find at Ofnet: two circles of nested, severed heads.

But matters are not so clear-cut on closer inspection. First, the skulls cannot be trophies, since they were located at the back of a very large cave, in a place so remote that they were left undisturbed until their discovery in 1908. Trophy heads, in comparison, are prominently displayed outside the victors' houses or on poles around a village. Second, we have no way of knowing whether the skulls were all collected and deposited after a single incident, or over a number of years, perhaps even over a series of decades. Clearly, the painting and arrangement of the heads attests ceremonial treatment, but the nature either of the killing or the ceremony is forever lost to us. Contexts other than warfare are just as conceivable and no less plausible—sacrifice, for instance. Intra-species killing this most certainly is, but warfare, well, all we can say is "perhaps."

Even more dramatic, and often cited as solid evidence for early warfare, is the mass and unceremonious burial at Jebel Sahaba in the Sudan, dating to about 12,000 years ago. Here were found the remains of 59 individuals, men, women and children, ranging in age from infants to seniors. No grave goods were found in association with these burials, and about half of the people had suffered violent deaths, some of them quite horrific. One young adult girl, for instance, had no less than 21 stone artifacts embedded in her body, in her head, spine, arms, legs, ribs, and pelvis. Others showed similar signs of multiple injuries. More so than Ofnet, Jebel Sahaba has been taken as unambiguous evidence for a mass burial after a massacre, probably after a raid, given the presence especially of infants, toddlers, women, and seniors—the population of the village, with the men folk off perhaps fighting the war themselves. The multiple injuries suggest to some a procedure called "pincushioning," whereby members of a raiding party each take a share in the kill in order to deflect guilt away from any one individual.

But, yet again, the situation is not so clear-cut on closer inspection. Recall that only half of the burials show signs of violent death. That means half do not. The burials were carried out singly or in small groups of four to eight. This is not a one-time burial of 59 individuals thrown into a communal pit. Over how long a period did the burials take place? The absence of grave goods makes dating them relative to each other virtually impossible. And how were the injuries inflicted? Why were they inflicted? The simple answer to all of these questions is, "we don't know."

The second class of archaeological evidence for early war is prehistoric weapons, principally axes, javelins, arrowheads, and so on. The problem here is that many such artifacts can also serve non-military, mundane functions. More instructive are tools with an exclusively military purpose. Examples of these include maces or daggers, neither of which are of much use in the hunt, or for other purposes, but are very, very good for killing people. Some scholars insist, however, that maces or daggers have long served as status symbols for chiefs. While certainly true, this observation in no way detracts from their essentially military nature, and so it can be set aside as largely irrelevant. Maces and daggers, let alone swords, are all relative late arrivals in the prehistoric toolbox, which might itself be an instructive observation.

Finally, there are monuments and iconography that seem to attest the practice of early war. From the Neolithic period we find impressive fortifications at Jericho in Israel, dating to about 7000 B.C; or from the prehistoric ring forts of Western Europe, or the pueblo-like defensive configuration of houses of the village at Çatal Hüyük in Turkey, dating to around 6500 B.C. Some of these fortifications can be very impressive. The walls of Jericho ran for 700 yards and still stand over 20 feet tall. The circuit also had a single tower, 30 feet high, built up against the inside of the wall, with a set of 22 interior steps leading up to the top. Does the sophistication of these fortifications imply a corresponding sophistication on the part of the attackers they were supposedly designed to repel? Can we infer, perhaps, tactical formations from the fear that induced the Jerichoans to such efforts?

Then again, Jericho is unique in the Neolithic Near East. It does not seem that other towns had walls like this. So might the walls be a product not of fear but of display, to telegraph power and wealth? Might they not be a statement of organization, order, and communal effort? Even if they were defensive, can we be absolutely sure they were warding off a human threat? If so, why didn't other settlements take the same precautions? Once more, uncertainty about context complicates interpretation.

Iconography is another class of ancient monument. Some cave paintings from Spain are particularly instructive. One appears to show armed men holding their bows over their heads, led by a "chief" marked by an elaborate headdress. The chief's headdress is bigger than the rest. But what are they doing? Now, one possibility is certainly that they're setting out on a war party, as some like to believe. But they could also be dancing, or they could be going on a hunt. Another depiction shows a fight between an army of four, so-called, and an army of three. Two of the four are moving in from the sides in an apparent flanking movement. Is this evidence of formations and tactical planning, as some would like to argue? Or is it an ambush or a raid? Or perhaps we don't have a clue what we're looking at, since the artistic conventions of the Neolithic are unknown to us. The same is true of a painting of a so-called "execution," in which a group of ten men armed with bows seems to be celebrating the death of a fallen figure who has precisely ten arrows sticking out of him or her. This is very clearly an act of "pincushioning" but we cannot tell under what circumstances it has taken place. It could be the execution of a malefactor, or the ambush of targeted wrongdoer, or part of a wider raid.

The problems of interpreting the archaeological record ought now to be clear. To an extent, these problems stem from the mute nature of archaeological evidence, which only gains meaning through interpretation. And here is where the danger of circular reasoning arises. Convinced that warfare is a very early phenomenon with particular characteristics, the eager scholar uses this conviction to identify mass burials or certain artifacts or images as significant, and then selectively interprets some features of these finds to validate the original conviction. In fact, an open interpretation of the finds leads to many plausible possibilities that, really, cannot be definitively resolved into a single right answer.

This is the main problem with interpreting physical remains alone. We must look at them largely divorced from their original cultural context. This opens up the danger of our imposing a context on them, and that imposition will most likely reflect whatever theoretical model we prefer. We therefore risk using a model to validate itself.

The foregoing ought not to lead to despair in treating the prehistoric evidence. A fair assessment of it does suggest that, at the very least, intra-species killing was not unknown to our ancestors. The difficulty lies in pinning down the character of that killing.

In the face of such interpretive difficulties with the prehistoric evidence itself, one approach has been to use ethnographic accounts of contemporary, so-called "primitive" peoples as a lens through which to view the archaeological evidence.

Anthropology offers a treasure trove of data on the prosecution of conflict among numerous, less-complex societies, as we saw with the Yanomamo or the Maring in the last lecture. So perhaps the conventions of modern traditional societies can shed light on prehistoric behavior and help guide our interpretations. We have seen this already with suggestions about trophy heads or other process of "pincushioning" as applied to the prehistoric evidence. Both of these suggestions derive from ethnographic comparanda.

Turney-High, for his part, simply assumed the applicability of ethnographic material to the past, and his analysis moves seamlessly between modern records of war among the Plains Indians, Africans, or Papua New Guineans and historical records of war among the ancient Scythians, Gauls, or Germans. On this perspective, "primitive war" is essentially all of a kind, wherever or whenever it was practiced, so that modern-day so-called "primitives" provide direct analogues for our Stone Age ancestors.

A more thoroughgoing application of this approach is found in Raymond Kelly's book, *Warless Societies and the Origins of War*. Kelly, as we saw in the previous lecture, which first establishes what is truly distinctive about warfare, namely the "calculus of social substitutability." He then charts this type of warfare between two neighboring tribes on the Andaman Islands in the Indian Ocean. Both warring societies had an unsegmented organization, but were very warlike due to their circumscribed habitat on islands, to their ethnic differences, and to intense competition over resources. The war was conducted in typical low-intensity "primitive" fashion. Individuals were shot and killed on sight when spotted in the jungle, and raids and counter-raids were organized against opposing villages.

From his initial definition, and then this ethnographic test case, Kelly formulates a model for conditions generating early war. War will be rare among unsegmented societies in conditions of low population density. Warfare might erupt between unrelated groups over competition for resources, such as hunting rights in a patch of jungle, for instance, especially if the population density is high and the environment circumscribed in such a way that rival groups cannot easily move away from each other, as on the Andaman Islands.

When we add into this model the increase in complexity of human societies and the appearance of segmental social orders, warfare can be surmised to have evolved only gradually over the Paleolithic period, between about 1,000,000 and 10,000 years ago, probably starting out as capital punishment and revenge killing, and then becoming more collective as the calculus of social substitutability was invoked. In all instances, in Kelly's view, warfare is a socially constructed activity, clearly demarcated from a state of peace by various rituals and ceremonies.

Finally, Kelly then applies this model to the archaeological evidence and locates the emergence of warfare as a gradual process in the Upper Paleolithic era—that is, between about 35,000 and 10,000 years ago. It only became, however, a regular and intense feature of human life in the subsequent Neolithic era. His whole procedure, then, is to construct a model of Stone Age conditions from modern ethnographic data and then use that model to interpret the archaeological evidence.

Critics however, maintain that modern ethnography throws little or no light on ancient conditions. An extreme version of this view consigns all ethnography to the dust heap by appealing to a sort of anthropological Heisenberg Uncertainty Principle. Physicist, Werner Heisenberg, as you probably know, deduced that quantum physics was hampered by the fact that conditions necessary for observation affected the way particles behaved. We therefore cannot be sure we are seeing the "natural" behavior of particles rather than some effect induced by the experimental protocol designed to observe them.

The anthropological version of this principle argues that the social behavior is altered by the very presence of anthropologists, who usually live among the people they are describing for months or even years at a time. Few, however, hold this view to be true. In the case of warfare, we would have to accept that otherwise peaceful people suddenly became warlike to impress a professor in a pith helmet.

A more cogent objection is that modern traditional cultures have not been frozen in time and bypassed by evolution. Rather, they too have evolved over the past 35,000 years, and they cannot be treated as living museum pieces from the Stone Age. Indeed, such an assumption is held to be deeply condescending to modern traditional societies. Influences from settled—and so, more warlike—societies may have corrupted the purity of their supposedly prehistoric behavior. At least so goes the argument.

The response to such objections is to be clear about what is being compared: types of social organization, not precise patterns of behavior. If unsegmented societies tend to be warless, this will be true both for modern and for ancient unsegmented societies. There is no need to think of modern "traditional" communities as frozen in time or bypassed by evolution. It is the social logic underlying actions rather than the actions themselves that is instructive for the prehistorian interested in the origins of war. Such, in any case, is the sort of response offered by the ethnographically inclined. But the debate goes on and it is far from resolved, and I'm not going to stick my head over the top of the trench and offer you an opinion.

We end by considering an entirely different line of inquiry into the origins of war that looks at factors even deeper than our social conventions: our genetic code.

The vast majority of known human societies, ancient and modern, simple or complex, practice some sort of identifiable warfare. On all continents in nearly every time period, evidence of inter-community violence can be found. This is a fact that demands explanation, and some find the cultural contextual emphasis of anthropological models insufficient and unsatisfying as a response to it. Can circumstance and context alone explain so wide a shadow as that cast by warfare over human affairs?

In fact, peaceful and non-warlike societies are the exception to the rule, whether they are ancient or modern. Even Kelly's study of warless societies makes this abundantly clear. Out of 563 documented human societies in the *Atlas of Human Cultures* of 1981, only 7 can be classed as peaceful, and some of those are entirely artificial, such as the Hutterites, a religious community expressly set up in protest against prevailing norms.

To some scholars, the near universality of warfare points to deep-seated roots, and culture-specific arguments begin to weaken in the face of the great diversity of communities practicing it. One approach has been to look to ethology: the study of animals. While ants or fish display intra-species aggression, particular attention has been paid to our evolutionary relatives among the primates, especially the chimpanzee, with which we share 98% of our genetic code. This approach deduces an evolutionary origin for patterns of male coalition to violence, which stands at the root of human warfare.

The classic study of chimp behavior was conducted by Jane Goodall for several decades, beginning in the 1960s at the Gombe Reserve in Tanzania. Here it was found that chimps, usually males, hunt in coordinated groups for meat, preferably monkeys. Their domestic interactions were marred by routine violence, as males batter and abuse females and fight among themselves over status in a hierarchy of dominance. Chimp bands at Gombe occupied particular territories, and groups of males went on border patrols. Even more remarkably, in the 1970s, it was found that such patrols, normally about 6-8 strong, would deliberately invade neighboring territory, advancing stealthily through the unknown country, hunting.

What they were hunting, however, was not monkeys but fellow chimps, usually a lone member of the neighboring band. If located, the alien chimp was attacked and brutally beaten, bitten, torn, battered, and left for dead. Disturbing evidence emerged of needless cruelty, such as the tearing off testicles or fingernails. Often, researchers would find only the aftermath of such assaults or notice injuries or disappearances among the observed chimp population. But on those rare occasions when the violence was actually observed directly, the attacking chimps became visibly excited during the assault, and continued to be so afterwards. They would beat the trees, pull down branches, and beat the ground. And they would go back home and they would be—what my undergraduates say—"pumped."

Eventually at Gombe, the more aggressive band entirely wiped out their neighbors and occupied their territory. But this brought them into contact with a new band, previously one territory removed, which now began raiding into the victorious band's range. Chimp wars raged on.

It is hardly rocket science to see how such observations have an impact on our understanding of the origins of human warfare. If a shared chimp-human ancestor, who lived sometime before 5 million years ago, when the chimpanzee and human lives diverged on the evolutionary tree, if that ancestor practiced the same sort of raiding observed in modern chimps and in some traditional human societies, then the roots of warfare extend deeper than the roots of our very species. Warfare, it seems, predates humanity itself.

This approach is termed sociobiology, in that it seeks to explain social action through biological means. Needless to say, it has its critics, and they have very cogent arguments in their arsenal. One will be obvious: how can we say that the behavior of chimps observed for only 40 years, in the time when their habitat is under severe pressure from human development, is the same as that of a chimp-human ancestor who lived more than 5 million years ago in an unrestricted environment? Is that assumption rather not a large leap of faith? In fact, since we know that environment influences behavior, is it not more likely that the violence observed in modern chimps is a recent development, a reaction to their being hunted by humans, to their forests being cut down and burned, and to their being squeezed into smaller and smaller ranges?

A recent discovery in the Congo is particularly damaging to the sociobiological view. Here, in 1999, a group of chimps was encountered in a remote part of the jungle, some 37 miles from the nearest human settlement. These chimps had never seen a human before, since they showed no signs of fear. Instead, they were curious and gathered about to examine what, to them, were strange-looking apes. These "naïve" chimps, as they are called, have so far shown no signs of violence, even between males within bands. If, indeed, they are peaceful chimps, then the violence observed at Gombe and elsewhere is product not of genes but of circumstance.

While this may be so, I personally find it nevertheless very significant and interesting that both chimps and humans react in such similar ways to constraint, resource competition, and circumscription—the very factors that we have seen are thought by some to have generated warfare in the first place. It is clearly the case that we are not genetically doomed to coalitional violence in all circumstances, but rather that certain environmental conditions elicit inter-group violence, both in humans and in chimps.

Yet there are those who insist categorically that warfare is strictly a human business and a product of human culture, in which genes play a negligible part, or no part at all. These scholars argue that the cultural aspects of human behavior are paramount and free us from the constraints of our biological proclivities. Examples of human urges constrained by culture are so numerous as to need no citation here. So even if we are inclined to aggression and war by our genes, it is our culture that shapes how these inclinations are manifested, if at all. In this sense, arguing from biology without culture entirely misses the point, and risks dangerous oversimplification.

To be sure, the addition of culture vastly complicates analogizing human and animal behavior. There is a risk of projecting onto animal actions, motives for actions, and ideas or motives that properly belong only in the human sphere. We cannot know the mind of an ape.

We can go further. If war and aggression are biologically hardwired into us, why do so many cultures recognize the inherent wrongness of killing by insisting on purificatory rituals for their warriors returning from battle? Why do armies in more complex societies need to be trained to kill, if aggression is our natural, default setting? And most people are observably nonviolent, and go through their whole lives without ever intentionally hurting, never mind actually killing, another person. Surely all this suggests that warfare is the aberration, a cultural construct foisted on an otherwise peaceful species? That's at least one line of argument. It is important to be clear on the evidence and the issues it generates, however. Emotions or politics ought not shape scientific conclusions.

In 1986, 20 prominent scientists issued the Seville Statement on Violence during UNESCO's International Year of Peace. The Statement is a noble one and expressly condemns any suggestion that aggression and warfare have genetic roots. It states, in part, and I quote, "It is scientifically incorrect to say that we have inherited a tendency to make war from our animal ancestors. Warfare is a peculiarly human phenomenon and does not occur in other animals. We conclude that biology does not condemn humanity to war, and that humanity can be freed from the bondage of biological pessimism."

The obvious fear of the authors, and many of its supporters, is that widespread acceptance of a biological aspect in war making will be used to exonerate any amount of awfulness as "natural behavior" that cannot be curtailed. Noble attempts to curb warfare would be stymied by such beliefs. Given how biological arguments have been misused in the past, and the sordid history of eugenics springs to mind, this fear is not unwarranted.

Yet in my personal opinion, despite its good intentions, the Seville Statement on Violence takes a step too far. It seeks for emotional reasons to shut down fiat lines of inquiry that it feels may carry dubious consequences. But it is incumbent on researchers, like detectives, to follow wherever the leads take them. It is not enough to say, "such-and-such an avenue is lined with threatening implications, we must eschew it."

Further, none of the sociobiologists seriously argue that we are doomed by our genes to a path of unrelenting butchery. Rather, they are fully cognizant of how complex the cultural aspects of human behavior are, war included. In the case of chimpanzees, for instance, the researchers are quite clear that human and chimp wars cannot be analogized in a facile manner; human wars, even among the most simplistic type, are infinitely more complex than anything chimps do. Rather, they believe that the possibility of identifying species-specific patterns of behavior that contribute to war's prevalence is significant, worthy of study, and may lead to a deeper understanding of the phenomenon.

On a broad historical and anthropological perspective, it remains the case that warless and peaceful societies are the exception to the rule. This generality of warfare demands explanation, and the sociobiological arguments offer an interesting and potentially useful avenue of investigation for explaining it. Cultural determinism grows weaker and more ad-hoc the greater the observed frequency of warfare in different places.

If, however, coalitional male violence is an ingrained proclivity practiced over millions of years of our evolutionary history and elicited by certain environmental conditions, then the generality of the phenomenon has been accounted for.

It is critical to be clear that coalitional male violence, as observed in chimps and people, is not a genetic destiny but an inherited proclivity brought out by circumstance. I don't think it is naïve or unethical to suggest that, just as triggering circumstances have been investigated intensely, so too ought the possibility of a genetic component in the phenomenon.

The identification of an evolutionary element in the origin of warfare does not require us to accept a sentence for our species of life without the possibility of peace. As the anthropologists so cogently demonstrate, cultural choices do indeed free us from the bondage of our biology. We can mould our culture to negate our worst impulses. Given this, surely the fullest possible understanding of what we are up against better equips us for that task.

Lecture Three
Sumer, Akkad, and Early Mesopotamian Warfare

Scope:

Whatever the case with the origins of warfare, there can be little doubt that by the time the first cities appeared in Sumer in c. 3000 B.C., warfare was already an established fact of life. The nature of warfare in the Early Dynastic Period (c. 3000–2350 B.C.) is attested only through a light dusting of evidence, but that material now crucially includes written records. From a variety of sources, it seems that warfare was endemic among the city-states of early Sumer. We examine the evidence in an attempt to reconstruct the conventions and conditions of warfare among the first cities, as well as the nature of Sumerian armies, their weapons, and battle tactics. We also explore what this evidence suggests about the organization of Sumerian society. The prevalence of warfare in Mesopotamia led to the regional ascendancy of Akkad in the period 2350–2100 B.C., under the conqueror Sargon and his grandson, Naram-Sin, who appears to have been worshipped as a god. The connection between warfare and empire is thus made clear at the outset of recorded history.

Outline

I. The establishment of the first cities in Sumer in c. 3000 B.C. marked the beginning of recorded history, when written evidence first became available to the scholar of ancient warfare.

   A. Cities provided several crucial requisites for the prosecution of wars.

      1. They had concentrated and settled populations to man the ranks.

      2. They provided complex political and social hierarchies to command armies.

      3. Their agricultural regions, boundaries, and surpluses were bases for dispute.

      4. Irrigation rights and water access were sources of competition.

B. The direct evidence of warfare for the first four centuries of the Early Dynastic period is nonexistent, perhaps due to the paucity of written evidence for this period.

    1. Yet the general considerations reviewed above make it unlikely that this very early period was warless, as some scholars like to believe.

    2. Resort to force was a common feature of later city-state polities (Greece or the Maya), when other forms of conflict resolution failed.

    3. By the time clear evidence of warfare did emerge (c. 2500 B.C.), weapons and military systems were already well advanced, suggesting a prior period of evolution through trial and error.

II. Evidence for warfare appeared indisputably in the Early Dynastic III period (2600–2350 B.C.). Four classes of evidence converge to attest warfare in this era.

    A. First, we have the discovery of actual weapons in the Royal Burials of Ur (c. 2500 B.C. and later).

        1. Maces, socket axes, daggers, and swords have been found.

        2. Chariots (or warcarts) are known from actual examples, models, and iconographic depictions.

        3. Chariots were already well-developed, two- or four-wheeled versions, but they were drawn by asses or onagers because domesticated horses were as yet unknown in the region.

        4. Bows are also known.

    B. Second, we consider iconographic evidence, in the form of figures, reliefs, or inlays.

        1. A sculpture fragment from Girsu in Iraq, dated to 2600 B.C., shows a bound victim being hit on the head with a mace. In all likelihood, he was a prisoner of war.

        2. The Royal Standard of Ur (2500 B.C.) depicts chariotry and infantry, the taking of prisoners, and their presentation to a leader and a council of his subordinates.

        3. Inlay figures from Mari (c. 2500–2400 B.C.) also attest to military developments.

    C. Third, military monuments in the form of city walls appear.

D. Finally, and most crucially, there is now written evidence.

  1. The *Sumerian King Lists* or the *Epic of Gilgamesh and Akka* assume fighting between cities was unexceptionable.

  2. Despite uncertainties of interpretation, administrative texts distinguish different types of leaders, some of them sacred (*en*) and others apparently military (*lugal* or *ensi*).

  3. Cuneiform tablets refer to the slaughtering of enemies and the heaping of their bodies and skeletons on the battlefield.

  4. Boundary stelae both depict and record in writing disputes between neighboring city-states.

III. The combination of this evidence allows for a reconstruction of the conditions and circumstances of early Mesopotamian warfare.

  A. The conflict between Umma and its southern neighbor Lagash over the borderland of Gu'eden between them offers the best attested example from this period.

  1. The Vulture Stela from Girsu in the territory of Lagash and later inscriptions from Lagash itself allow for a detailed reconstruction of events.

  2. A very early arbitrated settlement, recorded on the stela of Mesilim, was disregarded by Umma, and Gu'eden was annexed by force.

  3. As recorded on the Vulture Stela, Eanatum of Lagash invaded Umma and retook Gu'eden, cut irrigation canals, built shrines, erected stelae, and exacted annual tribute from Umma.

  4. The dispute continued long after the establishment of the Vulture Stela and escalated to include other neighboring city-states.

  B. Several features of this series of events are noteworthy.

  1. Between them, these texts record the earliest battles of recorded history; they do so, however, in very general terms and offer no details about the armies' tactical maneuvering or the fighting itself.

  2. We must envisage the battles as fought in the open between armies of chariotry and heavy infantry equipped with shields, spears, and socket axes and deployed in a dense phalanx formation.

3. The conflict was generational and indecisive in nature: It ended precisely as it began.

4. Motives for fighting were a mixture of tangible concerns for borderlands and water rights and the restoration of honor tainted by past wrongs and defeats.

5. Clearly, these battles were designed to decide a particular dispute, and despite their ultimate failure to do so, they can be classed as "decisive" engagements in a tactical sense.

6. The language of the accounts is religious, in which gods are credited with direct ownership of the disputed lands and their products, as well as the prosecution of the battles.

7. This language may reflect a genuine Mesopotamian conception of warfare as a religious activity, or the language may be attributable to the sacral nature of the records' context (as dedications to gods located chiefly in shrines or temples).

C. A recent suggestion that warfare in this period was not marked by field operations involving infantry and chariotry but was dominated by ineffectual sieges is untenable in the face of the evidence.

1. The Vulture Stela clearly depicts a formation of infantry in action.

2. The infantry on the stela, as well as that depicted in Mari and on the Royal Standard of Ur, all have standard dress and equipment.

3. The warcarts of this era, to be sure, were rather clumsy looking in comparison to later true chariots, and they were not drawn by horses, but relative inefficacy does not entail utter uselessness.

IV. The rise of Sargon of Akkad (a.k.a. Agade) established the first empire in history over the whole of Mesopotamia (Sumer, Babylonia, and the northern reaches of the two rivers, the Tigris and the Euphrates).

A. Sargon's life is known mostly from later romanticized accounts, but he was a genuine historical figure of great importance.

B. His conquest of Mesopotamia by force (c. 2350 B.C.) and the continuation of his family's rule by dynasty over a period of two centuries established the essential pattern for imperialists for millennia to come.

C. The Akkadian Empire, founded in war, set the pattern for later ages and demonstrated the inherent link between warfare and imperialism.

Essential Reading:

Cooper, *Reconstructing History from Inscriptions*.

Dawson, *The First Armies*, pp. 76–117.

Kuhrt, *The Ancient Near East*, 1.19–73.

Supplemental Reading:

Van De Mieroop, *History of the Near East*, pp. 1–79.

Winter, "After the Battle Is Over."

Yadin, *The Art of Warfare in Biblical Lands*, pp. 32–57.

Questions to Consider:

1. In what ways can the prosecution of warfare in early Mesopotamia be tied to our prior discussion of warfare's nature and origin? What specific benefits does the appearance of written evidence offer to our understanding?

2. If you were asked to choose five chief characteristics of early Mesopotamian warfare, what would they be? Justify your choices with reference to specific pieces of evidence.

Lecture Three—Transcript
Sumer, Akkad, and Early Mesopotamian Warfare

In the last lecture we saw how the issue of warfare's origins proved to be a methodological and evidentiary quagmire, where certainty proves elusive. This situation is due, in no small measure, to the prehistoric context in which warfare evolved, a time before writing. In this lecture, we enter the historical era, when written records first become available for study. Certainty is not ensured, but a greater degree of clarity certainly prevails.

The first cities appeared in Sumer, in southern Iraq, about 5,000 years ago. They were independent city-states, each with its own rulers, gods, laws, and administrative systems. These places provide us with our first written sources, but they also generated a fertile geopolitical context for wars. Cities housed people in concentrations not seen before. It is hard to arrive at firm figures, but the population of the typical Sumerian city-state certainly numbered in the tens of thousands. Such a pool of people offered rich pickings for the recruiter. The cities specialized labor, so that not everyone had to farm to survive. Certain craftsmen could therefore dedicate their time to making and improving military technologies. Also, cities fostered political and social hierarchies that would seek to create armies in the first place and, once mustered, provide an officer core to command them.

Finally, cities governed agricultural regions, shared boundaries with neighbors, and stored surpluses, all of which make for good reasons to go to war. In southern Iraq in particular, quarrels over irrigation rights and access to water sources are going to occur all but inevitably.

It has to be admitted that the direct evidence for warfare among the earliest Sumerian city-states in the first part of the era dubbed the Early Dynastic Period—roughly 3000 to 2600 B.C.—is virtually non-existent. For these very early centuries, there is very little written evidence. Yet the general considerations just reviewed, and the likelihood that warfare was already fairly common in the Neolithic era, make it unlikely that this early period in Sumer was warless, as some scholars would like us to believe.

It is noteworthy that, in general, resort to force is a common feature of other city-state political cultures, such as Classical Greece or the

Maya of Central America. More suggestive is that when clear evidence for warfare does emerge in Sumer, after about 2500 B.C., weapons and military systems are already well advanced. This points to a prior period of evolution through trial and error.

Unambiguous evidence for warfare appears in the period called Early Dynastic III, roughly 2600-2350 B.C. Four classes of evidence combine to attest warfare in this era.

First, actual weapons have been found in the Royal Burials at Ur, dating to around 2500 B.C. and onwards. Here, daggers, spears, maces, axes, and even chariots have been discovered. Chariots are seen to be well developed. They had two or four wheels, but they were drawn by asses, since domesticated horses were as yet unknown in the region.

As we shall see, iconographic evidence is clear that at least some of these chariots were used in warfare. Those chariots could also be used, of course, for racing or for hunting. Centuries later, the Greek historian Herodotus reports that Indian chariots in the service of the Persians were pulled by wild asses, so this appears to have remained a tradition in Eurasia long after Sumer had passed into history. Bows, when they are found, are of the straight-arc type; the more complex composite bow appears only during Akkadian empire of 2350 to about 2100 B.C., and we will consider that weapon towards the end of this lecture.

Aside from weapons, there is iconographic evidence, in the form of figures, reliefs, or inlays. A relief fragment from Girsu in Iraq, for instance, dated to about 2600, shows a bound victim being hit on the head with a mace. The mace is a peculiarly military weapon, as it serves no other useful purpose. The Girsu scene evokes the near-contemporary Egyptian depictions of Pharaoh clubbing prisoners of war to death with his mace, such as that on the Narmer Palette, which we review in the next lecture.

The bound victim in the Girsu relief is probably a prisoner of war as well, but we can't be sure, to be honest. From the same place and period comes an oversized ceremonial lancehead engraved with the inscription "Lugal, King of Kish." Now, *Lugal* means "king" or "head man," and "King of Kish", and is an obscure Sumerian title that appears in early Mesopotamia in connection with military leaders, and let's not forget, it is here carved onto a ceremonial lancehead, a facsimile of a weapon of war. Both of these Girsu artifacts therefore suggest that warfare was not unknown only a few centuries after the first cities had appeared.

One of the most remarkable objects from the Royal Burials at Ur, however, is the so-called Royal Standard, dating to about 2500 B.C. and now in the British Museum in London. It depicts chariotry, infantry, battle, the taking of prisoners, and their presentation to a leader and his subordinate officers.

Several features of the images stand out. The infantry are all depicted wearing uniform equipment: woolen skirts, hats or helmets with chin straps, and what appears to be an early form of armor in the form of studded cloaks. They also carry spears and socket axes of a type actually found in the Royal Burials. A socket axe, by the way, is a specifically military kind of axe. They fit over their shaft on the sockets and have a narrow, penetrating blade. They're not much use for cutting down trees, but they're very good for penetrating people. The exact correspondence between representation and known artifact gives confidence that these pictures strive for a realistic presentation of the military hardware then available.

Even more remarkable are the chariots, or more properly, "war carts." We shall discuss their possible uses shortly, but for the moment we note their uniformity of design and construction.

Inlay figures from the site of Mari in Syria, dating to about 2500 to 2400 B.C., also show uniformly equipped warriors. One figure wears a helmet, a war-cloak, carries a socket axe, and looks almost identical to the troops depicted on the Standard of Ur, a city over 300 miles away. The Mari warrior also carries a sickle sword, one of the earliest representations of a sword on record. Sickle swords were akin to sabers and were designed for slashing, cutting rather than stabbing. They were a popular weapon in the Near East and Egypt for more than 1,500 years.

Also from Mari comes an inlaid scene of a victory procession, where bound prisoners of war are paraded before standards and uniformly equipped soldiers wielding axes and spears. A war cart is depicted as well, and it is highly reminiscent of that shown on the Standard of Ur, again, 300 miles away.

What is really important in all the foregoing is the congruence of equipment and weaponry, which show a striking uniformity, even across regional borders.

The third class of evidence for warfare in this period are military monuments, such as city walls. We shall postpone consideration of these until our review of siege warfare in Lecture Eight.

The fourth and most crucial class of data is the written evidence. In the Sumerian king lists or the *Epic of Gilgamesh and Akka,* fighting between cities appears as a wholly unremarkable event.

For instance, the king lists, compiled around 2000 B.C., state that rulers competed intensely for the title High King, or *nam-lugal,* which moved from ruler to ruler. The High King is only declared after the current holder has been "smitten with weapons," as in "Uruk was smitten with weapons; its kingship was carried to Ur." The language is very laconic, and the prospect of retrojection of later conditions onto these very early periods cannot be wholly ruled out. In the *Epic of Gilgamesh and Akka*, Akka besieges King Gilgamesh in his city of Uruk. Hostilities end after a parley, and a treaty is arranged. Clearly, these sources assume warfare as a natural part of the geopolitics of Early Sumer.

Administrative texts distinguish among different types of leaders, some of them sacred, called the *sanga* or the *en*, others apparently military, such as *lugal* or *ensi*. The categories appear to be fluid, so that a precise demarcation of duties is unrecoverable, if it ever existed at all. In addition, there are references to wars conducted against neighboring peoples, like the Elamites of southwestern Iran, as well as campaigns by single rulers against multiple targets. Eanatum I, king of the city-state of Lagash, for instance, is hailed as "Eanatum, ruler of Lagash, who subjugates the foreign lands" or who "destroyed the foreign lands." The text goes on to list Eanatum's wars against nearly a dozen places across Iraq, Iran, and Syria.

We also read references to the slaughtering of enemies and the heaping up of their bodies and skeletons in burial mounds on the battlefield. Boundary stones both depict and record in writing disputes between neighboring city-states, and we shall examine one of these boundary stones in detail in just a moment.

Nothing in any of these sources intimates that warfare among the Sumerian city-states was considered egregious, uncivilized, or unusual. In one remarkable case, the circumstances generating early wars can be discerned with particular clarity. This is the boundary dispute between the city-states of Umma and Lagash, in what is today central Iraq.

The dispute is traceable from a variety of inscribed objects found at Girsu, one of the three cities that comprised the polity called Lagash. The city of Umma lay north of Lagash, and between them was a borderland called Gu'eden, which means "The Edge of the Plain." It is important to appreciate, before we delve into the sordid details, that we only have the Lagashite side of this story; the Ummaite perspective is entirely lost to us. We cannot therefore take what we read at face value, as a full and accurate record of what actually happened. It is clearly a biased account in which the Ummaites are consistently drawn as greedy and faithless scoundrels. That said, we can discern the course of the conflict for generations, from about 2600 B.C. down to 2300 B.C., and even beyond. But only its earliest phases need interest us here.

It seems that at some early time, a chap called Mesilim, who bore that elusive title "King of Kish," established a negotiated boundary between Lagash and Umma along the Gu'eden, which was a strip of borderland about 40 miles long and a few miles wide. This was generally thought to have happened around 2600 B.C. However, according to the Lagashites, the people of Umma later reneged on the deal, smashed the boundary markers, and occupied the disputed land. The people of Lagash, under their energetic king Eanatum, marched out and fought two battles with the Ummaites, winning both. Heaps of enemy corpses were piled up and buried, and a new boundary marker established. The Ummaite king was forced to swear humiliating oaths to stick to his agreements.

It just so happens that this boundary marker has survived in seven fragments. This is the so-called Vulture Stela, today in the Louvre in Paris, perhaps the most remarkable artifact to survive from Early Dynastic Sumer. It features a combination of inscribed texts and relief carvings, and dates to about 2450 B.C.

The texts trace the course of the border dispute up to the point that the texts were carved. And, of course, they do so from the Lagashite perspective. They relate the contents of a dream promising victory sent to Eanatum of Lagash by Ningirsu, the patron god of Lagash. Then they record the battles and their aftermath, and much space is devoted to the humiliating oaths forced on the defeated Ummaite king. It seems that a land-lease agreement was reached requiring Umma to pay rent to Lagash to use a portion of the debatable land in the Gu'eden. The reliefs show, on one side, Ningirsu ensnaring the Ummaites in his divine war net. On the other, we see the dream promising Eanatum victory. Eanatum is then depicted in his war cart leading ordered ranks of socket axe- and spear-wielding infantry out to battle.

Later, on foot and carrying what seems to be a sickle sword, he leads a tight formation of infantry with huge shields and bristling spears as they trample the corpses of the Ummaite villains. A burial mound is stacked with corpses, and overhead, vultures soar, carrying away the heads of the enemy in their beaks. It is this image of the vultures carrying the heads away that gives the monument its modern name of the Vulture Stela.

But the dispute did not end with Eanatum. Indeed, it became increasingly acrimonious and then escalated. In the generation after Eanatum, we are told that Umma defaulted on its payments and arrogantly used canals intended as boundary-markers to irrigate its own fields. Envoys were sent and rebuffed. Again there was a battle and again Umma was defeated. This time, the Ummaite leader was killed by his own people for his military failure, the ultimate vote of "no confidence." In later generations, we read of other city-states getting involved in the dispute, notably Uruk and Ur, both states that lay south of Lagash. The war was no longer confined to the borderland between Umma and Lagash, and seems to have been carried up to the very walls of Umma itself. Eventually, however, a king of Umma called Lugalzagesi, rose up and conquered much of southern Iraq, forming a sort of proto-empire in the region. His dominance did not last long, however, for a more threatening power was looming to the north.

Several features of this series of events between Umma and Lagash are noteworthy. Between them, these texts record the earliest battles of recorded history. They do so, however, in very general terms that offer no details about the armies' tactical movements or the course of the fighting. Of the battles themselves, we get only very laconic notices such as "He fought with him." And that's not a lot to go on.

The emphasis, rather, is on the slaughter, heaping up and burial of the defeated enemy. We get tantalizing notices of rulers recruiting from foreign lands, but it is unclear whether this means from other Sumerian city-states or from outside Sumer altogether. Whatever the case, such notices suggest an advanced level of military commerce and careful planning. Before setting out on campaign, Sumerian rulers sought to maximize their military resources.

Now, putting this meager body of written evidence, the flat nature of Mesopotamian terrain, and the depictions on the Vulture Stela and the Royal Standard of Ur, putting that altogether, we must envisage Sumerian battles as fought in the open field between armies of infantry deployed in tight ranks and armed with shields, spears, socket axes, and possibly sickle swords. There were also archers, since Eanatum was hit with an arrow during his second battle with the Ummaites and incapacitated. That's mentioned on the vogastele in the text. The war carts also played some role in the fighting, which we will consider more closely in just a minute.

Phrases in the written records leave no doubt that Sumerian armies fought in the open field. So we read, for instance, in the border dispute texts, and I quote, "He recruited foreigners and transgressed the boundary-channel of Ningirsu. The ruler of Lagash fought with him in the Ugiga-field, the field of Ningirsu." We should note briefly that it was the habit of the Sumerians to give names to tracts of land—here termed, for instance, Ugiga—and then refer to the tracts by those names. And in this instance, the battle is expressly stated to have taken place in an open field, and in this instance, the Ugiga field.

It is noteworthy that Umma-Lagash conflict is generational and indecisive in nature. In this respect, the dispute looks more like primitive war than real or true war. But true war it most certainly was, by any definition. This was organized violence, conducted by centralized states at a sophisticated level. The *casus belli* were a mixture of tangible concerns for borderlands and water rights, and the restoration of honor besmirched by past wrongs and defeats. The battles were intended to decide a particular dispute and, despite their ultimate failure to do so on the strategic level, they can be classed as "decisive" engagements in a tactical sense.

The language of the surviving accounts is religious, where gods are credited with direct ownership of the disputed lands—we just saw "the fields of Ningirsu," for instance—and also of their products. The gods also help prosecute the battles. They send dreams of victory or otherwise inspire the commanders. This language may reflect a real Mesopotamian conception of warfare as a genuinely religious activity, or it may be due to the sacral nature of the records' context. They're usually located in temples or shrines. Whatever the case, warfare seems to be folded into the religious life of these Sumerian city-states.

In sum then, the wars of the early Dynastic Sumerian city-states appear to have been sophisticated affairs, in which centrally-recruited and uniformly equipped armies contested in pitched battles to decide disputes between their polities.

Against this background, a recently suggested model for Sumerian warfare proves to be untenable. Doyne Dawson, in his 2001 book *The First Armies*, suggests that Sumerian armies, such as they were, were really mobs of peasant levies, poorly trained, and even more poorly organized and deployed. The military operations of such a rabble would not be too impressive, and so Sumerian warfare was not marked by complex field operations involving infantry and chariotry. Rather, warfare in this period was dominated by sieges. Since defenses far outstripped the capabilities of would-be attackers, these sieges were largely ineffectual. A sort of Cold War stalemate prevailed, and the boastful assertions of the royal inscriptions are the unique images, like those in the Vulture Stela, are not good guides to Sumerian military realities, at least goes Doyne Dawson's argument.

It seems to me that this model flies in the face of a fair assessment of the surviving evidence. It may be true that objects like the Standard of Ur or the Vulture Stela are unique, but they have survived by chance, and their close agreement on matters of military equipment is therefore all the more remarkable for that fact. Their value as evidence is, if anything, enhanced rather than diminished by their uniqueness. It would require very special pleading indeed to insist that, by a bizarre coincidence, the two most informative surviving iconographic representations of Sumerian warfare that we have both happen to be seriously misleading. When combined with the evidence from Mari, the opposite in fact seems to be the case.

As to battle mechanics, the Vulture Stela plainly depicts tight formation of infantry in action. The accompanying text and scenes of burial mounds set this image in the context of a battle in the open field. Indeed, there is no mention or depiction of sieges in this, or any of the Lagashite records about its dispute with Umma. This situation stands in sharp contrast with contemporary Egypt where, as we shall see in the next lecture, sieges are the commonest type of engagement recorded in Old Kingdom depictions. I am not suggesting that sieges did not take place in early Sumer, but rather that the contention that they were the only significant form of military engagement is not supported by the evidence.

As we have noted, the infantry on the Vulture Stela, as well as the troops depicted in the Mari inlays and on Royal Standard of Ur, all have notably standardized equipment. This observation alone suggests a considerable degree of organization and central control over warfare in general and over the manufacture of military hardware in particular. This is entirely consistent with other aspects of administration in these early city-states, which was heavily centralized and geared toward the collection, cataloging, and redistribution of goods.

A further inference may be made. The use of shock weapons such as socket axes and spears, and the wearing of helmets and protective clothing are surely signs that these troops expected to participate in close hand-to-hand combat. On the Standard of Ur, the infantry are in an ordered line; on the Vulture Stela, they march in serried ranks and fight in close formation. This is no rabble of conscripted peasants who fight as a formationless mob, showing off and firing arrows at each other from a distance on some sort of "primitive" model. This is serious, organized warfare.

The war carts of this era are, to be sure, problematic. The clearest depictions are on the Standard of Ur, but their design is recognizable also in the Vulture Stela and the Mari inlays. They are four-wheeled vehicles, pulled by asses steered with, of all things, nose-rings. The cabins, apparently made of hide stretched over a wooden frame, have a raised front fitted with a quiver for spears. There are two crewmembers, a driver and a weapon-wielder. The latter is invariably armed with an axe or a spear.

Now, just how these contraptions were actually used in battle is not at all apparent. Some, like Dawson, think that they would have been utterly useless. How could you control four asses by means of reins strung through their noses? The cumbersome design looks neither stable nor maneuverable. This argument derives primarily from comparison with the later, better-attested use of chariots as mobile firing platforms for archers or javelineers. But just because the Sumerians lacked the true chariot on the later model does not mean that their efforts were wholly futile. If the war carts were not used in warfare, then why are they shown in that context? Dismissing them as useless does not get us very far.

That said, the tactical function of the war carts remains problematic. They were not mobile firing platforms, since they don't have archers or javelineers in them. So perhaps they were used only to transport prestigious warriors, who then dismounted to fight on foot. The Vulture Stela, for instance, shows Eanatum in his war cart at the head of his marching troops, but leading his ranked infantry into battle on foot.

Other scholars see a very different function for these carts. The raised front of the cabin, the use of axes or spears by the warrior crewmember, as well as the protective covering discernible on the asses' chests, suggest to some that the carts were expected to plow into enemy ranks as shock weapons. Certainly, the carts on the Standard of Ur are pulled by running asses. Their legs became more and more animated from right to left; they are clearly galloping, if you'd like. They also careen over prostrate corpses, and in one case a crewmember leans out to spear a fallen foe.

In one near-contemporary text from the Umma-Lagash dispute we read that 60 teams of asses and crews were abandoned on a field of battle. All this certainly suggests some sort of active use in battle beyond mere transport. But what was it?

If I may be so bold, I would like to suggest here a possibility that I have not seen aired elsewhere. This is that the carts were employed in mopping-up operations, to run down a defeated enemy. This would explain their prominence on the battlefield, the galloping asses, the use of weapons like axe and spear, and the trampled enemy shown on the Standard of Ur. Indeed, I note with interest that the only standing enemy depicted on the Standard in connection with the war carts has his back to the vehicle, as if in flight. Such a function would not require a great degree of maneuverability on the part of the drivers, who just had to point the cart in the right direction and go to it.

Regardless of this detail, what all the available evidence tells us is that early Sumerian warfare was not restricted to ineffectual siege engagements. It was an organized, centralized, and planned activity of the state, folded into the ideology of leadership and religion, and conducted with a high degree of sophistication in open-field battles between ranked infantry, missile troops, and war carts. Sieges there undoubtedly were, but if so, they appear less obtrusively in the record.

We saw above how Umma appears to have prevailed in the border dispute with Lagash, when Lugalzagesi of Umma conquered the traditional realm of Sumer in southern Mesopotamia. But he was not to prevail for long, since from the north exploded the conqueror Sargon of Akkad, who established the first empire in history over all of Mesopotamia. That is over Sumer, Babylonia in central Mesopotamia and the northern reaches of the two rivers. This happened about 2350 B.C., and the Akkadian empire lasted a little over two centuries.

The city of Akkad or Agade has not been located. Some believe that it lies under modern Baghdad, so we can't expect it to be excavated anytime soon. But it was certainly located in central Mesopotamia, in the region generally called Babylonia. Sargon's life became the stuff of legend, and since his biography survives mostly from later romanticized accounts, the historical details often prove elusive. But it is clear that he was a genuine historical figure of great importance. He was the first to unify all of Mesopotamia under a single, centralized polity and he did so by military means.

In fact, we can go further. Sargon's conquests and the continuation of his family's rule over a centralized state by dynastic means established the essential pattern for Near Eastern imperialists for millennia to come. In later centuries, the Third Dynasty of Ur, the Old Babylonians under Hammurabi, the Middle and Neo-Assyrians, the Persians, and countless others in the region followed Sargon's prototype, with variations of course. For this reason, the Akkadian Empire is a pivotal moment in Mesopotamian history.

From the written and iconographic sources, it seems clear that the Akkadians were heavily militarized. Sargon was remembered above all as a great conqueror, and his successors likewise. His grandson, Naram-Sin, for instance, who ruled around 2250 B.C., left a great Victory Stela, which is now in the Louvre, which depicts him leading an army up a mountain to crush enemies. Naram-Sin himself is considerably bigger than his soldiers and wears a horned helmet, reflecting the divine status credited to him in some of his inscriptions. He also carries a battle-axe and a composite bow, one of the first appearances of this weapon on record.

The composite bow represents a major advance in military technology. It was made of several materials glued together: wood, bone, tendon, and sinew. This gave the bow such great tension that when unstrung, it bowed forward and to be strung it had to be bent all the way back again. Later Assyrian reliefs show it taking two men to string such a bow. Further, the bow's extreme tension meant that it could be relatively small, about a meter long, while still packing serious penetrative power over a range of between 500 and 600 feet, outstripping simple bows by 150 feet or more.

Some have suggested, in fact, that the Akkadians developed this weapon and conquered Mesopotamia with it. While others prefer to think of an Akkadian mastery of siegecraft as the key to their military success. Whatever the case, they certainly prosecuted wars more efficiently than their contemporaries, and this allowed them to conquer Mesopotamia.

Akkadian reliefs regularly show warriors, combat, and plenty of prisoners of war, which suggest that Akkad was militarized in a way that other states up to that point had not been. Their imperial ideology, recoverable from several sources, places a premium on the military qualities of their leaders. In inscriptions, the rulers are hailed for conquering cities, carrying Akkadian arms into regions outside Mesopotamia, and subduing the rebellious at home. One text praises Naram-Sin for winning nine battles in one year. But we cannot take on faith claims that all the regions attacked were permanently conquered. The fact that a series of Akkadian kings had to return to the same places suggests punitive raids rather than permanent, extra-Mesopotamian conquests with the order of the day. Naram-sin may have declared himself "king of the four corners of the universe" but that did not make it so.

The organization of the Akkadian army remains a little unclear, but we must imagine it drawing heavily on subject peoples. Access to a deeper pool of manpower is a perennial advantage of empire. Sargon himself seems to have had royal corps of 5,400 men, who are described as "eating daily in his presence," and so were maintained at state expense. This suggests a royal standing army, but its full extent and composition remain very obscure to us.

The Akkadian Empire exacted tribute from conquered cities and imposed a standard system of weights and measures and laws all across the realm. Local rulers were contracted into Akkadian service, and all official correspondence used the Akkadian language; local languages were used for local affairs. Imperial ideology was promulgated through inscriptions and monuments set up in the cities of the empire, such as the Victory Stela of Naram-Sin.

Eventually, the Akkadian Empire collapsed, around 2100 B.C., under pressure both from within and from without, but its legacy was towering. It had shown what could be achieved by military conquest. Sargon's empire now stood as a precedent for later generations to follow. Many kingdoms and polities tried to emulate it, but none more successfully than the Assyrian empire of the first millennium B.C. Before looking at the Assyrians, however, we must detour to Egypt and consider military developments along the banks of the Nile.

Lecture Four
Egyptian Warfare from the Old to New Kingdoms

Scope:

It used to be thought that Old Kingdom Egypt was relatively peaceful because overt evidence for warfare in this period was largely lacking: The tombs of Old Kingdom officials made scant reference to warfare, and military scenes rarely appeared in their decorative schemes. More recently, this somewhat utopian picture has changed as some crucial pieces of written evidence have been read against the background of the wider ideology of Old Kingdom Egyptians, particularly their view of foreigners and the outside world. Evidence of warfare for the Middle Kingdom is somewhat better and includes the massive fortress at Buhen in the south of Egypt, wall paintings on tomb walls, and even wooden models of soldiers. With the New Kingdom, the evidence becomes much more plentiful. The New Kingdom state was aggressive and imperialistic; pharaoh's role was increasingly that of a war leader; monuments, art, and texts extol the military virtues and achievements of pharaoh; and documents attest complex military organization and command structures. More than anything, however, Egyptian warfare was transformed by the introduction of the horse-pulled chariot. The precise way the chariot was used on the battlefield remains a matter of dispute.

Outline

I. Was the Old Kingdom a nonmilitary state?

    A. The absence of fortifications, overtly military imagery in art, and military terminology in texts suggested to many that the Old Kingdom (c. 2700–2180 B.C.), geographically remote and isolated, was a nonmilitary state.

    B. J. Keegan has suggested that depictions of Egyptian warriors imply highly ritualized, nonlethal warfare.

        1. Soldiers down to the New Kingdom are shown largely unarmored.

        2. Soldiers thus equipped will not rush into battle to face spear stabs and sword slashes.

3. Depictions of the "smiting pharaoh" remain constant from the Old to New Kingdoms.
4. All of this implies a highly ritualized form of warfare, perhaps like the later Aztec "flower wars."
5. But this model is probably incorrect.

C. On the other hand, the Predynastic Fortress Palette (3100 B.C.) and the Narmer Palette (c. 3000 B.C.) appear to depict assaults on fortified towns and warfare, respectively.

D. There are other very strong indications, however, that point to a less utopian view of the Old Kingdom.
1. Egyptian ideology was highly ethnocentric: Egypt and the pharaoh represented order and decency; foreigners represented chaos and vileness.
2. Geographic isolation may insulate a country from outside attack, but it may also lead to extreme ethnocentricity.

E. The Tomb of Weni (or Uni), c. 2350 B.C., records five campaigns against Asiatics and contains several interesting details.
1. Weni was the general of an army of units levied locally; there were also Nubians and Libyans, possibly mercenaries.
2. Weni's title and that of many officers was innocuous: He was "Chief Domain Supervisor of the Palace"; subcommanders were bureaucrats and carried similar civilian titles.
3. This suggests that military command may lie buried in such civilian titles as *nomarch* or "chief prophet of Upper Egypt."
4. Thus, the absence of military titles cannot be taken as evidence for the absence of militarism in the Old Kingdom.
5. Weni's campaigns, as presented in his texts, were not ritualistic and nonlethal encounters; on the contrary, they were total wars of genocidal intent.
6. Weni described going back to put down rebellions among the Sand-Dwellers; it is not clear if this language was literal or ideological.

      7. Weni's motives were wholly personal: to earn the pharaoh's favor, presumably in material and career terms.

  F. Four Old Kingdom tombs also include scenes of sieges, the technical details of which we will survey in Lecture Eight. There are also weapons to consider.

      1. Such stylized images are hard to "read" straightforwardly. What, exactly, are we looking at?

      2. Old Kingdom weapons included axes, maces, bows, daggers, and spears.

II. The First Intermediate Period (c. 2180–2040 B.C.) and Middle Kingdom (c. 2000–1650 B.C.) were more openly militaristic in tone.

  A. Collapse of central power saw a regionalization of Egypt as local *nomarchs* rose to prominence. Internal fighting made war respectable to talk about; thus, it appears in Middle Kingdom records more clearly than in the Old Kingdom.

      1. Depictions of warfare on Middle Kingdom tombs are more numerous than on Old Kingdom tombs (10 as opposed to 4).

      2. Weapons improved in quality, especially the composite bow and the axe-head.

      3. Model soldiers show us (possibly) what Egyptian warriors looked like.

      4. Known fortifications, such as Buhen in southern Egypt, show a high degree of sophistication

      5. There is mention in texts of a "Wall of the Prince" protecting the approaches to Lower Egypt across the Sinai.

  B. The *Story of Sinuhe* (c. 1960 B.C.) and the Stela of Khu-Sebek from Abydos (c. 1880 B.C.) reflect a complex world of war, diplomacy, and mercenary engagements between Egypt and Syria-Palestine.

      1. The *Story of Sinuhe* takes place against a backdrop of endemic warfare.

      2. Sinuhe, an official in the army of the dauphin Sen-Usert (r. c. 1971–1928 B.C.), goes into exile on the accession of his boss.

3. Among the Asiatics, he becomes a mercenary general and fights a "duel of champions" with a rival Asiatic ruler.
4. An emissary arrives from Egypt and recalls Sinuhe, who dies in honor at home.
5. The Stela of Khu-Sebek records the career of a fighter/commander.
6. Noteworthy is Khu-Sebek's advancement and enrichment.
7. Khu-Sebek's activities were against the Nubians to the south, as well as the Asiatics to the north.
8. The stela implies a military failure on the part of the pharaoh in Asia.

III. The Second Intermediate Period (a.k.a. the *Hyksos Invasion*, c. 1660–1570 B.C.) saw the Delta ruled by foreigners; the New Kingdom (c. 1570–1070 B.C.), forged in war, expanded its borders into Syria.

A. The collapse of pharaonic authority at the end of the Middle Kingdom saw Lower Egypt ruled by foreigners, the Hyksos, out of Avaris in the Delta.
1. The old belief that the Hyksos introduced chariots to Egyptian warfare no longer has much support.
2. Most scholars now believe that chariotry came to Egypt during the New Kingdom.

B. Over several generations, Egyptians in Upper Egypt subjugated the Delta and drove out (or subjected) the Hyksos.
1. Accounts of these campaigns are scant; a schoolboy tablet from Thebes and tomb inscriptions help to fill out the picture.
2. These texts contain interesting information about early New Kingdom warfare.
3. Pharaoh had a council of advisors.
4. Plunder and booty played a central role in the commemoration of warfare.
5. Chariots appeared on the Egyptian side and seem reserved for the upper classes; the rest fought on foot.
6. Long sieges are mentioned.
7. Finds of weapons fill out the picture.

IV. Evidence for New Kingdom military operations is the fullest yet; the chariot played a key, if problematic, role on the battlefield.

    A. Texts record a complex military organization with a substantial officer corps.

        1. The army was divided into chariotry and infantry, vaguely designated *hosts*.

        2. Infantry was divided into divisions named after gods (Seth, Ptah, and so on), subdivided into companies of 250, each with its own scribe.

        3. Infantry troops were conscripted locally and housed, fed, equipped, and trained by the state.

        4. Chariotry represented a separate division, organized into units of 10 up to a maximum of 50.

        5. Massive logistical effort was required to maintain this wing of the army.

    B. There are two views on how the chariot was used: It charged the enemy directly and took the main shock of battle, or it acted as a fire platform and screened infantry as it formed up.

        1. Egyptian chariots were light and two-horsed and carried a crew of two: a driver and a warrior armed with a composite bow and/or javelins.

        2. The nature of the chariot strongly suggests it was a fire platform, not a shock weapon.

        3. Chariots, then, were probably used in broad, mobile maneuvers to screen forming infantry units and to mop up enemy troops broken in combat.

        4. The chariot predominates in our accounts of New Kingdom warfare because it was the "prestige" weapon on the field and pharaoh rode in one.

Essential Reading:

Pritchard, *Ancient Near Eastern Texts*, pp. 18–22 ("Story of Sinuhe"); pp. 227–228 ("Tomb of Weni"); p. 230 ("Stela of Khu-Sebek"); pp. 232–233 ("War against the Hyksos," "Expulsion of Hyksos"); pp. 328–329 ("Execration of Asiatics").

Gnirs, "Ancient Egypt."

Spalinger, *War in Ancient Egypt.*

Yadin, *The Art of Warfare in Biblical Lands*, pp. 58–114.

Supplemental Reading:

Schulman, *Military Rank, Title and Organization in the Egyptian New Kingdom*.

Shaw, "Battle in Ancient Egypt."

Questions to Consider:

1. How does the nature of the available evidence limit our ability to understand Egyptian warfare? What specific issues are made more or less difficult by the paucity of evidence?

2. In what ways did Egyptian warfare differ from that practiced in Mesopotamia?

Lecture Four—Transcript
Egyptian Warfare from the Old to New Kingdoms

Last time, we examined military developments among the first cities in Mesopotamia. In this lecture and the next, we turn our attention to the situation in ancient Egypt and focus on the Old to the New Kingdoms, covering the period roughly from about 3100 to 1070 B.C.

It used to be believed that the Old Kingdom, stretching from about 2700–2180 B.C. was a largely warless place. The absence of fortifications, overtly military imagery in art, and military terminology in texts suggested to many that the Old Kingdom was a non-military state. Unlike the competitive environment facing the Sumerian city-states, Egypt was a unified polity, focused on its god-king and at peace with itself.

Also unlike Sumer, Egypt was geographically isolated, surrounded on three sides by open desert, and only accessible overland through the Sinai corridor to the northeast. The Old Kingdom Egyptians, it seemed, were largely left to their own devices by their neighbors and did not face serious external threats. All in all, then, there seemed good reason to suppose that this era of Egyptian history was largely warless.

The eminent military historian John Keegan has recently argued an extended version of the "warless Egypt" model. Keegan points out that Egyptian soldiers down to the New Kingdom era are shown armed only with bow, spear, sword, mace, and shield. They have no helmets and no body armor. Soldiers thus equipped will simply not rush into battle to face wounds inflicted with the spear, the sword, or the axe.

Also for a period of nearly 1,500 years, images of Pharaoh smiting enemies with the mace remained virtually unchanged, from which fact Keegan infers a highly ritualized form of warfare among the ancient Egyptians. As an analogy, he points to the "flower wars" of the Aztecs. In these strange encounters, Aztec and neighboring armies would converge on an agreed-upon site but exchange captives rather than fight a true battle. The armies met; there was much bravado and shouting, and perhaps an individual challenge or two. Then the field between the armies was scattered with red petals to symbolize blood—hence the "flowers" in flower wars—and the captives were exchanged, to be sacrificed later. Perhaps this is the meaning of the smiting Pharaoh's fixed image. It reflects a ritual of execution following non-lethal battles.

And so Keegan concludes: "The people of Egypt, over the space of 1,400 years, may very well have been spared the reality of war as other people later experienced it elsewhere, altogether."

The proposal carries considerable appeal, but it is probably incorrect. With the proper conditioning, warriors will indeed go into shock battles virtually naked. The ancient Gauls or the Zulus of the 19th and 18th centuries did so. The latter looked not too different from models of Egyptian troops, in being armed only with hide shields, loincloths, and stabbing spears called *assegai*. Semi-naked Zulu warriors like this fought many pitched battles with their neighbors and, later, with British Colonial forces. Their immense bravery and fearlessness in the face of death and injury are well documented. Indeed, in many warrior-cultures, contempt for wounds and death are the marks of a real man, and minimal personal protection readily demonstrated one's courage to peers. Egyptian soldiers could surely have been similarly conditioned, especially if seeking to impress their god-king or his battlefield commanders.

Secondly, one cannot read too much historical significance into the continuity of Egyptian artistic representations of Pharaoh. The artistic vocabulary developed in the Old Kingdom was retained for centuries, or, if it fell out of fashion from time to time, fads for archaism would revive it. So identical or similar-looking scenes of Pharaoh smiting enemies occurring centuries apart need say little or nothing about actual military practice. This same caution, by the way, applies to the depictions of common soldiers; even if they are shown minimally protected, they might not have looked like this in real life. Middle Kingdom weapons found in archaeological contexts, for instance, do not show up in the iconography, which retains this "traditional" look of the Old Kingdom depictions. So perhaps the very notion of the nearly-naked Egyptian warrior is itself the result of an overly naïve reading of the iconography.

None of this is to say that Egyptian battles lacked a ritualized element. All battle, as we have seen since the first lecture, is a cultural process marked by ritual. The issue, rather, is whether Egyptian warfare was as non-lethal as Keegan imagines, and on this point there is good reason to think not.

Indications of Egyptian militarism are to be found even in the Pre-Dynastic Period, before the Old Kingdom arose. An artifact called the Fortress or Cities Palette, dating to perhaps 3100 B.C., appears to show fortified towns. Depicted from a bird's eye perspective, the towns have circuit walls with projecting towers, which are clearly defensive features, since they allow fire to go down the side of the walls.

Further, these towns appear to be under attack by animals bearing what look like compasses. Based on later Egyptian artistic practice, the animals may symbolize army units and the "compasses", so-called, battering rams of some sort. Another Pre-Dynastic object, the Battlefield Palette, shows animals, representing leaders, attacking people, vultures pecking at corpses, and bound prisoners of war being marched off.

The famous Palette of about 3000 B.C. that honors Narmer, who unified Egypt and founded the first Dynasty, shows, on one side, Narmer smashing kneeling enemies on the head with a mace, in the pose that inspired Keegan's musings about ritualized non-lethal warfare. On the other, four men bearing animal-standards march before Narmer toward a line of headless corpses neatly stacked or laid out in a row. The standards can reasonably be taken to represent army units, the headless corpses, the consequences of battle, and the mace-wielding Narmer, the commander-in-chief. All of this suggests a warlike Egypt in the Old Kingdom.

Other considerations point in the same direction. In the first place, state ideology was highly ethnocentric. Egypt and the Pharaoh represented order and decency, foreigners chaos and vileness. Egypt's foreign enemies, in all eras, are referred to as "wretched" or "vile." Geographic isolation cuts both ways. It may help insulate a country from outside interference, but it may also lead to the sort of extreme ethnocentric outlook that fuels vicious wars. The latter appears to be the case in ancient Egypt.

We have positive evidence for all this in the Old Kingdom Tomb of Weni, or sometimes Uni, dating to about 2350 B.C. Here autobiographical inscriptions record five campaigns against Asiatics, "Who Are Upon The Sands," as the text has it.

Weni commanded an army of locally levied units, raised in regional administrative boroughs called nomes and commanded by the local big-men, called nomarchs. Such a method of muster mirrors how corvée labor gangs were raised to work on major royal projects like the pyramids. In fact, for many Egyptian levies, warfare was probably just another form of service demanded by the king. If so, this was no professional, standing army, though palace guards may have provided a corps of semi-professional troops.

Weni also mentions Nubians and Libyans in the Pharaoh's ranks. Whether these were captives forced into service or soldiers of fortune out for hire, is impossible to say. Weni numbers his army vaguely, as "many ten-thousands."

More significant is Weni's title: he is "Chief Domain Supervisor of the Palace." Sub-commanders are identified as civic bureaucrats who carry similar titles: "Seal-Bearers of the King," or "nomarchs and mayors of Upper and Lower Egypt," or the "Chief Prophet of Upper Egypt." It seems that such people fulfilled both civilian and military functions, which explains the absence of clear military titles in most Old Kingdom texts. Military command was only one part of an official's duties, and so lies concealed behind innocuous-sounding civilian designations.

If so, then army service may have been seen as somehow lacking in social prestige. So in their tombs, officials stressed their civilian titles and duties over their military service, Weni being the whistle-blowing exception. Therefore, the absence of a military vocabulary cannot be read, as it often has, as evidence for the absence of warfare in Old Kingdom Egypt.

When Weni describes his campaigns against the Asiatics, there is nothing ritualistic and non-lethal about them. On the contrary, they are presented, even celebrated, as practically genocidal. And I quote:

> The army returned in safety, after it had hacked up the land of the Sand-Dwellers. The army returned in safety, after it had crushed the land of the Sand-Dwellers. The army returned in safety, after it had thrown down its enclosures. The army returned in safety, after it had cut down its fig trees and its vines. The army returned in safety, after it had cast fire into all its dwellings. The army returned in safety, after it had killed troops in it by the ten thousands. The army returned in safety, after it had taken troops in it, a great multitude, as living captives.

The form of this, by the way, suggests it may have been a prayer or litany of some sort recited upon the return of the army from its campaign.

Now, it is immediately evident that the so-called Sand-Dwellers are not nomads, but settled agriculturalists. They have enclosures, dwellings, vines, and figs. The very term "Sand-Dwellers" then is itself an example of the ethnocentric worldview of the Old Kingdom and a warning that labels and titles in these texts ought not to be read at face value. These are propagandistic documents, and not objective wartime reports. This doesn't mean that they are outright false, only that caution is needed in interpreting their content, particularly when that content has an overtly political purpose, here to glorify Pharaoh.

A good example of what I mean is Weni's comment that he had to go back five times to put down rebellions among the Sand-Dwellers. Is this language literal? Had pacts been made and broken? Or is it ideological? Are the Egyptians claiming suzerainty over unconquered territory, in the way the Spanish did in the New World? For Weni's part, his motives are presented as wholly personal, and he says, "I acted with regard to that for which his majesty would show me favor." No doubt, Pharaoh's favor was made manifest in innumerable material ways. So a key message buried in the text, and one repeated throughout the ancient Mediterranean Basin, is "war pays."

Aside from Weni's inscription, four Old Kingdom tombs are decorated with siege scenes, the technical details of which we will survey in Lecture Eight. We merely note here that such stylized images are hard to "read" straightforwardly. Were sieges the prime mode of Old Kingdom warfare, as some scholars have concluded? Or did sieges mark the climax of a campaign, and thus come to dominate the Old Kingdom representations of war? Indeed, do these scenes accurately depict specific encounters at all? None of this is evident from the images alone.

Finally, we have finds of actual weapons. Maces and clubs were popular in Old Kingdom Egypt, even though a mace is effectively countered with a helmet. Whereas the Mesopotamians developed helmets early on, and also socket-axes to penetrate them, the Egyptians did not clearly adopt helmets until the New Kingdom. So maces retained their usefulness in Egypt long after they had been relegated to status symbols elsewhere. Instead of penetrating, narrow-bladed socket-axes, the Egyptians preferred a wider-bladed slashing weapon, called "epsilon axe," so named for its similarity to the Greek letter epsilon. Daggers, spears, and bows have also been found, or are depicted in the siege scenes.

All in all, then, the evidence suggests that Old Kingdom Egypt was not as warless as was once thought, or as Keegan's more recent model suggests. Frequency is impossible to quantify, but if Weni's inscription is anything to go by, Pharaoh had regular and ruthless dealings with the despised Asiatics to the north. Despite the propagandistic purposes of Weni's inscription, this detail smacks of the truth. In general, wars between ethnically distinct groups are more vicious and brutal than wars fought among people who feel some affinity for each other. Studies of soldiers' outlooks in World War II suggested American troops in Europe felt some sympathy for German captives, who were white Europeans like themselves, although in the Pacific theater, tended to harbor less forgiving attitudes toward their Japanese opponents and visa versa of course. So, might it have been in Old Kingdom Egypt, where Asiatics were a target of outright contempt as well as repeated expeditions that dealt out death and destruction in spades.

The collapse of central authority at the end of the Old Kingdom initiated a poorly documented period of disunity called the First Intermediate Period, that stretched more or less from 2180–2040 B.C. This era saw Egypt regionalized as local nomarchs rose to prominence and ruled over their nomes. Internal fighting made war "respectable" to talk about, so warfare appears in the records of the subsequent Middle Kingdom, roughly 2000–1650 B.C., more obtrusively than it did in the Old Kingdom.

Depictions of warfare in tombs of the Middle Kingdom era are more numerous than they are for the Old Kingdom. There are ten for the Middle Kingdom as opposed to only four for the Old. These depictions are, again, overwhelmingly of sieges. Weapons improve in quality. The composite bow was introduced from Asia, but it was not widely used. Instead a type called the double-convex bow predominated, with an effective range of about 150 yards or so. Improvements were made to the epsilon axe-head to give it greater penetrating power.

Slings, spears, and javelins were also attested. Swords first appear in this period but only come into widespread use in the subsequent New Kingdom. But it seems from all this that the armory of the Middle Kingdom Egyptians had been enlarged and diversified by the internal conflicts that marked the First Intermediate Period.

The Middle Kingdom also preserves model units of Egyptian soldiery. The troops are depicted in organized ranks, trained and disciplined. They are clearly of different racial stocks, with care taken to distinguish the darker-skinned Nubians from the lighter-brown Egyptians. The Egyptian army, therefore, appears to have been a multi-ethnic force, very much like Weni's army of the preceding Old Kingdom, with its local Egyptian levies, Libyans, and Nubians, you remember.

More striking still is the evidence from fortifications. At Buhen in Southern or Upper Egypt, as its sometimes called, a fort of the 20th and 19th centuries B.C., built as a bastion against the Nubians, and it has been discovered unexcavated. It shows a surprisingly high degree of sophistication. The fort, home to a garrison of a few hundred men, had mud-brick walls almost 30 ft high, with narrow piers every few feet to allow a wooden overhang to be stretched between them. From this overhang rocks could be dropped down on those attacking the wall below. The walls were built with reed mats between the brick courses for extra stability and strength, and they had a glacis, that is, a sloping, thickened lower section to deter sapping and battering—that is to say, attempts to bore through the wall either with machines or with poles.

The gatehouse had massive towers that projected internally and externally to create a 70-foot long corridor down which would-be attackers would have to fight to gain entry. More remarkably, the whole fort was surrounded by an outer rampart with projecting semicircular bastions equipped with downward-facing firing slots. Beyond this outer wall was a ditch 24 feet wide and 20 feet deep.

The complexities of the Buhen fortress reveal not only the advanced engineering capabilities of the Middle Kingdom military architects, but also the sophistication they expected from would-be attackers. Buhen was designed and built not to deter unruly barbarian mobs, but to repel well-orchestrated assaults. What is preserved at Buhen therefore infers much about what is not.

There are other Middle Kingdom fortifications of note, such as the so-called "Wall of the Ruler" that protected the northern approaches to Egypt from across the Sinai. Little has been found of this entrenchment, leading many to suppose that it was a chain of forts, rather like the ones to the south, rather than a contiguous curtain on the model of the Great Wall of China or Hadrian's Wall in Britain. Written evidence lends support to this conclusion.

We find reflected in Middle Kingdom texts a complex world of war, commerce, diplomacy, and mercenary engagements between Egypt and Syria-Palestine. The *Story of Sinuhe,* set in the mid-20th century B.C., stands out. This may be a genuine autobiography, or a work of fiction. Either way, it tells us much about military matters in the Middle Kingdom era.

Sinuhe is a senior officer in the service of the dauphin, Sen-Usert. When the prince succeeds to the throne as Sen-Usert I, who ruled from 1971–1928 B.C., Sinuhe overhears a conversation that frightens him. Now, we're never told what he heard, but it causes him to flee Egypt altogether. So he slips past the forts of the Wall of the Ruler, "made to oppose the Asiatics and to crush the Sand-Dwellers," as the text has it, and goes to live in a place called Retenu, which was in Canaan. Here he makes a living as a mercenary commander, training the native troops and earning the respect and loyalty of an Asiatic prince. He is granted honor, status, and wealth. He marries, has a family, and raises them to adulthood.

One day, Sinuhe is challenged to a duel by the best warrior in a rival Asiatic army. A David-and-Goliath-like single combat follows. The two men advance on each other. Sinuhe dodges the champion's arrows, then hits him in the neck with an arrow of his own before finishing him off with a battle-axe. He gloats over his fallen foe and strips his armor. Later, an Egyptian emissary arrives and summons Sinuhe home, where he is reconciled with Pharaoh and dies an honored man in his homeland.

The story shows that relations between Egypt and the Asiatics were far more complex than the official propaganda might suggest. Further, there appears to be a market for mercenaries, and warfare is seen to offer a ready path to riches, respect, and status, even for an outcast like Sinuhe. War pays. The duel scene contains useful details of how different weapons were used. Sinuhe is equally adept with missile and shock weapons, though we cannot be absolutely sure that all Egyptian soldiers were similarly well trained. Sinuhe may be an exception. He is a commander, a man of special talents—at least so he says himself.

Another informative text is the *Stela of Khu-Sebek* from Abydos, which dates to about 1880 B.C. The Stela records the career of a fighter and commander of what appear to be elite troops around the Pharaoh, who fight in squadrons of seven or eight men. Khu-Sebek goes on campaigns against the Asiatics to the north and Nubians to the south. He is advanced and enriched by displaying his valor in battle under the gaze of Pharaoh. He receives rewards of gold and promotions for his deeds. Need I say it? War pays.

The Stela contains an interesting detail. In one Asiatic campaign, Khu-Sebek proudly proclaims that he fought with the rearguard, "without deviating from the fight, for my face was forward and I did not turn my back to the Asiatic." If a fighting retreat were required, it would appear that this expedition was not entirely successful. If this inference is correct, here is a good example of how these inscriptions twist the truth without betraying it entirely. We cannot expect them to state openly that Pharaoh's campaign failed. Rather, the negative, the retreat, is presented as a positive, Khu-Sebek's bravery, but without an outright lie claiming a success that wasn't there. It is left to the reader to infer what happened from the slanted language.

The Middle Kingdom came to an end in the early mid-17th century B.C., ushering in the so-called Second Intermediate Period, also known as "The Hyksos Invasion," which ran more or less from 1660 to 1570 B.C.

The Hyksos were foreigners of uncertain origin who ruled Lower Egypt from their capital, Avaris, in the Nile Delta. I should explain here that Lower Egypt means the northern part of Egypt and Upper Egypt means the southern part of Egypt because the Nile flows from south to north. So when you go up river, you are going south. Hyksos only controlled the lower part of the Nile Delta in the north. It used to be believed that the Hyksos introduced the chariot to the Egyptians, but this view does not have archaeological support. No definite finds of Hyksos chariots have turned up in decades of excavation in Egypt. As a result, many scholars now think that chariotry, in the sense of organized chariot units deployed *en masse* on the battlefield, only came to Egypt in the New Kingdom, not with the Hyksos. Individual chariots might well have appeared earlier, but they were not used in the tactical sense just outlined.

The New Kingdom, which stretched from about 1570 to 1070 B.C., was formed after several generations of warfare against the Hyksos in the 17th and 16th centuries B.C. Equipped with an ideology of liberation from foreign domination, the New Kingdom was an aggressive military state that expanded its borders north into Syria-Palestine and south into Nubia.

Accounts of the early campaigns against the Hyksos are scant. One of the fullest is a schoolboy tablet from Thebes, the so-called Carnavon Tablet I, the text of which seems to be based on contemporary historical inscriptions. Tomb inscriptions help fill out the picture to some degree. These texts contain interesting information about early New Kingdom warfare.

We read that Pharaoh had council of noble advisors whom he consulted about strategy. The advisors act as foils to Pharaoh's wisdom. Their plan is presented, and then rejected by the king. Plunder and booty play a central role in the commemoration of warfare: "My soldiers were as lions are," goes the text, "with their spoil, having serfs, cattle, milk, fat, and honey, dividing up their property their hearts gay." The property of course being the enemies' property. Another text details how hands were cut off enemy corpses as proof of kills, and rewards were granted in the form of gold from the Pharaoh. There was even a specific military award, called "The Gold of Valor." People were part of the spoils, enslaved and granted to their captors by the king.

In these texts, chariots appear on the Egyptian side, but they are reserved for the King or the nobles; the rest fight on foot. So the chariot in the early New Kingdom was not yet the important armament it was to be a century later. These texts also mention long sieges, one lasting three years.

As to New Kingdom weaponry, the old toolbox remained in use with two major innovations: the composite bow and the sword. The composite bow, as reviewed in the previous lecture, was particularly well suited to chariot warfare, which came to dominate the New Kingdom's military practice. Its small size but great range and penetrating power made it ideal for use in the confined space of a chariot carriage. Swords, known since the Middle Kingdom, now became more common, particularly the sickle sword. Helmets were finally introduced to Egypt during the New Kingdom period, though they make only rare appearances in the iconography.

Evidence for New Kingdom military operations is extensive. Texts record a complex military organization with a substantial officer corps. The army is divided into chariotry and infantry, and vaguely designated "hosts." The infantry was organized into contingents of 50. These were grouped into companies of 250, and the companies grouped into four divisions of 5,000, each named after a god: Amun, Re, Ptah, and Seth. Each of the 20 companies that made up a division had a commander and a scribe, and a variety of officers were ranged below these. A full Egyptian mobilization could therefore field 20,000 infantry alone. Infantry, so far as we can tell, were conscripted locally, and housed, fed, equipped, and trained by the state.

By around 1500 B.C., chariotry is found as a separate division of the Egyptian army, with its own officer corps and titulature. The chariots were organized into units of 10, up to a maximum of 50, and attached to the infantry divisions. A massive logistical effort was needed to maintain this wing of the army, since each chariot was drawn by two horses that needed to be housed, fed, trained, and maintained by specialist staff. Administrative records reveal that a typical chariot was equipped with one or two composite bows, two or four quivers that held up to 80 arrows, a spear and/or a javelin, a shield, and an axe. All of this material, as well as the carriage itself, required artisans to build and repair, and crews to maintain. As we shall see in the next lecture, the battles of Megiddo and Kadesh suggest that the number of chariots in the New Kingdom's armies stretched into the thousands, although we may expect some exaggeration on this point. But nevertheless, the administrative effort needed to maintain several thousand horses and perhaps a 1,000 or so chariots was truly gargantuan, and stands as a testament to the impressive organizational abilities of the ancient Egyptians.

There are two main camps of opinion on how the Egyptian chariot was used in battle. One was it charged into enemy units as a shock weapon. The other was that it acted as a fire platform and screened infantry as it formed up.

The chariots and their armaments surely provide the best clues as to their use. Egyptian chariots were light, two-horsed vehicles that carried a crew of two: a driver, and a warrior armed with a composite bow or a javelin. The light nature of the vehicle strongly suggests it was a fire platform, not a shock weapon. Charging into disciplined infantry is something horses in any age will usually refuse to do. In any case, the shock of such an impact was just as likely to prove fatal to the charioteers as to their targets. The horses would be disabled, the vehicle rendered immobile, and the crew would be sitting ducks.

In the main, then, Egyptian chariots were probably used to lay down a screen of fire as infantry units formed up and to harass the enemy as they approached. They may have also been used also to chase broken enemy troops. This indeed was one of the chief functions of cavalry in later eras. I would also suggest that a charge of massed chariots, even if aborted before the actual shock, would have been a hugely intimidating psychological experience for enemy infantrymen, all the more so if they were untrained conscripts. Such a charge could have been especially effective either at the opening of an engagement, to get the enemy to flee without a fight, or as a mental hammer blow against infantry on the verge of breaking.

Finally, the shock weapons in the chariot need to be accounted for. They were either there as weapons of last resort, were employed to cut down fleeing enemies, or the warrior crew member could dismount and fight with them—the axe and so on—on foot. Pharaoh was depicted as doing just that in some New Kingdom reliefs. But the shock weapons were secondary elements in the chariot's armory. Its main function was that of a mobile firing platform.

It would take considerable training to fire a bow from a moving chariot, and this is likely part of the reason that the chariot remained the prestige weapon of the Egyptian army in the New Kingdom, crewed by princes, noblemen, and other people of superior socio-economic status. This, again, is paralleled in the cavalry forces of later eras. The chariot was not the tank of the Late Bronze Age battlefield. It was the Lamborgini.

The prestige value of the chariot also explains why in surviving Egyptian battle accounts that vehicle dominates the narrative. This was the weapon on the field, owned and operated by the important people, including Pharaoh himself. We should not therefore conclude from the textual focus on the chariot, as some have done, that infantry was either tactically irrelevant or even non-existent on the Egyptian battlefield. That would be too hasty a judgment to make on the basis of slanted evidence.

So in the next lecture, we will turn our attention to two Egyptian battle narratives and see what they can tell us about the specifics of how the New Kingdom army functioned on the field.

Lecture Five
The Battles of Megiddo and Kadesh

Scope:

With the New Kingdom, we get the first fully recorded battle in history: the Battle of Megiddo between Pharaoh Thutmose III and a coalition of Syrian lords, fought outside the walls of a town in Palestine. Detailed accounts of the battle were carved into Egyptian monuments, and these accounts form the basis of our analysis. Such accounts, being royal propaganda, are not without problems of interpretation, but they reveal many interesting details about Egyptian warfare as practiced 35 centuries ago. The sophistication at all levels in this period shines through in the events of Megiddo. Thutmose III, victor at Megiddo, was a great conqueror and helped set New Kingdom Egypt on the road to empire. Once more, the connection between war and empire requires some consideration: Why did the New Kingdom Egyptians embark on wars? Were they motivated by greed, by religious devotion, by xenophobia, or a combination of all three? As seen in the last lecture, the chariot was central to warfare in this period. The Battle of Megiddo bears this out, as does the later Battle of Kadesh between Pharaoh Ramesses II (the Great) and the Hittite king Muwatallis. Once more, accounts of this battle are full and plentiful, but the use of chariots here is considered by some to be atypical.

Outline

I. The background to Megiddo is New Kingdom imperial aggression against Asiatics; Thutmose III (r. c. 1504–1452 B.C.) was one of the empire's founders.

   A. Having ousted the Hyksos and Nubians from their territory and reunited Egypt, the pharaohs turned their attention to expansion abroad.

   B. Thutmose III, the first 20 years of whose rule had been usurped by his stepmother Hatshepsut, led yearly campaigns into Palestine for 17 years.

      1. The motives for the campaigns are unclear: They could have been personal and political, expansionist, economic, religious, or a blend of all of the above.

2. In the first campaign, in year 23 of Thutmose's reign (he counted the 20 years of Hatshepsut's usurpation as his own), the Battle of Megiddo was fought.

3. This would put it in April or May, sometime between 1479 and 1468 B.C., depending on which version of Egyptian chronology one favors.

II. The events of Megiddo are instructive and worth considering in detail.

A. The battle was recorded in inscriptions, principally carved onto the temple walls at Karnak but also known from other places.

1. The different accounts are largely consistent with each other; it seems they came from scribes attached to the units involved.

2. Consistency does not necessarily equal reliability; with royal records, we must be cautious about what we read.

3. Pharaoh is everywhere dominant and decisive; this may reflect the realities of command by a despot, but it may also be pure propaganda.

B. The events of the battle are well documented, but uncertainties remain.

1. A coalition of Asian lords, numbered at 330 in one account, assembled under the chief of Kadesh, occupied Megiddo and waited for the Egyptians to come and fight.

2. There were three approaches to Megiddo: a road through a narrow pass from the town of Aruna directly toward Megiddo and two more circuitous routes to the north and south.

3. Egyptian intelligence showed that the Syrian coalition was arrayed before the town; the Syrians appear to have expected the Egyptians from the south.

4. After a war council, Thutmose led the vanguard of his army into the plain; the rear was still at Aruna, some nine miles away.

5. The Syrians were surprised, and Thutmose camped on the plain.

6. The next day, both armies faced off in battle, and the Syrian army broke on the first Egyptian charge and fled to Megiddo.

7. Thutmose's army devoted itself to looting the spoils of the battlefield and failed to follow up the victory.
8. Megiddo was besieged for seven months, at the end of which it surrendered.

C. Several observations can be made about this battle.
1. The battle was mutually agreed: The Syrians specifically waited at Megiddo for a decisive engagement with the Egyptians.
2. Intelligence was gathered by the Egyptians; little or no scouting was done by the Syrians.
3. On two occasions, pharaoh acted after consultation with a war council.
4. The marching order of the army was recorded.
5. Thutmose's stated reason for taking the Aruna road was neither strategic nor tactical but personal—that he not lose face.
6. The Syrians were remarkably complacent.
7. The Egyptian camp illustrated the sophistication of warfare at this time.
8. Strategic and tactical details are hazy.
9. The accounts do not cast clear light on the martial use of the chariots.
10. Casualties can only be estimated. There is mention of 83 hands taken (hands were typically taken by soldiers as proof of a kill).
11. There is great emphasis on loot taken and tribute exacted.
12. This is the first properly recorded campaign and pitched battle in our historical records.

D. Thutmose III and his successors continued to fight in Syria-Palestine against local coalitions and foreign rivals.
1. Thutmose's campaigns established the Egyptian empire in Syria-Palestine, but total conquest was impossible and diplomacy was necessary.
2. The Hittites were Egypt's main rival in the region. Conflict with them culminated in the Battle of Kadesh, c. 1285/1275 B.C.

III. Ramesses II (the Great) was the New Kingdom's greatest pharaoh and ruled for 66 years (c. 1279–1213 B.C.); the Battle of Kadesh is celebrated as his greatest achievement.

A. Ramesses's long reign ensured that his monuments are among the most numerous from ancient Egypt.

    1. From the sheer profusion of accounts of the Battle of Kadesh, Ramesses clearly regarded it as his greatest achievement.

    2. As with Megiddo, therefore, we have plenty of evidence. Unlike Megiddo, however, we also have the outline of an account from the other side, the Hittites.

    3. It is clear from these accounts that Ramesses did not win a terrific victory but, rather, saved his army from total annihilation by a display of personal valor.

B. Kadesh stands as the greatest chariot engagement on record.

    1. Ramesses approached from the south, with his army marching in four divisions.

    2. Duplicitous Bedouins fed misinformation to Ramesses, who was deceived as to Hittite dispositions.

    3. The Hittite king, Muwatallis II, was hidden to the east of Kadesh, allegedly in command of some 2,500 chariots.

    4. Ramesses, at the head of the column, moved west of Kadesh and established a camp.

    5. As the second division approached, the Hittite chariots swarmed out around Kadesh and attacked the Egyptians unprepared.

    6. Ramesses saved the day by charging into the Hittites and driving them off.

    7. Clearly, our account is not credible as it is. Various scenarios have been constructed to make sense of it.

    8. The Hittites then attacked the Egyptian camp, but the arrival of another Egyptian corps put them to flight.

C. Kadesh was a stalemate, as both sides claimed victory and the battle led to the signing of a nonaggression pact by the two realms.

IV. These two battles lead to several important observations about military affairs at the very outset of full historical records.

    A. Pitched battles in the open field between well-organized forces were already a feature of warfare.

    B. The battles were agreed upon by both sides and were intended to be decisive in that they aimed to settle an issue once and for all.

    C. Infantry featured heavily in these armies, but our records focus on the prestige armament of the chariot, driven by the rulers in both cases.

    D. Precise details of the actual fighting remain unclear, as do casualty figures.

Essential Reading:

Gabriel and Boose, *The Great Battles of Antiquity*, pp. 40–87.

Goedicke, *The Battle of Megiddo*.

————, *Perspectives on the Battle of Kadesh*, especially pp. 77–121.

Lichtheim, *Ancient Egyptian Literature*, 2.29–35 (Megiddo) and 2.57–71 (Kadesh).

Supplemental Reading:

Pritchard, *Ancient Near Eastern Texts*, pp. 234–241 (evidence for the Battle of Megiddo and Thutmose III's Asian campaigns) and pp. 199–203 (Egyptian and Hittite treaties after Kadesh).

Cline, *Battles of Armageddon*.

Spalinger, *War in Ancient Egypt*, pp. 83-100 (Megiddo) and 209-234 (Kadesh).

Questions to Consider:

1. Which features of the surviving records of Megiddo and Kadesh seem reliable and which do not? How can acceptance or rejection of specifics be justified in methodological terms?

2. What aspects of these battles do you find the most militarily impressive? Why? In what terms would you characterize these engagements: direct, shock battle; freewheeling fights of maneuver; or a combination of the two?

Lecture Five—Transcript
The Battles of Megiddo and Kadesh

Last time we examined the development of Egyptian warfare from the Old to the New Kingdoms. Here we turn to our first specific engagements. The Egyptian records about the battles of Megiddo in the 15th century and of Kadesh in the 13th century B.C. are the first examples of battle narratives we have to read, insofar as they describe the background, the lead-up to the battle, how the armies behaved, and the aftermath. However, gaps remain, as we shall see.

Imperial aggression by New Kingdom Egypt against Asiatics provides the background for Megiddo. Thutmose III, who ruled between 1504 and 1452 B.C., was one of the empire's founders. The New Kingdom had been forged in war; it was to persist in the celebration of the martial ethos for its entire duration. So having reunited Egypt after the Hyksos domination, the pharaohs turned their attention to expansion abroad. For the first 22 years of his reign, the young Thutmose was usurped by the dowager queen Hatshepsut. But after a brief period of joint rule, Thutmose emerged as sole ruler and led annual campaigns into Palestine for the following 17 years. The motives for these campaigns are not obvious. The official version claims that the first campaign was launched against "those plotting to attack Egypt's borders." In other words, the campaign is presented as defensive in intent.

But there are other possible motives to consider too. Thutmose faced personal and political imperatives, principally to establish his distinct reputation in the wake of Hatshepsut's dominance. Having lived in the shadow of a woman for so long, Thutmose needed to display his pharaonic virility.

As a rule, Egyptian records characterize the Asiatic enemy as "treacherous" or "in rebellion," but how or when prior suzerainty had been established over them is left rather fuzzy. It is more likely that this language glosses a naked brand of imperialism. Certainly, the expansion of Egypt's frontiers is stated as a benefit of war. Greed cannot be ruled out as a motivation either. We are told that Thutmose campaigned "to give things to those who were loyal to him," and the recording of captured loot is stated as the reason for carving the royal annals on the walls of the temple at Karnak. There is a religious factor also; the sun-god Amun-Re commands Pharaoh to act and gives him victories; expansion returns Egypt to its condition under the legendary rule of the gods; and the standards of Amun-Re are carried at the head of the army. None of the foregoing are mutually exclusive motives of course. Indeed, a blend of benefits may have impelled Thutmose into Palestine and the battle at Megiddo.

The battle was fought in Thutmose's first campaign, initiated only three months into the 23rd year of his reign. Since he counted the 22 years of Hatshepsut's usurpation as his own, this means that Thutmose went on campaign almost immediately upon assuming sole power. Chronological indications in the official account would place the battle sometime in April or May.

The year is more difficult to determine, since Egyptian chronology is hotly disputed among scholars, but a year somewhere between 1479 and 1468 B.C. is widely accepted. By the way, the speed with which Thutmose set out on this campaign tends to undermine the purely defensive motives for it stated in the official accounts. Three months seems a very insufficient span for Thutmose to hear of foreign threats, muster and supply an expeditionary army, and set out to counter those threats. It seems more likely that an aggressive campaign had been planned for some time.

The battle is recorded in inscriptions, principally those carved on the walls of the Temple of Amun-Re at Karnak, but it is also attested in other sources from Thutmose's reign. The different accounts are largely consistent with each other and may derive from the reports of scribes attached to army units. A tomb of one such scribe, called Tjaneni, has been discovered, and he declares, "I was the one who set down the victories which he achieved over every foreign country, put into writing as it was done." The Karnak texts also speak of records kept by individual troop commanders, so we could be dealing with eyewitness evidence in some of these accounts.

Consistency, however, does not equal reliability. Royal records demand interpretive care. The texts give us good reason for caution when, for instance, they number the enemy at "millions and hundred-thousands of men" or record the battle "for the magnification of his victories, to cause that his deeds of valor be related for millions of years to come, apart from the deeds of heroism which his majesty did at all times. If they were to be related all together with their names, they would be too numerous to put them in writing." "Indeed," is the only response I have for that.

Throughout the text, Pharaoh is everywhere dominant and decisive, the center of the action. This situation may reflect the realities of command by a despot, but it may also be pure propaganda.

The situation confronting Thutmose was as follows: a coalition of Asian lords, numbered at 330 in one account, many of them supposedly renegades from Egyptian fealty, had assembled in Palestine under the Chief of Kadesh, who is never named. These forces occupied Megiddo and waited there for the Egyptians. A decisive battle in the open field was sought by both sides. The stage was set.

The official records state that there were three approaches to Megiddo: a road through a narrow pass from the town of Aruna directly toward Megiddo; and two, more circuitous routes to the north and south respectively. Scouts reported that the Asiatics were deployed in front of the town. Most analysts agree that the main Asiatic force was blocking the road from the south, which they expected the Egyptians to take, naturally enough coming from the south, and the rest were arrayed in the arc around Megiddo facing west.

At a place called Yehem, Thutmose held war council. The army, presumably meaning his generals, advised him to take one of the circuitous routes on strategic and tactical grounds. Taking the more direct but narrow road through Aruna risked destruction in detail as the army emerged from the pass in front of Megiddo. "Do not make us go on that difficult road!" they pleaded.

In the official accounts, Thutmose listens to them but ignores their concerns and elects to take the direct, narrower route, which in parts was only 30 feet wide. His generals, of course, agree, "for a servant will be after his lord," as the annals have it.

The road was so narrow that as the vanguard emerged onto the plain before Megiddo, the rear was still at Aruna some nine miles away. The Egyptians, led by Thutmose, then proceeded to set up camp on the plain. We are told that the vanguard reached the plain when the shadow turned, or around noon, and Thutmose took up his position on the plain "as the 7th hour was in its course in the day," presumably seven hours later. So the Aruna road was sufficiently narrow that the Egyptian army took at least seven hours to decant into the plain. The generals again became worried, and pleaded with Thutmose to wait for the arrival of his full force before engaging the enemy. This time, he heeded their advice.

The Egyptian camp was to the south of Megiddo, probably on the north side of a creek, which ran across the plain. The text now becomes a series of staccato, diary-like entries, as if transcribed directly from field notes: "Providing for the officials. Issuing rations to the retinue. Posting sentries of the army. Saying to them, 'Be steadfast! Be steadfast! Be vigilant! Be vigilant!'" In the camp, the troops rest, feed, prepare their weapons, and wait. The Chief of Kadesh would have taken this opportunity to reunite his forces and prepare for the coming battle.

The next day both armies faced off on the plain. The Egyptian battle order is given, the Asiatic order ignored. Thutmose occupied the center of the Egyptian line in his fine chariot, armor, and equipment. Northern and southern attack forces were stationed on his flanks. The battle of Megiddo was often seen as primarily a chariot battle, but while many Asiatic chariots are mentioned, only one Egyptian chariot ever appears explicitly in the text: the fine vehicle of Thutmose himself. Another view therefore, is that the Egyptian army was mostly infantry. However, there is mention of many horses in the march along the Aruna road, and these must be attached to chariots, since genuine cavalry were unknown in this early era. In all likelihood, the Egyptian army was a mixed force, but the proportions of chariotry to infantry are no long recoverable. Arrayed in their battle formation, the Egyptians advanced on the Asiatics.

Of the battle itself, a minimal account is given. The Asiatic coalition broke at the mere sight of Thutmose's majesty. And this is what the text says: "Thereupon his majesty prevailed over them at the head of his army. Then they saw his majesty prevailing over them, and they fled headlong to Megiddo, with faces of fear." Abandoning their chariots, the Asiatics were hauled up over the walls by their clothes. Their escape was facilitated by the indiscipline of the Egyptian troops, who were looting the enemy camp.

So if this account is to be believed, there was little no real fighting at Megiddo at all, just an effective show of force that induced one side to yield instantly. Many ancient battles indeed must have turned out this way. But it is possible that, in the Near Eastern tradition, the actual fighting has been glossed over, as the account hastens to the point where the enemy breaks and runs. The text, however, later indicates that only 340 live prisoners and 83 hands were taken; that is, 83 Asiatics were confirmed killed. And there is no mention of course of Egyptian casualties. These are miniscule losses for a losing army. We shall consider explanations for them in a moment.

Since the Egyptians had missed the opportunity to annihilate their foe by looting the Asiatic camp, Megiddo had to be besieged for seven months before surrendering. A detailed list of loot closes out the official account.

Several observations are worth making about this sequence events. The battle was a mutually agreed encounter: the Asiatics specifically waited at Megiddo for a decisive engagement with the Egyptians, and Thutmose rises to their challenge. The Syrians are presented as saying, "I shall wait here in Megiddo to fight against his majesty," or, in a different account, we are told that the Asiatics "had come to engage with my majesty." Megiddo was a pre-arranged encounter, intended to settle a dispute.

While the generals give the wrong advice about which road to take and Pharaoh picks the correct option, they were allowed to speak freely, and none of them was executed or otherwise punished for proposing a plan that the Pharaoh disliked. That this first council was not pure window-dressing is shown by Thutmose taking the generals' advice on a second occasion, though their suggestion that he wait for the army to emerge from the narrow road before engaging the enemy is rather obvious. Though a despot, it does seem that Thutmose does not command in a wholly despotic manner.

The marching order of the army is recorded: "horse goes after horse" in the van, as the text has it, which must denote chariotry; and the infantry, dubbed vaguely as, "the people," are in the middle and rear. Pharaoh of course is at the very front with the standard of Amun-Re. Such a marching order would allow the chariots to screen the infantry as it emerged from the pass, adding to the Asiatics' difficulties.

Some read into Thutmose's decision to take the shorter but more perilous Aruna road clever strategic and tactical reasoning. But Thutmose states the basis for his decision very clearly, and it is as follows: "'Behold' they will say, these enemies whom Re abominates, 'has his majesty set out on another road because he has become afraid of us' —so they shall speak!" In other words, Thutmose's decision was personal and political rather than strategic or tactical. He took the narrow road to save face.

The complacency of the Chief of Kadesh is remarkable. He doesn't seem to have scouted the Egyptian approach, and he deployed his army on the basis of an assumption, that the Egyptians would approach from the south. Asiatic complacency extended even into allowing Thutmose to bring his full force onto the plain, despite it taking several hours for his whole army to emerge from the pass. They even allow the Egyptians to build a camp without interference.

Now, perhaps the Egyptian records are leaving out vital details. But the annals state that the Asiatic forces were split. One force was stationed outside Megiddo, the other along the southern road. So they were tactically in no position to interfere with the Egyptians' movements. While it remains inexplicable that no scouts were sent out to locate and observe the Egyptian approach, and no efforts were made to prevent it, it would not be the last time that complacency or overconfidence has lost a battle.

The Egyptian camp shows the sophistication of warfare at this time; orders are issued to various units; weapons are greased and polished; food is rationed and distributed; and sentries are posted.

Finally, strategic and tactical details are very hazy. We are told only that the Egyptians issued forth into the plain. We are not given the Syrian battle order, or even the composition of their troops. We are not told the nature of the Egyptian force or how it performed on the field.

The accounts of Megiddo do not cast any light on the use of the chariots and infantry. What form the fighting took we are not told, which has allowed scholars to project onto Megiddo their preferred model of combat for this era, with freewheeling chariot gyrations being the most popular model. This view, however, seems to me to be a retrojection from the later Battle of Kadesh, which probably did feature large chariot forces, as we'll be seeing in a moment. Rather, an agnostic stance is the fairest to the evidence. We honestly don't know exactly how Megiddo was fought.

The casualty figures may offer a clue however. Eighty-three Asiatic deaths and 340 captives suggest either the fighting was very limited in scope or duration, or that little killing was done once the Syrians broke for Megiddo, since the Egyptians devoted themselves to looting their camp. A third possibility is that the armies involved were very small. Scholar Hans Goedicke, for instance, envisions a pharaonic army of not more than 1,000 strong, though most scholars would set that figure 10 or 15 times larger. So a wide variation in modern interpretations reflects the uncertainties presented in the source material itself.

There is great emphasis on the loot captured and tribute exacted, all of which is enumerated in terrific detail down to specific items, which suggests on-site counting of the goodies by a scribe. So we get, for instance, "340 living prisoners and 83 hands; 2,041 horses, 191 foals, 6 stallions; 1 chariot worked with gold, with a body of gold, belonging to that enemy; 1 fine chariot worked with gold belonging to the Prince of Megiddo; and 892 chariots of his wretched army - total: 924; 1 fine bronze coat of mail belonging to that enemy," and so on. Over 2,000 horses and nearly 1,000 captured Asiatic chariots, by the way, argue sharply against Goedicke's view that the battle was on a very small scale.

So much then for the battle of Megiddo, the first properly recorded campaign and pitched battle in our historical records. But the uncertainties that persist in this encounter nicely illustrate the problems with the ancient data. While they appear so full and informative in some respects, they leave a lot unsaid or assumed in others, so that we know what road the Egyptians' took, what form their deliberations took, what their camp was like, and so on, but we do not know how the army functioned in the field, or how it gained its victory. We will have to wait until the Greeks, in fact, for the emergence of the fully developed battle narrative that include some indication of the course of the actual fighting. But that is some way off yet.

Let us know turn our attention now to the second great Egyptian battle on record, the Battle of Kadesh in the early 13th century B.C. Thutmose III's campaigns in Syria-Palestine established an Egyptian presence there, but total conquest proved impossible, and diplomacy with nearby foreign powers, namely the kingdom of the Mitanni in Mesopotamia and the Hittites in Turkey, remained a necessity. The

Hittites were Egypt's main rival in the region. They were a sophisticated empire based in central Anatolia and had interests in Syria. Egyptian tensions with them came to a head at the Battle of Kadesh, fought sometime between 1285 and 1275 B.C., depending on which chronological scheme each one favors.

Ramesses II, also known as Ramesses the Great, was the New Kingdom's greatest Pharaoh, who ruled 66 years, between about 1279 and 1213 B.C. Ramesses' long reign means that his monuments are among the most numerous from ancient Egypt. From the sheer profusion of accounts of it, Ramesses clearly regarded the battle of Kadesh as one of his greatest achievements. As with the Battle of Megiddo, therefore, we have plenty of evidence. But unlike Megiddo, we also have an account from the other side, the Hittites. It is clear from these accounts that Ramesses did not win a terrific victory, but he rather saved his army from total annihilation by a display of personal valor. Strategically, in fact, he lost Kadesh.

Once more, the essentially personal focus of the Egyptian texts is noticeable. Ramesses is at the center of attention, always at the heart of the action. At this stage, we should expect nothing else from pharaonic records. But it is very interesting that a reconstruction of events, not very complimentary to Ramesses, is possible on the basis of the information he himself provides us. Once more, propaganda does not entirely drown out the facts, though it does try to spin them positively.

As presented, the battle of Kadesh stands as the greatest chariot engagement on record. In May, Ramesses approached Kadesh from the south, his army divided into four divisions named after the gods: Amun in the van, commanded by the Pharaoh himself; Re following behind that; Ptah behind Re, and Seth well to the rear. Each division appears to have been 5,000 strong, a mixture of chariotry and infantry. He crossed the River Orontes some way south of Kadesh and moved toward the plain west of the town. It is highly likely, though not stated in the sources, that the Hittites and the Egyptians had agreed on Kadesh as the place to settle their dispute. This would be consistent with what we saw at Megiddo.

Two Bedouins were then brought before Pharaoh and reported, duplicitously, that the Hittite King Muwatallis II and his forces were far distant, over 100 miles away. They appealed to Ramesses' vanity here, saying, "He fears because of Pharaoh to come southward." In fact, the Hittites were lying in ambush only a few miles distant, northeast of Kadesh and so screened from the Egyptians by the city's mass. Muwatallis commanded a force of 2,500 three-man chariots, along with unnumbered infantry.

The Egyptian records report that these two Bedouins were really Hittite agents, deliberately feeding misinformation to Ramesses to grease the trap. It may be so, or it may be that Ramesses was complacent in accepting an erroneous but honest report uncritically. Neither scenario redounds to Pharaoh's credit. As the Egyptian camp was being set up, two Hittite scouts were captured, beaten, and then brought before the Pharaoh. These scouts divulged the true whereabouts of their force and its huge size, "more numerous are they than the sand of the shore," they said, as the official account puts it.

So Ramesses must now have realized that he was in deep trouble: caught in the open, unready and outnumbered, and facing an enemy arrayed for battle. He called a council of his generals and, in a bizarre non sequitur, lectured them about bad intelligence and incompetent subordinates. He surely had more pressing concerns to face. Nevertheless, orders were issued to hurry the rest of his army along.

Meanwhile, the division of Re was some way behind, approaching the Egyptian camp on the west side of the Orontes. What happened next is debated by scholars. One side, the dominant, prevalent view, has the Hittites seeing an opening and launching a massed chariot charge across a ford on the Orontes against this division "while," as the records have it, "they were marching, and not expecting it." The other sees the battle starting accidentally, when a large party of Hittite chariots on reconnaissance happened upon the Re corps coming north. The Egyptians, taken off guard, panicked and ran for their camp. There was no surprise attack at Kadesh, goes this line of argument, only a chance encounter.

Whatever the case, it seems unlikely that all 2,500 Hittite chariots took part in this initial engagement, as most commentators assume. For them to have done so would have required too long to cross the ford on the Orontes and still be in a position to surprise the division of Re. But in either of these scenarios, and whatever the size of the Hittite force that did actually attack Re corps, the Egyptians were now in really serious trouble, with 25% of their army routed. The Re corps, broken, ran in the face of this charge.

Ramesses donned his armor, mounted his chariot, and went out to rescue the division of Re. He claims quite clearly to have done this alone, wholly without support, and I quote:

> I charged all countries, while I was alone, my infantry and my chariotry having forsaken me. Not one among them stood to turn around. I swear, as Re loves me, as my father, Atum, favors me, that, as for every matter which his majesty has stated, I did it in truth, in the presence of my infantry and my chariotry.

He rallied the troops and reminded them of all the benefits he had conferred on them. The texts are strident in stressing the themes of abandonment and cowardice on the part of the army, and of unique courage on the part of Ramesses. The Pharaoh presents himself like a superhero from a comic book, who puts on a costume and single handedly saves the day.

Now, most commentators have dismissed this portrayal of events as the worst sort of pharaonic bombast. They suggest either a huge cover-up, but if so, why did Ramesses plaster Kadesh all over his monuments, sometimes even decades later? Or they suggest a suppression of pertinent facts, such as the actual presence of substantial support. Now Ramesses probably had, at the very least, his royal guard with him, whom he could justifiably omit from mention as they accompanied him everywhere. The whole issue may be one of perspective. From Ramesses viewpoint, he was alone facing the Hittites and in a very unready position. An astonishing display of pharaonic courage would also explain why this rather equivocal battle became a centerpiece in Ramesside commemoration. And, of course, the lone Ramesses did not charge 2,500 Hittite chariots, as many think he claims to have done. He never actually says that. Rather, he probably went after the smaller chariot force harassing the Re corps, or attacked only a part of the larger Hittite force.

As all this was happening, Muwatallis, the Hittite King, ensconced inside Kadesh and watching the battle from the walls, did nothing. He committed no further forces to the developing battle. Whether out of command paralysis, vacillation or a respect for the conventions of

Bronze Age warfare, which expected battles to be arranged—whatever the case, he held his main forces back at this crucial moment. Had he committed them, Kadesh would undoubtedly have been a decisive Hittite victory, and Ramesses' reign a very short one.

Meanwhile, the Hittites had penetrated into Ramesses' camp. At this juncture a corps of the Egyptian army arrived from the west—they are dubbed the *net arene*, "the youths" and were possibly drawn from local allies in the region—and this corps slaughtered the Hittites in the Egyptian camp. The next day, Ramesses withdrew.

So ended the clash at Kadesh. The scale of this engagement is debated. Some see it as a huge encounter involving many thousands of chariots, others as a couple of rather small-scale skirmishes followed by a standoff and a negotiated settlement. Once more, apparently fulsome evidence from ancient times is open to diametrically opposite interpretations.

It is clear that Kadesh was a stalemate. The Hittite records, more fragmentary than the Egyptian, state that Muwatallis defeated the Egyptians; they just make that claim outright, that "we defeated the Egyptians." The Egyptian texts, in contrast, do not so much claim outright victory as imply it. One gets the impression from Ramesses' exploits that the Egyptians came off on top. However, looked at in any way objectively, the edge has to go to the Hittites. Ramesses' objective was to capture Kadesh, but he never got to fire so much as a single arrow into the place. This is because he was too busy rescuing his army from a situation that was fast developing into an utter disaster. At the strategic level, then, Kadesh was a Hittite victory. But it was not completely decisive, which led to a negotiated settlement with the next Hittite king. Remarkably, both Egyptian and Hittite versions of the non-aggression treaty that emerged from Kadesh survive, and show that international posturing is not a modern preserve.

These two battles offer interesting insights into military affairs at these early dates. First, pitched battles between states marshalling well-organized forces are already a feature of warfare. There is no reason to think that they only appeared in the 15th century B.C. at Megiddo. This was a pattern of behavior with a long prior history. In my view, it is traceable back to the Vulture Stela in Sumer, which itself suggests an even earlier, Stone-Age heritage. Though it must be said that the Vulture Stela doesn't state that any of the battles between Umma and Lagash were actually prearranged. But one can infer that perhaps they were. Pitched battles in fact, I would say, at predate, are written in historical records.

Second, battles are agreed upon by both sides, and were intended to be decisive, in that they aimed to settle an issue once and for all. It has been argued, for instance, that Muwatallis did not commit his chariot reserves to finish Ramesses off, since that would have contravened the accepted rules of war in the Late Bronze Age. If so, we are dealing with a sophisticated, international scene, as is reflected in all sorts of ways in the Late Bronze Age, near east, and the Asian. And this comes in the form of, for instance, correspondence between rulers—letters back and forth—marriage alliances, treaties, trade, and so forth. Warfare and battles were just one mode among many in which these early states interacted. But it is clear that the decisive battle was part of this world, and not an invention of 7th century B.C. Greeks, as some insist.

Third, infantry feature heavily in these armies. At Kadesh, the Hittite infantry played no part in the actual fighting; and in general, accounts of infantry actions in this early era are certainly vague. This has led some to believe that infantry was either underdeveloped, or even possibly absent from the battlefield entirely. But this would be a mistake. Our records focus on chariots, since these were the prestige armament of the era, driven by nobles and by kings. They were also prized items of plunder, and so they are highlighted and even described in the records, as we have seen.

But infantry, dubbed "the people", were there, and they were there in force. This is clear in the case of Megiddo, where it took several hours for the army to emerge into the plain; and we are told that the "horses"—that is, the chariots—were at the front, and the people followed behind in column. The written focus on the prestigious chariot ought not to be read literally to imply that only chariots took part in these engagements.

Finally, precise details of the actual fighting remain unclear, as do casualty figures. The reports generally tend to bypass the undecided fighting and cut straight to the rout and slaughter of the enemy. This is a consistent pattern in Near Eastern and Egyptian records, and was to remain so for millennia. We'll be seeing it again with the Assyrians in a couple of lectures.

So really, we are left in the dark about how these armies functioned tactically. While various combat models have been suggested by modern scholars, we should be clear that any such model is really an interpretation founded in inference rather than on hard fact, because the ancient sources are simply not there to tell us exactly how, say, chariots and infantry worked together on the battlefield. The focus is on the chariots because they're the interesting and the prestige; and so the vehicles and the infantry are either not mentioned or passed over in virtual silence. So it's important to beware that these modern scholars' models of ancient combat in these early eras are really inferences rather than hard fact. I'm not saying that these models are nonsense; it's just that their tentative nature needs to be fully appreciated.

Next we turn to even more tentative matters: the Trojan War and so-called Homeric warfare.

Lecture Six
The Trojan War and Homeric Warfare

Scope:

The battle for Troy provided Greek mythology with one of its foundational themes. It is the background for the great Homeric epics, *The Iliad* and *The Odyssey*, and it served as inspiration for many later Greek tragedies and works of art. As illustrated by Virgil's *Aeneid*, the saga of Troy also occupies a central place in the mythical underpinnings of Rome. Given its importance, the reality of the Trojan War has been debated since ancient times. In this lecture, we address the so-called Homeric question and survey the archaeological evidence for Troy and for warfare among the mainland Greeks, called Mycenaeans. In particular, the heated scholarly debate surrounding the nature of Homeric warfare—whether even such a thing existed at all—is examined. Interpretations range from the purely literary (Homeric warfare, as described by the poet, is a literary fiction) to the more literal (Homeric portrayals of warfare are logical and plausible when the poet is properly interpreted). This discussion offers essential background for material to be covered in Lecture Nine.

Outline

I.   The historicity of the Trojan War, as well as the practice of a distinctly Homeric form of warfare, is closely tied to interpretive uncertainties surrounding our chief source for both: the Homeric poems. Others sources are not terribly helpful.

    A. The so-called Homeric question (or, more properly, the Homeric questions) affects all planes of interpreting the poems *Iliad* and *Odyssey*.

        1. Practically all aspects of the Homeric poems are controversial: whether Homer ever existed as an individual artist, whether the poems show the imprint of a single talent, when and where the poems took their current form, and so on.

        2. For the historian, two issues are paramount: Do the poems enshrine a historical reality (or realities)? If so, what is their chronological point of reference?

3. There are no ready responses to these issues, but points of consensus are as follows:
    a. The poems are a product of oral transmission, which preserved snippets of information about different eras as they were passed down by the generations of bards who sang them.
    b. The oral process can be traced for several centuries back from the generally accepted time of final composition (c. 750–700 B.C.).
    c. What all this might or might not say about the historicity of the Trojan War remains moot, but confronting these interpretive difficulties must be the starting point of any analysis.
B. External sources are of limited usefulness in illuminating the supposed historicity of the Trojan War.
    1. The site of Troy was discovered in northwestern Turkey in the 19th century.
    2. Yet excavations, although suggestive, have failed to demonstrate categorically the reality of the Trojan War; such a demonstration is a fundamentally unrealistic expectation of what archaeology has to offer.
    3. Discovery of the Hittite Empire in the 19th century and the reading of its extensive archives opened up some tantalizing possibilities, but again, none are decisive in establishing the historicity of the Trojan War.
C. Several ground rules can be established and must be borne in mind in assessing all this material.
    1. Homer was a poet, not a historian. Being historically accurate was not his main concern, nor that of the tradition to which he belonged.
    2. The poetic tradition clearly magnifies and glorifies the events it describes.
    3. If there really was a historical Trojan War, it was likely a rather minor event that, for whatever reason, obtained a towering cultural status among the Greeks.

II. A major controversy swirls around the issue of Homeric warfare as a distinct and historical entity in its own right.
    A. Battle scenes in the *Iliad* are of a type.
        1. Heroes fight in one-to-one duels.

2. Missiles are thrown (and miss), warriors run about and clash with spear and sword, and chariots patrol the battlefield.
   3. Homeric warfare is, thus, loose and open-cast, apparently fought by heavily armed "fighters in front" (*promachoi*).
B. A terrific spectrum of scholarly opinion exists on how such scenes are to be read.
   1. Some argue that Homeric warfare is a poetic fiction, unreflective of any form of warfare ever actually practiced.
   2. The fact that Homer appears to be confused in some military details—notably, the proper use of chariots or heavily armed men running around an open field—suggests to some that his portrayal of battle is largely fictitious.
   3. Even among those who accept that Homeric warfare did take place in reality, a wide variety of opinion is evident.
   4. Some accept Homeric descriptions at face value and seek to find parallels in ethnographic records of fighting among New Guinean tribesmen or *samurai* warriors in Japan.
   5. Another view emphasizes the massed ranks in Homer's battle descriptions to argue that the later form of Greek warfare—heavily armed infantry ranked into close formations—was already in place in Homer's day.
   6. The apparent inconsistency of Homeric battle descriptions, with massed ranks in some parts, individual fighters in others, and long-range missile exchanges in others, has been explained by some as a product of phases of battle.
   7. Others see Homeric warfare as consistently portrayed once a judicious interpretive stance with regard to the poems and what Homer sought to do is adopted.
C. Given the performative nature of the Homeric tradition, it seems most unlikely that the style of warfare depicted therein is wholly fictitious; the descriptions of battle had to resonate with the audience to be effective.
D. But it is much more difficult to determine which elements of Homeric warfare are real and which are elaborations.

Essential Reading:

Homer, *The Iliad* (a useful selection of passages is found in Sage, *Warfare in Ancient Greece*, pp. 1–18).

Latacz, *Troy and Homer.*

Supplemental Reading:

Powell, *Homer*, chapter 2.

Van Wees, "Homeric Warfare."

Questions to Consider:

1. What chief obstacles, methodological or circumstantial, stand in the way of establishing the Trojan War as a historical reality? Can these obstacles be overcome?

2. Was Homeric warfare a reality or a figment of the poet's imagination? What are the deciding factors in leading you to decide as you do on this question?

Lecture Six—Transcript
The Trojan War and Homeric Warfare

Thus far we have concerned ourselves with the earliest civilizations in the Near East and Egypt. Now we turn, for the first time, westward, or at least partly westward, to the coast of Asia Minor. The Trojan War was the foundational motif of Greek civilization, providing as it did the dramatic backdrop for the two epic poems by Homer, the *Iliad* and the *Odyssey*. Although there was a tradition independent of Homer about the Trojan War and the heroes who actually fought in it, these two poems—especially the *Iliad*, which takes place entirely at Troy—represent our fullest and richest representations of the event. As such, we must precede our consideration of the Trojan War with an appreciation of what exactly we are dealing with in these two fabulous works of literature.

For the past 200 years, practically every aspect of the Homeric poems has generated scholarly controversy: whether Homer ever existed as an individual; whether the poems show the imprint of a single talent; whether they are the work of one man, two men, or a sequence of authors working in different times and places; when and where the poems took the form they currently have. On and on it goes.

Most of these Homeric controversies are well beyond the scope of this course, but two issues are paramount for the possibility of using the poems as an historical source. First, do the poems enshrine an historical reality or realities? And second, if so, what is the chronological point of reference for that reality or realities? We will consider each in turn.

Most today would accept that the Homeric epics were written down between 750 and 700 B.C. But they self-consciously refer to a bygone Age of Heroes, when men were bigger, stronger, and communed freely with the gods. In this sense, the poems are overtly fictive. But is the heroic world a complete fantasy, or does a historical reality inform it? Are we dealing, perhaps, with a garbled memory of a real past, overlaid with fantastical elements? And if so, how do we disentangle the memory from the fantasy?

There are no ready responses to these questions, and much depends on what views one holds on the even most basic questions about

Homer and the Homeric corpus just mentioned. A broad consensus, however, exists on the following issues.

Following the work of Harvard professors Milman Parry and Albert Lord in the mid-20th century, it is all but universally accepted that the poems as we have them are a product of an oral epic tradition, passed down the ages before Homer from bard to bard. Epic was a performative medium, sung with musical accompaniment before an audience. The tradition was not enshrined in a fixed text; rather, it was a flexible and malleable collection of narrative modules that could be creatively combined as the circumstances of performance required.

The *Iliad*, as we have it, is really a collation and amalgam of modules revolving around different heroes, probably initially performed separately, but here retold under the umbrella of an overarching story about the anger of Achilles and its consequences outside Troy. The formulaic nature of oral epic poetry—with its rhythmic meter and fixed epithets, lines and even whole passages— meant that as the tales were sung and resung down the generations before Homer, bits and pieces were added or dropped out as need be. So the poems do not refer to a particular time and place, but represent a palimpsest of eras and settings, freely mixed and mingled by the requirements of the genre to evoke the quasi-mythical world of the heroes. This world was real and familiar to an ancient Greek audience at one level, but clearly fantastical and fictional on another.

Like prehistoric insects caught and encased in once-fluid amber, slices of ancient reality could become embedded in the epic tradition as it passed by. These slices will likely pertain to "things" rather than to social customs or political practices, because, to keep the tradition lively and relevant, the latter needed constant upgrading to remain germane to each generation's audience; while unfamiliar objects only added color to the exotic world of the heroes. And this is precisely what many analysts see in the poems: a largely 8th century social and cultural world of Homer's day studded with bits of earlier, even Bronze Age, material culture.

Thus, the heroes all use bronze weapons, even though in Homer's day iron weaponry was the norm. In one passage, Homer describes a curious helmet made from boars' tusks sewn onto a felt cap. Helmets just like this are archaeologically attested down to the end of the

Bronze Age, around 1100 B.C., but not afterwards. Homer's audience did not use them, and probably didn't know of them. Likewise, a minor hero in the *Iliad* uses a huge shield that reaches down to his ankles and can be slung over his shoulder as he runs away.

The Trojan champion Hector kills this hero when he trips over his shield and falls over, so that the shield is a key element in his death-scene. Such shields are known from Greece, but only before the 15th century B.C. So not only was this so-called tower shield alien to Homer's audience, it would have been alien even to later Bronze Age audiences. And it is important to note that the tradition preserves not just the appearance of the shield, but how it was used as well. So some items in the heroes' world appear to have solid historical analogs in ages long before Homer. And note—they are all objects.

The process of oral transmission possibly reaches back from the time of final composition—we'll say around 700 B.C., —back into the Mycenaean Period in the Greek Bronze Age, which stretched roughly from 1600 to 1100 B.C. Now what all this might say or might not say about the historicity of the Trojan War, which is traditionally dated to 1183 B.C. remains moot. But confronting these interpretive issues in Homer must be the starting point of any analysis. Time now to see what non-Homeric sources may contribute to the issue.

First, archeology. Troy, also known as Ilium, was unearthed in 1870 by Heinrich Schliemann at Hisarlik in northwestern Turkey and has been explored in dozens of excavation campaigns ever since. The site has yielded a complex archaeological history with at least nine distinct occupation levels going back before 3,000 B.C. This was clearly a popular spot for settlement in ancient times. There are two candidates for the Troy of King Priam and the Trojan War: Troy VI, with a broad boulevard and massive walls, towers, and gates, but of a date around 1250 B.C., a little too early to fit the Trojan War, and Troy VIIa, a shadow of Troy VI's former glory but better fitted to the date of the supposed War.

The site has provided ammunition for those who support or deny the reality of the War itself. Supporters point to the fact that archaeology has confirmed the existence of a place formerly considered purely legendary. It occupied a very advantageous location; it was rich and powerful, and "well-walled," as one Homeric epithet puts it, with massive gates and towers of the highest quality construction. Skeptics point to many things, not least the site's small size. At about 20,000 square meters, this is hardly the vast city of towering monuments and expansive palaces described in Homer.

As one German scholar of ancient cities has put it, "Troy VI and VIIa, which might be considered a chronological match for Homer's Troy, were wretched little settlements with could make no serious claim to the title of city." If there ever was a war over this insignificant place, it must have been a pretty minor tussle—hardly the stuff of epic tradition.

It is precisely about the issue of scale that recent excavations by Manfred Korfmann, starting in 1988 and still ongoing, have caused such a firestorm. Korfmann has found evidence that the compact citadel tourists visit today was only the acropolis of a much larger city that ranged widely over the plain around it, enclosing perhaps 200,000 square meters; that is, ten times larger than previously thought. This larger Troy would have been much more worthy of a serious war, as it was probably a major regional power that controlled key trade routes and access to the Anatolian plateau, home of the powerful Hittite Empire. Furthermore, the evidence has been interpreted to suggest that this "Greater Troy," as we might call it, had connections to the Hittites, led a league of local states, and was destroyed violently, possibly in a trade war with the Greeks.

A new Trojan War exploded over these claims, when an ancient historian and colleague of Korfmann's at Tübingen University in Germany, Frank Kolb, the very man who had dubbed Troy VI and VII "wretched little settlements," accused Korfmann of fantasizing in print. The dispute became so vicious and heated that it even made into the pages of the *New York Times*, a rarity for any academic spiff, never mind one taking place in Germany.

Kolb's objections center on two issues. First, evidence that Troy was a trade hub at the time of the Trojan War is virtually non-existent. Indeed, evidence for major commercial activity in the Bronze Aegean and Black Sea as whole is very weak, and virtually nothing from these regions has been found at the site of Troy itself. Second, Kolb maintains that Korfmann's claims for a Greater Troy are overblown and don't bear close scrutiny.

This debate aside, the fundamental truth is that the physical remains at Troy and elsewhere, while suggestive, have failed to demonstrate categorically the reality of the Trojan War. For instance, pottery made by Bronze Age Greeks, termed "Mycenaeans" by modern scholars, has been found all along the western Turkish coast and at Troy itself. Further, tablets from the Greek mainland inscribed with the Mycenaean script make mention of female workers marked as coming from various western Turkish locations. The connections between Mycenaean Greece and the region around Troy are therefore not in doubt. But the material record would suggest that those connections were not terribly strong: 99% of all pottery found at Troy VI and Troy VII is of local style and manufacture. So while such finds may be illuminative of its context, they do not prove that the Trojan War itself actually happened.

At the site, Troy VI and Troy VIIa seem to have suffered violent destruction. There is evidence of burning and tumbled walls. In particular, Troy VIIa features many small dwellings packed up against the citadel's walls, and much space devoted to storage. An arrowhead of Mycenaean type was found in one of its streets. Is this evidence for people coming inside the walls to escape besiegers, and does the arrowhead point to the Greek identity of those besiegers? Possibly. But a single arrowhead is a slim basis indeed on which to posit the occurrence of a whole war, and an earthquake can just as easily account for the tumbled walls and fires. Famine-ravaged rustics could have packed into Troy VIIa to receive sustenance from the royal store-rooms; and a single arrowhead could drop into a Trojan street as easily from a Greek traveler's bag as from a Greek besieger's bow.

All in all, given the solid evidence drawn from other ancient siege sites—and we can compare here the evidence found at Lachish in Israel, which will be discussed in Lecture Eight—there is much that is lacking at Troy by way of hard evidence for a war, let alone an epoch-making conflict of the sort Homer seems to commemorate.

In my view, the deeper issue is this: short of weapons and armor inscribed with "Achilles was here" or "I belong to Hector," what could archaeology possibly unearth that would "verify" the stories told about the Trojan War—Paris taking Helen from Sparta, the Expedition to Troy, Achilles' fight with Agamemnon, the deaths of Patroclus or Hector, or the Trojan Horse? These motifs surely exist wholly in the realm of legend, and no amount of physical evidence will ever confirm them. We just have to accept that.

So there were high hopes when a different line of inquiry was initiated by the discovery of the Hittite Empire in Anatolia in the 19th century. Extensive archives were found, and study of them opened up some intriguing possibilities.

Now, we have already met the Hittites, as they challenged Ramesses the Great for control of Syria-Palestine at Kadesh in the 13th century B.C. At this time, they were the lords of Asia Minor. Their records, uncovered and read, make mention of places called *Wilusa* and *Truwisa* to the west; the former ruled by a king named *Alaksandu*; and people-dubbed *Ahhiyawa* also lay the west. Many have heard in these appellations echoes of the Greek names for Troy: "Ilios", for instance, which would have been pronounced "wilios" in pre-Homeric Greek, for the Hittite term, *Wilusa*; or "Troia" for the Hittite term *Truwisa*. And *Alaksandu* echoes *Alexandros*, an alternate name in Homer for Paris, prince of Troy. And *Ahhiyawa* sounds like one of Homer's words for the Greeks at Troy, *Achaeoi*. Likewise, contemporary Egyptian records mention *Danaya*. Are these the "Danaoi," another of Homer's labels for the Greeks?

Even if these identifications are all sound—and they are debated—they only go to establish that Egyptians and Hittites were aware of people from the Greek mainland and of a place possibly called Ilios or Troy. The Hittite records do not put them together to report a War on *Wilusa* by the *Ahhiyawa*, or indeed any major military incursion by these westerners into Turkey. Once more, a potentially hot line of inquiry cools on closer scrutiny.

It is best if we establish several "ground rules" in assessing all this material. First, Homer was a poet, not an historian. Being historically accurate was not his main concern, nor that of the tradition to which he belonged. Second, the bardic epic tradition clearly magnified and glorified the events it described. Third, if there really was a historical "Trojan War," it was likely a rather minor event that didn't merit notice even by the neighboring Hittites. But, for whatever reason, it acquired a towering cultural status among the Greeks. And that status is not in the least impugned by the actuality, or not, of the war itself.

Parallels are provided by the Battle of Little Bighorn, also known as "Custer's Last Stand" in America, or the *Song of Roland* in France.

In military historical terms, these were minor engagements involving only a few hundred U.S. Cavalrymen and Frankish warriors respectively. In artistic and cultural terms, of course, they took on quite different dimensions as cornerstones of national mythologies. While sober historical analysis can re-evaluate the realities of such conflicts, their value as cultural capital stands unimpaired. This is no less the case with the Homeric poems.

Their power and attraction lies not in their historicity or lack thereof, but in what they tell us about the human condition, the nature of duty, honor, friendship, and death. This is why people still read Homer today, almost 3,000 years after the oral tradition was first set down to papyrus. Whether any of it ever actually happened is, in a very real sense, quite secondary.

In one respect, however, the *Iliad* may provide vital information for the military historian: the way early Greek warfare was fought. You will not be surprised to hear that major scholarly controversy swirls around this issue too, as various models for so-called "Homeric warfare" as a distinct and historical practice have been proposed and challenged. For the rest of this lecture, we turn attention to this issue. What is discussed here lays vital groundwork for the material to be addressed in Lecture Nine.

Battle scenes in the *Iliad* are all of a type. The focus is firmly on individual heroes, who are nearly always named, even if they appear only for a few lines to get speared or hacked to death. So, typically, and I quote:

> There, he killed Asynous, then Hypiron, a frontline captain. One he stabbed with a bronze lance above the nipple, the other his heavy sword hacked at the collarbone, right on the shoulder, cleaving the whole shoulder clear of neck and back.

The main characters fight it out in duels, which are presented as taking place in front of their respective armies; indeed, they are often termed *promachoi*, which means "fighter in front." The *promachoi* show up clad in bronze armor and use spears, swords, and stones. Usually, the fight opens with a spear cast or occasionally a huge boulder, which, as Homer has it, "no two men could lift, weak as men are now." Another spear is held in reserve for closer work, if the throw misses. As a last resort, the sword can be drawn. Lengthy speechifying sometimes precedes the clash, as heroes recall past encounters, taunt opponents, and vaunt their own capabilities.

There is room enough in the combat zone for hurled spears or stones to miss their targets and hit open ground, for the wounded or dead to be withdrawn by groups of followers, and for heroes to advance and retreat freely. Indeed there is enough room for chariots to patrol the field, delivering fresh fighters or picking up those who are tired out or injured. Occasionally, massed, tightly packed ranks appear, sometimes likened in similes to walls. Longer range combat with arrows, stones, and spears is also referred to, but really in a secondary role, since the main work of the heroes is conducted at close quarters with spear and sword.

Putting it all together, Homeric battles seem to be fought by a few, heavily armored men out front, between lines of larger masses of men who throw stones and fire arrows at each other. The free movement of fighters and chariots demonstrates that open cast combat is what's envisioned, spread out over a wide area. This model was the "standard view" up until recently, when new research has cast the whole matter back into dispute.

Today, a terrific spectrum of scholarly opinion exists about how the Homeric battle scenes should be interpreted. To some, Homeric warfare is a poetic fiction, unreflective of any form of warfare that was ever actually practiced. In this view, Homeric battle is an amalgamation of features and details drawn from various phases of the epic tradition's development. Some parts would be familiar to Homer's audience, so that the scenes make sense to them; some would be unfamiliar, to emphasize the heroic context.

Homer's interest was in entertaining the audience and in exploring the human issues central to the poem's themes, not with being accurate and rigorously consistent in his portrayal of combat modes.

The fact that Homer appears to be confused about some military details would tend to support this view of Homeric battle as largely fictitious. For instance, in Homer, chariots are used to move prominent men to and from the front. The vehicles have a driver and a warrior, and the warrior invariably dismounts to engage the enemy on foot, although some unfortunates are speared right out of their vehicles. In reality, as we've seen, chariots were properly used in the

Bronze Age in large formations as firing platforms for javelineers or for archers.

Since Homer hadn't a clue how chariot warfare was actually conducted, but since he had inherited a tradition that featured chariots, he created a fictional role for them as battlefield taxis. Likewise, bronze-clad warriors are unlikely to sprint about the way Homer's heroes do, throwing spears, dodging missiles, and chasing down fleeing enemies. Features like this suggest that Homer's warfare is a warfare of the imagination, not of reality.

Others see things very differently, and argue, for instance, that the mere presence of chariots on the Homeric battlefield itself represents a memory of their one-time use in warfare, but in a manner the bardic tradition has seriously distorted. So their presence suggests not outright fiction, but garbled memory of an erstwhile reality. Even among those who believe that Homeric warfare reflects a reality, however, there is a wide variety of opinion.

Some accept that the Homeric descriptions should be read at face value, and argue that the model of the *promachoi*, the "fighters in front," operating between lines of lighter-armed, socially inferior followers, finds parallels in ethnographic records of fighting among New Guinean tribesmen or the samurai warriors in Japan. On the basis of such better-documented parallels, Homeric warfare ought to be considered as a historical reality, pretty much as it is presented. But it is not exactly clear how an amalgam of loose parallels from widely divergent contexts proves the historicity of Homer's descriptions. This to me is a big problem with it. Parallels are at best suggestive, but they're never probative.

Another view rejects the standard model of Homeric warfare altogether and stresses the passages where massed ranks appear, such as this:

> A wall of them bulked together, spear-by-spear, shield-by-shield, the rims overlapping, buckler-to-buckler, helm-to-helm, man-to-man massed tight, and the horsehair crests on glittering helmet horns brushed as they tossed their heads, the battalions bulked so dense, shoulder-to-shoulder close.

Not much room for heroic dueling or for the open-order combat. So massed ranked combat, it is argued, is actually decisive in Homer's battles. Since we know that later Greeks fought in tight formations of bronze-clad spearmen, proponents of this view hold that Homer refers to this later type of fighting, with some embellishments for dramatic effect.

Yet, the duels of the *promachoi* are still unquestionably a major part of Homeric combat. So how do they jibe with the massed-rank passages? The answer is to propose phases in the combat: an opening exchange of missiles that leads to a fight among duelists in open order, which in turn gives way to massed combat of packed ranks; or the massed ranks clash first, which leads to missile exchanges and is then followed by duels of the *promachoi*. The order of the phases is thus malleable. Since it was proposed in 1977, this massed-ranked model of the Homeric warfare has become so popular that it is today the new standard view.

The problem with the model is that the alleged phases are not nearly as distinct from one another in the poetry as their champions would have us believe. The massed ranks, for instance, only emerge occasionally, and in particular circumstances, such as when a hero is in trouble and calls for support, or when a fight develops over the corpse of a fallen comrade. The massing of ranks, in other words, is not a distinct, never mind a decisive, phase of Homeric battles. It is an occasional resort. This is strikingly different from the later Greek warfare the poems are supposed to reflect. In these later battles, as we shall see in Lecture Nine, the armored warriors went into battle *en masse* in tight formation and maintained that formation true to the end.

Further, there is no distinct missile "phase" in the Homeric poems. Rather, missiles are constantly being fired or hurled as the fighting proceeds. And let's not forget that we have these chariots roaming around. The phased model of Homeric combat, while very cleverly argued, thus relies on a selective reading of select passages and cannot be sustained after a close reading of what Homer actually describes.

So yet another approach is to take as a starting point a consistent reading of all Homeric battle passages, not just bits and pieces of them. Once a judicious interpretive stance is adopted, goes this argument, battle turns out to be rather consistently represented in the poems.

Homer depicts battles in a cinematic fashion. He sometimes offers a panorama, or sometimes a close-up of heroes battling it out. The idea of "phases" fails to appreciate this poetic mode of depiction, at least goes the stand of argument. The text simply moves from one plane to another, as the poet's attention is drawn to a close-up or a wide-angle view. Given the legendary world of epic, there are of course fantastical elements on display, such as the massive, gold-encrusted weapons, or the direct intervention of gods into the combat, or extended verbal exchanges in the heat of battle. But, goes the argument, Homer's audience would have recognized the reality of the battle scenes while simultaneously discerning the fantastical in them.

A parallel might be how combat in the *Star Wars* movies is familiar-looking to modern audiences, even as we also know that the weapons and the hardware are all fairly unrealistic. Once the clearly fictional elements have been stripped away, an internally consistent and not implausible form of warfare is discernible in Homer.

On this view then, Homeric warfare is reconstructed as largely open-order combat among *promachoi*; but massed ranks could be formed under pressure, and missile exchanges were constantly going on as the fighting proceeded. Chariots were less military in function, and more status symbols, as was the heavy armor worn by the main fighters. Just because Homeric Greeks did not use chariots the same way the Egyptians or Hittites did, does not mean Homer was clueless about how chariots performed in battle; and it was the Greek use of the chariots that seems to be at least consistent and plausible. Homeric warfare then, on this view, is a consistent entity and probably reflects an historical form of combat.

So we have several models of what Homer is describing when he describes warfare, ranging from a New Guinean-*samurai* amalgam to a denial that there ever was such a thing in the first place. There seems little room to maneuver in this densely contested scholarly battlefield, and the continuously underlying problem of making sense of the Homeric poetry as an historical source adds immeasurably to the complexity of the debate.

For what it's worth, my views are as follows: the performative nature of epic poetry seems to me a critical factor. In order for epic combat to resonate with the live audience, they must have been able to recognize what was going on. To depict a form of fighting that was completely fictitious risked losing their interest. To my mind, this is enough to establish that Homeric warfare must have a basis in historical reality.

The space battles in the *Star Wars* films were actually modeled on footage of real World War II aerial engagements. By choreographing the movements of fantastical-looking spaceships from real combat airplanes, the familiar was embedded within the imaginary, and a bridge was built to the audience's world. So even *Stars Wars* combat, it can be argued, is founded in some form of historical reality. I believe the same is true of Homeric warfare.

Figuring out what that reality might have been is far more difficult. I favor the view that, once stripped of their clearly fantastical elements, Homeric battle scenes are internally consistent. I see no reason why the open-order warfare found in Homer was not the norm in the 8th century and earlier. In vase paintings of this very era from the Dipylon cemetery in Athens, we see, in geometric silhouette, warriors armed with large shields, crested helmets, two spears, and swords. Some even climb off the back of chariots, driven by a comrade. The echoes with Homeric warfare in these scenes are striking, although it cannot be ruled out that the images are in fact inspired by the epic tradition itself.

But, in my more romantic moments—they are few and far between— I like to think of the influence running in the opposite direction. I imagine a group of these "Dipylon Warriors," as these vase-painted fighters have been dubbed, gathered around a hearth, spellbound by a bardic performance about fighting heroes before the walls of Troy; and then going out to take part in battles fought in a fashion very close to that enshrined in the verses still ringing in their ears.

I'd like to end on a slightly different note and address the issue of violence in the Homeric poems. Homer's *Iliad* is replete with gruesome images of violent death, so much so that even my modern students are sometimes appalled by it. People get stabbed through the face, the spear point severing their tongues as it explodes out the back of their heads; their limbs are cleaved from their bodies; blood spurts and gushes and pours; screams pierce the air; and the dying writhe in the dust and claw the earth. This aspect of warfare must have been familiar to any Greek or indeed any military audience in any era. The dead and the mutilated are the constants of warfare in all ages.

But a particular feature of this brutal violence is emphasized in Homer, which raises his poetry to its well-deserved level of classic. The consequences are unsparingly presented. Minor characters show up to be straightaway gored by a spear, but they are often given a personal history. For example, in Book Four, a Trojan called Simoisius appears for less than a dozen lines. But listen to how he is presented:

> And Telemonian Ajax struck Anthemion's son, the hardy stripling Simoisius, still unwed. His mother had borne him along the Simois's banks, when she trailed her parents down the slopes of Ida to tend their flocks, so they called him Simoisius. But never would he repay his loving parents now for the gift of rearing — his life cut short so soon, brought down by the spear of lionhearted Ajax. At the first charge he slashed his right nipple, clear through the shoulder went the brazen point and down in the dust he fell.

And here are Homer's lines about a pair of Trojan brothers slaughtered by Diomedes, son of Tydeus, in a single encounter:

> The son of Tydeus killed the two of them on the spot; he ripped the dear life out of both and left their father tears and wrenching grief. Now he'd never welcome his two sons home from war, alive in the flesh, and distant kin would carve apart their birthright.

Homer's attitude toward war is therefore deeply ambiguous. He recognizes the glory and courage and the opportunities of the battlefield. But the tragedy of young people dying in combat is not lost on him. Everyone has a mother, a father, wives, and kids at home. Each killing ripples across the pool of human misery. It is well to remember, with Homer, that the brutality of war has deeply personal consequences.

Lecture Seven
The Assyrian War Machine

Scope:

In the late Bronze Age (1350–1100 B.C.), the kingdom of Assyria, located in the northern reaches of Mesopotamia, emerged as a major regional power on the back of a powerful military machine. Its initial territorial acquisitions were washed away in the great upheavals that brought the Bronze Age to an end in c. 1100 B.C. The core of the Assyrian kingdom, however, survived when other states (the Hittites, Mitanni, and Mycenaeans) collapsed. In the 9th century B.C., the Assyrians began to expand their realm once more and eventually created the vast Neo-Assyrian Empire, which for the first time in history, united the Near East and Upper Egypt under a single polity. The military machine of the neo-Assyrian kings was a ferocious opponent, as revealed by the often brutal contents of the Assyrian Royal Records and reliefs carved onto the walls of palaces. Through these records, we contemplate the nature of the Assyrian army, the unique features of the empire it created, and the place of warfare in Assyrian imperial ideology. The Assyrian military model of multiethnic, highly mobile armies relying on missile weaponry and chariots was to be stock for major Near Eastern powers for centuries to come.

Outline

I. Assyrian history falls into two distinct phases: the so-called Middle Assyrian period (c. 1350–1100 B.C.) and the Neo-Assyrian Empire (c. 900–612 B.C.). Most of our military information derives from the neo-Assyrian period.

A. In the 14th century B.C., the mountain kingdom of Assyria emerged as a regional power in Mesopotamia and Syria.

1. A series of energetic kings expanded Assyrian control south into Mesopotamia and westward toward the Mediterranean.

2. This proto-Assyrian empire was washed away in the widespread upheavals at the end of the Late Bronze Age (c. 1200–1000 B.C.).

3. The Assyrian heartland remained intact, however.

B. Another series of energetic kings, beginning with Ashurnasirpal II (r. 883–859 B.C.), re-extended Assyrian control over the Near East and expanded it into the first true imperial system in history.

    1. In the guise of reclaiming a lost inheritance, Ashurnasirpal II began conquering the Middle Assyrian lands. His successors extended the empire by annual campaigning.

    2. The Assyrians distinguished between the homeland and the conquered territories, which were organized into provinces under governors appointed by the kings.

    3. This arrangement marks Assyria as the first genuine imperial system known to history.

II. The empire was forged by the Assyrian army, an awesome military machine deployed with utter ruthlessness by the kings.

  A. Sources for the army are provided by written records and from the detailed relief sculptures found at the Assyrian cities of Nimrud, Nineveh, Assur, and Khorsabad.

    1. Evidence for the Assyrian army comes from the Royal Records of Assyria and bas-reliefs carved on palace walls.

    2. The army was organized around units of 10 and 50, with a complex officer corps reaching up to the king.

    3. The organization of the officers suggests the existence of an elite unit, the Royal Guard (*sab sharri*), combined with units drawn from conquered and allied peoples.

    4. The bas-reliefs from royal palaces show us various contingents, armed differently and carefully identified as foreign auxiliaries by dress and equipment.

    5. The Assyrian army consisted of chariotry, cavalry (first developed systematically by the Assyrians), archers, slingers, heavy infantry, and light infantry. As we shall see in the next lecture, siege warfare was a specialty of this impressive fighting force.

  B. There is disagreement among modern commentators about how this army functioned in the field.

    1. In the long tradition of Mesopotamia, the Assyrian Royal Records are bombastic exercises in self-aggrandizement. There is little detail about how the army actually fought.

2. This vagueness in the source material has left the tactical system of the Assyrian army a matter of uncertainty.

3. There are three main proposals on the table.

    a. The Assyrian army was primarily a chariot force, in the ancient tradition of Egypt and the Near East. The Assyrians were just particularly good at chariot warfare.

    b. The Assyrian army was primarily an infantry army; in fact, it was the first true infantry army in history. This accounts for its success.

    c. The Assyrians developed the world's first integrated operational army, which deployed multiple specialist troops in mutually supporting roles.

4. Of these reconstructions, the evidence of the reliefs supports the latter best.

5. Reliefs of open battle and the hunt suggest that coordinated action among varied units was the key to the Assyrian tactical system.

C. The Assyrians inflicted the most hideous cruelties on defeated rebels or recalcitrant enemies, as recorded with apparent relish by both the archives and the reliefs.

1. A deliberate policy of extreme violence was evidently in effect.

2. A common reaction to such vileness has been to declare the Assyrians inordinately cruel by nature. Such judgments are valueless as historical explanations.

3. A much more productive approach is to interpret such actions as acts of psychological warfare.

III. In the stated reasons for their wars, we can discern the shape of Assyrian imperial ideology.

A. The Assyrian Royal Records offer various reasons for warfare.

1. Of these, religious reasons were the most common. The king, as the representative of Assur and Marduk, was impelled to war by the oath-breaking disloyalty of dishonest enemies.

2. In the neo-Assyrian period, the Bronze Age holdings of Assyria were used as justification for (re)conquest.
3. Revenge featured heavily as a motif also, for wrongs actual, ancestral, or perceived.
4. Economic motives are evident in the long lists of loot taken from conquered peoples, but they are rarely acknowledged as the *causes* of war; rather, they are presented as the natural *results* of success.
5. This last point alone is reason to be cautious in accepting what the Assyrians themselves say about why they fought so much. The prospect of loot has long been a motive for aggression.

B. In all this, aspects of Assyrian imperial ideology are to be discerned. A passage in Sargon's records describing his eighth campaign is particularly instructive.

C. The Assyrians overstretched themselves in Egypt and, facing multiple revolts, finally succumbed to an alliance of Medes, Babylonians, and Scythians in 612 B.C.
1. Assyrian control over Egypt was never better than sporadic.
2. Other parts of the empire took advantage of Assyrian troubles in Egypt to revolt.
3. A major coalition of enemies, both internal (Babylon) and external (Medes and Scythians) finally overthrew Assyrian power by sacking Nineveh in 612 B.C.
4. The name of Assyria passed from history and its homeland returned to being a realm of shepherds and goatherds.

Essential Reading:

Dawson, *First Armies*, pp. 158–209.

Luckenbill, *Ancient Records of Assyria*, various passages, especially in volume 2.

Supplemental Reading:

Oded, *Mass Deportations*.

———, *War, Peace, and Empire*.

Wiseman, "The Assyrians," in Hackett, *Warfare*, pp. 36–53.

Questions to Consider:

1. Which model of the Assyrian army's tactical system seems the most convincing to you? Why?

2. What is the connection between warfare and empire in ancient Assyria? To what degree can we call Assyria a *militarized society*? What do we mean by *militarism* in the first place?

Lecture Seven—Transcript
The Assyrian War Machine

After our brief excursion to Troy and Greece, we now turn our attention back to the Near East and the Empire of Assyria, which dominated the entire region from roughly 900 to 612 B.C. The Assyrians commanded one of the fiercest military machines developed in the ancient world, and the sources for it are sufficiently full to allow us, for the first time, to appreciate an ancient army in very close detail.

On a broad perspective, Assyrian history falls into two distinct phases: the so-called Middle Assyrian period in the Late Bronze Age, roughly 1350 to 1100 B.C.; and the Neo-Assyrian Empire of the early Iron Age of about 900 to 612 B.C. Most of our military information derives from the later period.

In the 14th century B.C., the mountain kingdom of Assyria, located in what is today northern Iraq, emerged as a regional power in Mesopotamia and Syria. Spearheaded by a series of energetic kings, the Assyrians expanded their control south into Mesopotamia and westward toward the Mediterranean Sea. The degree to which these activities were lasting conquests, or more transitory raids glossed by Assyrian claims of permanence, is disputed among scholars. Whatever its nature, this proto-Assyrian empire was washed away in the widespread upheavals that racked the Near East and the Aegean at the end of Late Bronze Age, between 1200 and about 1000 B.C.

But the heartland of Assyria remained largely unscathed, even as the Hittite Empire, the kingdom of the Mitanni, and Mycenaean Greece all succumbed. From their mountain fastnesses the Assyrians were to re-emerge in the early Iron Age, stronger and more aggressive than before.

Beginning in the 9th century B.C., another series of energetic kings, starting with Ashurnasirpal II, who ruled from 883 to 859 B.C., re-extended Assyrian control over the Near East. The Bronze Age Assyrian claims to these regions greased the cogs of conquest, since the neo-Assyrians could present themselves as doing no more than reclaiming their lost inheritance. But whereas Ashurnasirpal II began by re-conquering the Middle Assyrian lands, his successors extended the empire far outside these initial realms in a series of annual campaigns.

In organizing their conquests, the Assyrians distinguished between the homeland and the conquered territories, which were organized into provinces under governors appointed by, and answerable, to the King. For this reason, many regard the Assyrians as establishing the first true empire in history, since this was the model followed by all subsequent territorial empires.

At its height, the Assyrian Empire embraced northern Mesopotamia, Babylonia, Sumeria, Syria, and Palestine; and it even maintained a rather spotty control over Egypt. Never before had the region seen a polity of this size and complexity. But to fashion it, massive violence had to be administered, and the Assyrians evolved a formidable tool for doing just that—the Assyrian Royal Army.

The sources for the Assyrian army are, by the standards we have so far seen, embarrassingly plentiful. First, there are written sources in the form of the Assyrian Royal Records. These are a series of texts inscribed on stone and clay that record the military and the construction activities of the kings in annalistic fashion, one year after the next. They are of unclear function but have a definite propagandistic intent, to praise the king and vaunt his conquests. In this respect, all the caveats that applied to the inscriptions of Thutmose or Ramesses apply here too. In addition to the Royal Records, there are the marvelous, if brutally frank, relief sculptures that once decorated the palace walls of the Assyrian capital cities, principally Nineveh and Nimrud. For the most part these were excavated, or, should I say, crudely hacked out of their context, in the mid-19th century, and are housed today in the great museums of Europe, principally the British Museum in London. From these two sources, the Assyrian Royal Army comes to life for us in a way that no prior ancient army can.

The army was organized around basic units of 10 and 50. When on campaign, the king was naturally the commander-in-chief, but second-in-command were two field marshals dubbed *turtanu*, and below them ranged a series of officers down to the commanders of ten. This command system alone was more complex than anything that preceded it and provided a firm backbone for the rest of the army. The organization of the officers suggests the existence of an elite unit, the Royal Guard, called *sab sharri*. Most interestingly, it is clear that many units were drawn not only from allied peoples, but also from among the conquered.

Following Roman terminology, we can dub these units auxiliaries. The army, therefore, incarnated the empire itself, as former opponents now fought for their Assyrian overlords. In this respect, too, the army has a strikingly modern imperial character—think of the Nepalese, Indian, Australian, or Irish units in the British Imperial Army.

The reliefs from the royal palaces confirm these deductions from the written evidence and reveal what the troops actually looked like. Great care is taken in these images to distinguish various contingents, some clearly identified as foreign by their dress and their equipment. From the reliefs, we see that the army consisted of chariotry, cavalry, archers, slingers, heavy infantry, and light infantry. The heavy infantry were clad in scale-armor shirts, wore distinctive conical iron helmets, and carried a shield, the shape of which changes over time but it always large. These shields were usually curved, affording maximum protection to their bearers; they could stand inside them almost. The shield curved around the body.

The heavy infantryman also carried an iron sword and a stabbing spear, perhaps seven to nine feet long, if the dimensions on the reliefs are to be trusted. Sometimes, these troops carry composite bows on their backs, so they could also double-up as archers. Light infantry appear to have been mostly auxiliaries, and so are armed variously according to their native custom, usually with lighter, round shields and spears. They wore little armor, if anything, sometimes just a pectoral plate over the vitals of the chest, strapped on—sort of cross straps.

As far as we can tell, the Assyrians were the first to exploit systematically the full potential of cavalry as a distinct military wing. On the reliefs, the Assyrian cavalry come in one of two varieties: lancers and horse-mounted archers. Our earliest depictions of Assyrian horsemen, from the 9th century B.C., show two riders on two horses, apparently harnessed together. One rider reins the horses, while the other wields his weapon. It has been reasonably argued that such early cavalry emerged from chariots, with the team of horses decoupled from the vehicle and now ridden by individual horsemen. The riders also sit rather far back on the horse, not quite yet comfortable in the more forward and familiar saddle position. And they have no saddles and no stirrups; they grip the horse with their ties in sort of a squatting position.

Now other Near Eastern powers had employed horsemen earlier than this, but the resources available to the Assyrian kings allowed them to do so on a scale and in a systematic manner that was unprecedented. The written records show that great effort was put into locating, training, and maintaining stables of horses. It fell under the jurisdiction of the governors to do so, in fact, and reports were expected by the King. A Royal Guard of horsemen accompanied the king in all his movements, in war and in peace. The advanced use of cavalry by the Assyrians probably gave them a tactical advantage over their opponents, at least initially.

Finally, as we shall see in the next lecture, siege warfare was a specialty of the Assyrian army. All in all, then, the Assyrians fielded a complex and diverse army, but there is no clear agreement among modern commentators about how it functioned at the tactical level. In the longstanding tradition of the ancient Near East, the Assyrian Royal Records are bombastic exercises in self-aggrandizement, rather than strictly accurate historical records. There is little in them on how the army actually fought.

The Records follow the course of the king's annual campaigns in vivid and brutal language. For example, in the records of Ashurnasirpal II we read: "While I stayed in Aribua, I conquered the towns of Luhuti, defeating their inhabitants in many bloody battles. I destroyed them, tore down the walls, and burned the towns with fire; I caught the survivors and impaled them on stakes in front of their towns." Similarly, the records of Shalmaneser III, who ruled between 858 and 824 B.C., recount the great battle of Karkar, fought in 853 between the Assyrians and a coalition of Syrians led by the King of Damascus.

Shalmaneser records the huge army facing him, numbered at 40,000 infantry, 2,000 cavalry, and 4,000 chariots, all drawn from 12 kingdoms; and he continues, "They rose against me for a decisive battle. I fought with them with the support of the mighty forces of Ashur. I did inflict a great defeat upon them between the towns of Karkar and Gilzau. I slew 14,000 of their soldiers with the sword, descending upon them like Adad when he makes a rainstorm pour down. I spread their corpses everywhere, filling the entire plain with their widely scattered fleeing soldiers," and so on.

Battles are therefore routs and massacres rather than hard-fought contests, as cowardly enemies are crushed and their cities sacked. Specifics about what the Assyrian army was actually doing as battle proceeded are virtually non-existent. About the most detailed information we get on the course of a battle comes from the records of Sargon II, who ruled between 721 and 705 B.C. In his sixth campaign in 714, Sargon launched an attack into Armenia. In the process, he fought two kings there, Ursa the Armenian, and Metatti, of the polity called Zikirtu. These two renegades took up position in a mountain defile and sent a challenge via messenger to Sargon. After a difficult crossing of the mountains, Sargon's army approached. And, as the records put it:

> I was not afraid of his masses of troops, I despised his horses, I did not cast a glance at the multitude of his mail-clad warriors. With my single chariot and the horsemen who go at my side, who never leave me either in hostile or friendly region, I plunged into his midst like a swift javelin, I defeated him, I turned back his advance; I killed large numbers of his troops, the bodies of his warriors I cut down like millet, filling the mountain valleys with them. I made their blood run down the ravines and precipices like a river, I cut down their army and broke up their organization.

You get the picture. Remember this is about the most detailed account of fighting we have.

We can tell that Sargon attacked with cavalry alone. His infantry were too tired to participate, he tells us in a passage immediately before this. He himself rode in a chariot. But how, exactly, his horsemen broke up and defeated the enemy's army, packed densely into a defile, is not at all clear. "I plunged into his midst like a swift javelin" doesn't convey a heck of a lot.

The language of massacre and butchery does not leave us then much to work with in the Assyrian Royal Records. We get no indication of tactics, and little of strategy; no turning points are charted and no plans laid out and discussed. Instead, the Assyrians just slaughter their enemies like dogs. In this, the records stand in the august tradition of Sumer and Egypt.

The vagueness in the source material has left the tactical *modus operandi* of the Assyrian army an open question. There are three main proposals on the table. Each can be tested against both the written evidence and the reliefs.

The first is that the Assyrian army was primarily a chariot force, in the ancient tradition of Egypt and the Near East. The Assyrians were just particularly good at it. This, for instance, is the view of John Keegan in his 1993 book, *The History of Warfare*. To be sure, war chariots appear in the reliefs, and we've just seen Sargon riding his chariot into battle against the Armenians. The chariots are shown to get heavier and heavier over time, from rather light-looking, two-man vehicles in the 9th century to massive, four-man carriages with huge wheels in the 7th. But their role as the decisive tactical arm in the open field is far less clear. More on this in a minute.

The second proposition is that the Assyrian army was primarily an infantry force, in fact, it was the first true infantry army in history, and this accounts for its success. This is the view of Doyne Dawson in his book, *The First Armies*. This notion however is untenable in the face of the evidence. Our earliest sources from Sumer, as we saw in Lecture Three, depict well-ordered infantry. There is no reason to think that infantry were effectively a rabble until the Assyrians organized genuine units. However, there may have been something about the way the Assyrians used their infantry that is significant.

Which leads us to the third proposal: that the Assyrian army was the world's first integrated operational force, which deployed multiple specialist units in mutually supporting roles. This is Arther Ferrill's argument, in his book *The Origins of War*.

Of these three suggestions, the combined written and iconographic evidence of the release best supports the integrated-force view. We have already seen the great variety of troops the Assyrians had to hand: archers, slingers, heavy spearmen, light skirmishers, chariots, lancers, and horse archers. Surely this alone speaks to variety as the key to the success of the Assyrian army, rather than its reliance on one arm over all the others. But how did this army fight? How were the units coordinated?

Depictions of open-field battles are rare. A good example, however, is offered by the reliefs of the Battle of Til-Tuba, fought either in 663 or 653 B.C., in which king Ashurbanipal, who ruled from 668 to 627, defeated the Elamites of southwestern Iran under their defiant king, Teumman. Teumman had made the serious mistake of sending insulting letters to Ashurbanipal. The Assyrian king came after him and won a great victory at Til-Tuba, on the Ulai River. He celebrated this success with captioned reliefs on the walls of his royal palace at Nineveh. And these reliefs are now splendidly displayed in the British Museum in London.

The scenes show the Assyrians advancing from the right with archers, spearmen, chariots, and cavalrymen working in close concert. Infantry wield spears and very large shields; the cavalrymen have lances; four-man Assyrian chariots chase down primitive-looking Elamite war-carts. The Elamites are driven into the Ulai River, which is shown gorged with their bodies and the detritus of battle. Teumman's fate is traced in a series of scenes. And these scenes, by the way, have captions, almost like cartoon scenes, so that we know exactly what's happening. Teumman is chased in his war cart first. Then his cart crashes and he is hit in the back with an arrow. He flees on foot with his son, but then himself and his son are surrounded by Assyrian archers and infantry wielding spears, axes, and maces.

They are killed with maces and Teumman's head is cut off. The head is then transported to a tent full of captive Elamite nobles for identification, actually shown a series of heads. There's a pile of heads, and the nobles are shown looking, and Teumman's head, which has a very distinctive hairline, has been displayed to them. They're saying, "Yep, that's him." Then the head is taken off in a chariot to be displayed to Ashurbanipal.

Elsewhere, Teumman's son-in-law is shown wounded and begging an Assyrian officer for death. Again, that scene is actually captioned by such. The message of the reliefs is therefore very clear: not only are the Elamites crushed, but also the house of Teumman has been extirpated.

However, there is one interesting feature, noticeable also in the few other Assyrian depictions of open battle: the large-shielded spearmen work closely with archers, often in pairs. The archer takes cover behind the shield and fires, while the spearman wards off assailants or stabs fleeing enemies. Along with the initial charge of multiple types of units, this points to the sort of coordinated mutual support that characterizes integrated armies.

One caveat must be borne in mind, however. Like the Royal Records, there is an emphasis in the reliefs on the combat's aftermath, with the enemy fleeing and slaughtered, the Assyrians carrying away the loot while the scribes take notes, or individual soldiers rewarded for their confirmed kills by presenting officers and scribes with severed heads. They thus present battle as a rout and a massacre, the enemy already defeated and in flight. How the Assyrian army fought to reach this point, when the outcome was still in doubt, is not depicted directly. So we cannot be absolutely sure that what we are looking represents how the army was deployed before the battle and during the fighting.

I would argue, however, that since any ancient army's tactical cohesion would tend to break down as it pursued a broken and fleeing foe, any sign we do get of coordinated effort in these scenes only reinforces the idea of mutual support among the varied forces as the hallmark of the Assyrian tactical system.

I reiterate that we don't have a lot to go on, either in the Royal Records or in the reliefs. So this suggestion is tentative and open to revision. The Battle of Til-Tuba aside, war scenes in the reliefs are dominated by sieges, which we will examine in some detail in the next lecture. Some scholars have made the mistake of concluding from this fact that Assyrian warfare was conducted overwhelmingly as sieges. But the Royal Records are clear that battles in the open field were an essential part of the Assyrian army's activities. The predominance of sieges in the reliefs may be partly artistic, in that sieges, which have a fixed point of focus, are easier to depict than the more dispersed operations in the field. Perhaps, also, sieges were more prestigious; anyone could put a bunch of warriors into the field, but not everyone had the logistical, organizational, and technological know-how to prosecute a successful siege.

Finally, the propagandistic purpose of the reliefs ought not to be overlooked here. Think of a foreign embassy waiting in a hallway or in an antechamber for an audience with the King. What psychological effect, do you think, would scene after scene of towns assaulted, captured, looted, and destroyed have on them?

The images of the Royal Hunt may also reflect Assyrian military practices. Hunting and warfare shared a connection since the Paleolithic era. In such hunt scenes, we see archers and large-shielded spearmen acting in concert, precisely as depicted in the battle scenes. The hunts also have mounted archers, and chariots with crews armed with bows and spears. The hunt scenes, therefore, may well show us *how* the Assyrian army fought: spearmen and archers advanced in concert; mounted bowmen charged, wheeled, and fired; chariots massed in order to keep enemy formations within the optimal firing zone. Once the enemy broke, lancers and chariots charged in for the kill, and the spearmen likewise. Archers could pull their swords, or wield maces and axes to join the slaughter of the routed opponent. The whole machine acted with devastating efficiency, and coordinated its armaments to maximum effect.

The royal records offer one final contribution to this already impressive picture: the corps of engineers who built roads and bridges for the army as it moved through difficult terrain. Once more, this is a feature of fully integrated armies, acting on a military philosophy of specialist units working together to benefit the whole.

If this view is right, then the Assyrian army ought to take its place alongside the Macedonian army of Alexander the Great and the Roman Imperial legions as one of the most effective and sophisticated fighting forces of antiquity. And, what is more, the Assyrians were the first to deploy such a force. No wonder they forged the largest empire the ancient world had seen to that point.

A feature of the Royal Records that has long struck commentators is their reveling, not only in the violence of battle, but also in the most hideous cruelties inflicted on defeated rebels or particularly recalcitrant enemies. Clearly, a deliberate policy of what can only be termed terrorism was in effect. In the records of Ashurnasirpal, for instance, we read:

> Many captives from among them I burned with fire, and many I took as living captives. From some I cut off their hands and their fingers, from others I cut off their noses, their ears, and their fingers, of many I put out their eyes. I made one pillar of the living, and another of heads, and I bound their heads to posts around about the city. Their young men and maidens I burned in the fire and elsewhere I formed a pillar of the living and of heads over and against the city gate and 700 men I impaled on stakes over and against the city gate.

Scenes like this are confirmed in Assyrian art. We see people staked down, their tongues pulled out, and then flayed alive; severed heads heaped in piles; people having their hands and feet cut off, impaled on stakes; and trophy heads nailed to city walls. The plight of refugees is unflinchingly depicted: women and small children led off on carts and camels to exile and hard labor. In one particular scene from Nineveh, Chaldaean captives are shown being beaten and forced to grind the exhumed bones of their ancestors. The level of vindictiveness is startling: the destruction not only of living people, but of their past as well.

A common reaction to such vileness has been to declare the Assyrians inordinately cruel by nature. Such judgments are, in my opinion, utterly valueless as historical explanations. Given recent history, we moderns are hardly in a position to sit in judgment on the Assyrians and their cruelty. Warfare is always very unpleasant, and populations are often badly maltreated by soldiers. What really matters is whether the perpetrators are willing to talk about it or not. Usually, they are not. The Assyrians, in contrast, appear to have had no qualms about trumpeting the destructiveness of warfare and their violent treatment of captives. The question therefore is, why?

A more realistic approach is to interpret such actions as acts of psychological warfare. Potential enemies or rebels would take note, and embassies to the king in his palace would be confronted by a stark visual record of what happened to those who defied the will of the Assyrian king. It is noteworthy that harsh treatment was not normally meted out to the newly conquered, though they could be deported, but was reserved for rebels and insurgents. That is, people who had already accepted Assyrian suzerainty but then had had second thoughts and reneged. The atrocities were distinctly punitive in function and intent; they were not sadism for its own sake.

The psychological-warfare interpretation of Assyrian cruelty makes much more sense than mere moral condemnation, well earned though it may be. One scene from the Til-Tuba reliefs, I think, is extremely instructive. At the victory parade after the battle, ambassadors from the region of Urartu in modern Armenia, who are identifiable by their peculiar hats and clothing, and are in position of supplication, with their hands clasped in front of their chests and crouched down slightly, bowing before the king. These guys are being shown the insulting tablets that the Elamite king Teumman had sent to Ashurbanipal.

This foolish act, remember, initiated the war which had resulted in the destruction of Teumann's people and of his royal line. In a related scene, the same ambassadors are shown witnessing captives being flayed alive. They're staked out on the ground and guys are working on them with peelers. So while we may be repelled by such cruelty, there was a method in Assyrians savagery, and the Royal Records document its efficacy. Time and again, towns and even whole regions are said to have surrendered merely on hearing of the Assyrian army's approach. "I poured terror out over the land" is a phrase that we find in the royal records to describe the approach of the army. This generally marks the surrender of this whole region as soon as they hear that the Assyrians are coming. So people had good reason to be afraid I think. In the ancient Near East it seems terror was an effective instrument of policy. That seems to remain so unfortunately to this day.

The Assyrian Royal Records offer several reasons for wars, which allow us to discern the broad shape of imperial ideology. The reasons of religion are the most commonly offered. The king, as the representative of the gods Ashur and Marduk, is often impelled to war by faithless and dishonest enemies. The religious flavor of Assyrian campaigns is persistent: armies can be described as commanded directly by gods; armies are called "the people of Ashur" or "Ashur's hosts"—Ashur being the chief god of the Assyrians and also the chief city of the Assyrians. The king is the god's earthly representative. Many campaigns are presented almost as divine rescue missions, to punish oath-breaking enemies and restore dignity to their gods, often by transferring them to Assyrian cities, where they'll be properly treated.

However, the role of religion in justifying war *post hoc* is not the same as its role in causing it. The notion that the Assyrians fought crusades or jihads against their neighbors relies on too literal and uncritical a reading of their pronouncements. Other more temporal reasons are readily traceable in the record.

As we've already seen, Assyria's Late Bronze Age holdings were used to justify, at least initially, the neo-Assyrian conquests. In this way, all resistance could be classed as rebellion.

Another prominent motif is revenge for wrongs whether actual, ancestral, or perceived. Vengeance could be invoked to right actual wrongs, such as Teumman of Elam sending insulting tablets to Ashurbanipal; or because sovereignty had been claimed over a region, but then denied by its recalcitrant inhabitants; or against people having the insolence and temerity to reject a demand of submission. In all cases, the Assyrians present themselves as the wronged party, extracting by force what should have been theirs by right.

Economic motives for war shine through in the long and often minutely detailed lists of loot taken from conquered peoples, but these lists are never acknowledged as the causes of war; rather, they are presented as the natural results of success. Examples of these lists are numerous, repetitive, and rather tedious, but they can be quite extraordinary in their detail. I just want to give you a flavor of what they're like by this sample taken more or less at random from Sargon's 8th campaign:

> 1 ivory couch; a bed of silver, for the repose of his divine majesty, covered with jewels and gold; 139 ivory staves; ivory tables; ivory vegetable baskets; ivory daggers. 10 boxwood tables, house chairs made of boxwood, whose inlay is gold and silver.

On and on it goes, line after line. The loot had clearly been gathered, categorized, and then inventoried.

The likely, but unacknowledged, economic motive for warfare is reason enough to be cautious in accepting what the Assyrians themselves say about why they fought so many wars. In all eras, the prospect of loot has been a constant motive for war and aggression, if rarely acknowledged as such. Greed is not pretty, and best kept in the background.

Two passages in Sargon's records of his 8th campaign are particularly instructive for making out the Assyrian imperial worldview. The first concerns Sargon himself, who modestly proclaims: "I, Sargon, king of the four regions of the world, ruler of Assyria, who carefully observes the law of Shamash, of the stock of Ashur, city of learning, quick of wit, who waits reverently upon the word of the great gods, never violating their ordinances, the rightful king, whose words are gracious, whose abomination is falsehood, from whose mouth words bringing evil and harm do not emanate," and so on.

The second passage characterizes Ursa the Armenian in the following terms: "Ursa, the Armenian, who does not respect the word of Ashur and Marduk, who does not fear the curse of the lord of lords—a mountaineer, of murderous seed, who was without judgment, whose speech was evil, whose lips kept bawling indecencies, who had no respect for the honored name of Shamash, supreme judge of the gods, and who was forever, without let-up, overstepping his bounds."

So Sargon is pure of heart and intention, an educated and cultured man, at one with the gods whose loyal servant he is. His enemies are repugnant oath-breakers, lacking judgment and wits, and above all, disrespectful toward the gods. Thus, the Assyrian Empire represented the natural order of things on earth, the state of affairs desired by the gods and ordained from on high. It was an earthly reflection of the divine order of the cosmos. Consequently, those who opposed the empire could only represent the forces of chaos and disorder. They were heretics and rogues who wouldn't accept the gods' will.

In the end, the Assyrians overstretched themselves in Egypt. Other parts of the empire took the opportunity presented by Assyrian troubles there to revolt. After the reign of Ashurbanipal, a major coalition of enemies, both internal and external, finally overthrew Assyrian power and sacked Nineveh in 612 B.C. The name of Assyria passed from history, and its homeland returned to being a realm of shepherds and goatherds.

But their achievement in creating the world's first integrated fighting force was immense. To unite the Near East, it had been necessary to mete out horrific violence all around. And although the Assyrian empire, like all empires, finally crumbled, it showed what was possible and so set a precedent that would not be lost on future generations in the region.

Lecture Eight
The Sieges of Lachish and Jerusalem

Scope:

One aspect of warfare we have not closely examined thus far is sieges. The Assyrians, unlike any before them, were masters of this most demanding form of conflict. We examine first the background of ancient siege warfare, and then the Assyrian skill at it by considering two great sieges in the third campaign of Sennacherib (701 B.C.). The sources are particularly good for these events given that we have Assyrian written and iconographic records, the accounts in the Bible, and the evidence of archaeology to work with. The imposing Judean fortress of Lachish was a main target of Sennacherib's efforts in this campaign, as is reflected by the personal supervision of the siege by the king himself. So proud was he of his success at Lachish that he decorated a room of his palace at Nineveh with scenes from this battle. These scenes offer excellent evidence of the Assyrian army doing its deadly work. Meanwhile, Sennacherib's forces were also besieging the Judean capital of Jerusalem, described in passages of 2 Kings 18 and 19 and, to a lesser extent, 2 Chronicles 32. The Assyrian account of this conflict, naturally, differs considerably.

Outline

I. Before the Assyrians, the development of siege warfare in the ancient world is not terribly clear.

    A. The Neolithic sites of Jericho and Çatal Hüyük were clearly constructed with defense in mind, but that does not demonstrate that sieges were prosecuted against them at this early date.

        1. Sieges are complex procedures, demanding advanced planning, command and control, technical and technological know-how, significant manpower, and sophisticated logistics.

        2. There is little evidence that Neolithic chiefdoms or proto-states deployed such resources in warfare.

        3. The first cities in Mesopotamia also had impressive walls.

B. Evidence for early siege warfare is sparse. The best material comes from Egypt.

    1. The Predynastic Fortress Palette shows walled cities with towers apparently being attacked by animals (representing gods? kings? regions?).

    2. The tombs of Inti at Deshasheh and Kaemheset at Saqqara (both c. 2300 B.C.) show Asiatic cities assaulted by Egyptians.

    3. The tomb of Khety at Beni Hasan (c. 2000 B.C.) shows the first definite siege engine, a hut covering three men who wield a long pole and approach a besieged town.

    4. We have no comparable iconographic depictions from Mesopotamia until the Assyrian reliefs of the first millennium B.C.

II. Whatever its beginnings, the neo-Assyrians took siege warfare to a high level of competence.

    A. The principles of siegecraft are easily appreciated. Essentially, a siege can be conducted actively or passively.

        1. Active prosecution of a siege involves going over the walls (*escalade*) or going under or through them (*sapping* and *battering*). Gates, ever the weakest spots, are ideal targets for assault.

        2. Passive sieges involve investing a town and starving it out.

    B. Both siege methods are best employed in combination: A passive siege can be employed until such time as the attacker feels that the defenders are sufficiently weakened to succumb to an assault.

III. The sieges of Lachish and Jerusalem, both conducted by the Assyrian king Sennacherib during his third campaign (701 B.C.) to crush rebels within his empire, are particularly well attested and can serve as templates for the sophistication of Assyrian siege techniques.

    A. The siege of Lachish is attested by written evidence from Assyria, archaeological discoveries at the site, and the remarkable reliefs from Sennacherib's palace in Nineveh.

        1. Two copies of cuneiform tablets record Sennacherib's official version of events.

2. Although Lachish is not mentioned by name, it undoubtedly is among the "46 strong, walled cities" Sennacherib mentions as taking.

3. There are details that can be checked by excavation at the site, where much confirming evidence has been found.

4. Dramatic as the archaeological evidence is, perhaps even more so are the reliefs from Sennacherib's palace depicting this siege and the king's supervision of it. They reveal the intensity of the assault and its aftermath, with thousands of deportees led away to captivity.

B. The siege of Jerusalem is known mostly from Sennacherib's account and from that in the Bible.

1. Sennacherib's account is interestingly disingenuous. It gives the impression of subjecting Jerusalem to his power, but clearly, he did not take the city.

2. The Bible's account in 2 Kings 18 and 19 is rather different and gives a terrific insight into an otherwise unattested aspect of Assyrian siegecraft: psychological warfare.

3. The level of sophistication in psychological warfare displayed by the Assyrians is remarkable. They used the carrot and stick in their communications with the defenders of the city: Come out to a comfortable deportation or resist and suffer.

4. What followed in this darkest of hours, of course, was divine intervention.

5. There are several possibilities to explain what happened, but both the Assyrian and biblical accounts are clear that Jerusalem was not taken.

C. From all this evidence, we may piece together a composite picture of Assyrian siege techniques.

1. A camp was set up within sight of the target city.

2. Envoys threatened and cajoled the defenders to give up, using their native language.

3. Passive siege techniques were employed to keep the defenders within the zone of operations.

4. When circumstances were right, active siege techniques were employed.

5. The Assyrians had a broad array of special assault methods and equipment at their disposal: specially trained assault troops who could climb ladders armed; sappers; siege engines, sometimes prefabricated; and missile troops.
6. Overall, the Assyrians had achieved a degree of mastery in siege warfare that was to be unparalleled until Hellenistic and Roman times.
7. Armed with these methods and given the complexity of their military system overall, it is little wonder that the Assyrians conquered the whole of the Near East.

Essential Reading:

Kern, *Ancient Siege Warfare*, pp. 1–85.

Ussishkin, *The Conquest of Lachish*.

Yadin, *The Art of Warfare in Biblical Lands*, pp. 291–328.

Supplemental Reading:

Gabriel and Boose, *The Great Battles of Antiquity*, pp. 90–120.

Oded, *Mass Deportations*.

Questions to Consider:

1. What best explains the extreme violence meted out to Assyria's enemies? What examples can you locate in the Royal Records? Was such violence necessary in forging the world's first true empire?

2. In what ways was siegecraft an essential buttress of empire in the ancient world? Why do you think the Assyrians were so good at it?

Lecture Eight—Transcript
The Sieges of Lachish and Jerusalem

We've had occasions already to mention the art of siege warfare. But the time has come now to devote our attention to it in more detail. The matter has been delayed up to this point, since the first well documented besiegers of ancient world were the Assyrians, whose impressive war machine we reviewed in the previous lecture. But, for all that army's formidable capabilities in the open field, it is true to say that without effective siegecraft, the Assyrians could not have built the empire they did. In fact, the ability to deny your enemy a safe haven was instrumental in building an empire. If they can simply hide behind their walls, you won't get far in dominating them. So siege warfare was a cornerstone of ancient imperialism, and all the great ancient empires were experts at it. In this respect, the Assyrians too were pioneers.

In this lecture, we first survey the siege warfare prior to the rise of the Assyrians, and then illustrate Assyrian capabilities by looking at two particularly clear examples, both of which were prosecuted in the same year: the sieges of Lachish and Jerusalem in 701 B.C. First, however, we turn to pre-Assyrian siegecraft.

The development of siege warfare prior to the emergence of the Assyrians is a little indistinct. Simple fortifications such as those at Jericho in Israel, or Çatal Hüyük and Yalangach in Turkey, were clearly constructed with a defense in mind, but that alone does not demonstrate that organized sieges were prosecuted against them at this very early date. By their nature, sieges are complex procedures, demanding advanced planning, command and control, technical and technological know-how, significant manpower, and sophisticated logistics. There is little hard evidence that Neolithic chiefdoms or proto-states marshaled such resources in fighting their wars.

The walls of Yalangach in Turkey, dating to around 5000 B.C., have round towers that face outwards—a sure sign that they the occupants feared attack. This is because projecting towers serve as firing platforms to enfilade adjacent walls; that is, to fire along the lengths of the walls at the attackers. But the methods employed by those attackers remain unknown to us.

Following the same line of reasoning, it is significant that the first cities in Mesopotamia also had impressive walls. Those at Early

Dynastic Ur for instance, are excellent examples. The walls were made from sun-dried mud-bricks, and were up to 100 feet thick. Since the ratio of thickness to height had to be either 3:1 or 3:2 for such simple mud-brick walls to retain their stability, the walls stood anywhere between 30 and 60 feet high. Ur's walls were also built in independently standing modules, so that if one section collapsed, it did not bring down the entire length with it. They also had balconies and projecting towers, which allowed defenders to drop weights on attackers and to enfilade the curtain wall respectively.

It is not unreasonable to deduce from these facts that the Sumerians of the Early Dynastic era expected their attackers to bring some skill to bear in sieges, or else such elaborate fortifications would not have been necessary.

On the whole, direct evidence for early siege techniques is sparse. The best material comes from Egypt. As we saw in Lecture Four, the Predynastic Fortress, or Cities Palette, of around 3100 B.C., shows walled cities with towers apparently being attacked by animals. The animals representing gods, kings, or possibly regions. The animals wield compass-like tools that seem to penetrate the walls. Does this suggest the use of battering rams, as some had suggested? The evidently metaphorical and symbolic representation, however, makes so literal an interpretation of these images rather dubious.

Far clearer is a fresco from the Old Kingdom Tomb of Inti at Deshasheh in Egypt, which dates to around 2300 B.C. Here, an Asiatic city's walls are presented from a bird's eye perspective. The walls are shown to have projecting round towers, designed for defense. Inside the city, various desperate scenes unfold: defenders kill each other and, possibly, their families; a family beseeches the statue of a god. The reason for their desperation is shown outside the walls, where Egyptian troops battle Asiatics with bows and epsilon axes, while soldiers push ladders against the wall under covering fire from archers. In one corner, Egyptian troops equipped with poles bore into the corner of the wall. The near-contemporary Tomb of Kaemheset at Saqqara shows an interesting variation: a rather precarious-looking ladder on wheels, the first tenth of a step toward siege engines.

A little later, the Middle Kingdom tomb of Khety at Beni Hasan, dating to around 2000 B.C., shows the first definite siege engine, which is little more than a hut covering three men who wield a long pole to poke at the wall of a besieged town. Unfortunately, we have no comparable iconographic depictions from Mesopotamia or, indeed, anywhere, until the fabulous Assyrian reliefs of the first millennium B.C.

There is, therefore, no way to know for sure if the sorts of techniques shown in these Egyptian sources were used also in the Sumerian or Akkadian eras. It scarcely seems credible, however, that rulers with imperial ambitions would make no efforts to improve siege techniques. Some scholars suggest, in fact, that advances in the art of siege warfare are what allowed Sargon of Akkad to conquer the whole region of Sumeria at the end of the 3rd millennium B.C. It is a reasonable and plausible proposition. But, thus far, direct evidence from Akkadian times is lacking to confirm the hypothesis.

Whatever about its beginnings, there is no doubt that the Neo-Assyrians took siege warfare to a new level of effectiveness. The principles of siegecraft are easily summarized. A siege can be conducted either actively or passively. Active prosecution involves going over the walls with ladders, called escalade, or going under or through them by sapping or battering. Sapping involves either tunneling underneath the walls, and so undermining them that they collapse, or boring into the lower reaches of a wall overground, which also induces collapse. Battering is a little less subtle; one smashes into a fortification by brute force. Gates, being effectively prefabricated holes in the wall, are the juiciest targets for assault. But they are also, of course, particularly well defended.

All of these methods, however, are difficult and costly in lives and resources. Ladders, for instance, have to be exactly the right height: too high and the ladder can be easily pushed away by defenders on the walls; too low and the attackers are sitting ducks. And sapping, particularly mining, requires impressive technical skill: too deep and the sapping tunnel is rendered useless; too shallow and there is a risk of premature collapse. In all cases, of course, the attackers have to get close to the wall, usually under fire from above. So large scale shielding is also demanded if the besieger wishes to avoid the massacre of his force. All in all, prosecuting active sieges is a difficult and risky business, and requires pretty advanced levels of engineering skill to pull off successfully.

Passive methods involve sealing a town off from the outside world, and then waiting for the inhabitants to starve and suffer to the point of surrender. This is often termed "investing" a town. In the ancient Near Eastern sources we read of blockades enforced by chariotry and cavalry, or by the more laborious means of circumvallation, which means walling in the besieged by building a circuit of fortifications around them. Such techniques require extreme patience, and great order and discipline on the part of the besieger. Passive sieges can drag on for a long time, depending on the resources available to the besieged. The passive besieger must be prepared to wait it out, all the while keeping a substantial force in the field, fed and equipped.

Passive and active methods are best employed in combination. A place can be invested passively until such a time as the attacker feels that the defenders are sufficiently weakened to succumb to an assault.

And since assault is so much more interesting a visual subject than starving defenders and waiting attackers, it is hardly surprising that we only see active sieges in the ancient iconography, such as the Egyptian tomb paintings just surveyed. But that passive sieges took place is quite clear from the written evidence, which records sieges that last for weeks, months, or even years.

Now to the sieges of Lachish and Jerusalem. In 701 B.C., the Assyrian King Sennacherib's third campaign saw him descend into Palestine to crush a nest of rebels who had formed a regional alliance with Egypt. Among these rebels was King Hezekiah of Judah, with his royal seat at Jerusalem. The northern kingdom of Israel had been taken over by the Assyrians in 722 B.C., and Judah was now a quasi-independent state.

After defeating an allied army in the field, Sennacherib personally oversaw the siege of the fortress at Lachish, and sent subordinates to deal with Jerusalem. These two sieges are particularly well attested, and so can serve as templates for the sophistication of Assyrian siege techniques.

The siege of Lachish is attested by written evidence from Assyria, archaeological discoveries at the site itself, and the remarkable reliefs carved onto the walls of Sennacherib's palace in Nineveh. Two cuneiform tablets record Sennarherib's official version of events. The Taylor Prism, now in the British Museum, and the Oriental

Institute Prism in Chicago, both dated to about 690 B.C., record the same course of events. Sennacherib, we are told, made his way into Judah via Syria and Phonecia—roughly modern Lebanon—winning many victories and accepting many offers of submission. He then turned south to Ashkelon and captured it after a siege.

Next, hearing that Hezekiah had deposed one of his puppet kings in the region, Sennacherib headed further south. A field battle was fought with allied Egyptian rebels—but no details about that battle, of course, provided—that led to the puppet being reinstated. Then Sennacherib turned on, as he himself says in his records:

> Hezekiah, the Jew, who did not submit to my yoke. Forty-six of his strong, walled cities, as well as the small cities in their neighborhood, which were without number—by escalade and by bringing up siege engines, by attacking and storming on foot, by mines, tunnels and breaches—I besieged and took those. Two hundred thousand-one hundred fifty people, great and small, male and female, horses, mules, asses, camels, cattle and sheep, without number, I brought away from them and counted as spoil.

Although Lachish is not mentioned by name in this particular summation, it undoubtedly was among the 46 strong, walled cities of Hezekiah's that Sennacherib took. The real value of the report lies in the recorded siege methods mentioned: assault, escalade, bringing up siege engines, and sapping. These are details that can be checked by excavation at the site, where much confirming evidence has been found.

Lachish was second only to Jerusalem in the strength of its fortifications. It would therefore be a natural target for Sennacherib, indeed an essential one to demonstrate the futility of resistance to Assyrian arms. Excavations show that 8th-century Lachish stood atop a plateau, with massive walls and a glacis, towers and bastions, a heavily defended gatehouse, and a fortified redoubt astride the city's highest point inside. It was a formidable place to assault.

Excavations turned up major evidence of the Assyrian siege in Level III at the site, the archaeological stratum corresponding to the date of Sennacherib's visit. The single most impressive feature was a siege ramp discovered near the gatehouse in the Southwest corner of the fortress. The oldest known siege ramp, it was a complex structure, a conglomerate of stones and mortar piled on top of a solid base of boulders. The ramp allowed Assyrian siege engines to gain access to the wall. Inside, Level III is marked by burned mud-bricks from the upper reaches of the walls at Lachish.

Hundreds of Assyrian-style arrowheads were found in this layer, some still embedded between the fallen and burnt mud-bricks. Slingshots of flint were found in profusion around the gatehouse. Slingers were especially useful for sieges, since their shots flew in a straight trajectory at the defenders; and, as we shall see, we know for a fact that the Assyrians used slingers at Lachish. Scales from Assyrian armor and the crest of an Assyrian auxiliary's helmet were also found. By way of a footnote, I would just ask you to compare all of that evidence with the scant and meager evidence at Troy for similar sieges.

Skeletons and valuables were not found in the city. This would conform to the Assyrian standard practice of burying the dead, deporting the survivors, and looting captured towns before burning them. But three nearby caves yielded the remains of 1,500 people: men, women, and children. The skeletons were disarticulated, and some were burned.

Dramatic as this archaeological evidence is, perhaps even more so are the reliefs from Sennacherib's palace at Nineveh, which in fact depict the siege and the king's supervision of it. The Palace of Sennacherib at Nineveh, which the today is located near Mosul in northern Iraq, was crudely excavated between 1846 and 1851 by Austen Henry Layard. Layard unearthed 71 halls with relief decoration, much of which was cut out and shipped back to England. These reliefs today are displayed in the British Museum in London, and among them are the Lachish reliefs.

The reliefs, which are labeled as depicting Lachish, show the Assyrians approaching under covering fire from slingers and archers. These troops are ethnically distinguished, as usual, by their styles of dress and their headgear. Siege ramps are clearly shown, thrown up against the wall on both sides of the gatehouse. Log tracks are embedded into the upper surfaces of these ramps, and up these lanes move no less than seven siege engines. The engines are prefabricated in sections, and so were brought to Lachish rather than built on site.

The engines, of a single design with raised fronts, spoke wheels, and projecting rams, work away at the walls and the gatehouse as two archers shoot out from their roofs. Behind the rams advance ranks of archers and spearmen, crouched behind huge wicker shields. The scale in the images is not uniform, so it is difficult to gauge the size of the engines, but they must have had a crew of at least five: two archers, two ram operators, and a water-pourer—more about the water-pourer in a second.

The attackers operate under a hail of projectiles hurled from the walls: stones, cartwheels, shields, a broken ladder, and a welter of burning torches. And this is where the water-pourer comes in, because the Assyrian rams have a water ladle projecting out front which douses the ram and the front of the engine to counter these torches. Corpses of defenders tumble from the walls. The reliefs starkly, and in a very powerful fashion, convey the intensity of the assault.

There are all sorts of convergences between these scenes and the finds at the site itself. The reliefs seem to show a concentrated effort by the Assyrians at one part of the wall only, in the area around the gatehouse. This corresponds with the topography of the site, where the natural plateau is at its lowest near the gatehouse, and where access was easiest. And it is exactly this spot that the siege ramp was found by the archaeologists. As already noted, slingshots, arrowheads, lanceheads, the crest of a helmet, scaled armor—all are shown in the reliefs and all were found at the site.

One scholar has proposed that the reliefs can be read as a sort of cinematic portrayal of the actual events of the siege, and were based on royal artists' drawings made in the field. But it is not at all obvious how much concern there really was at Nineveh for precision in depicting events that had transpired so far away. The reliefs themselves give cause for pause. Lachish looks very like any of the towns and cities depicted in Assyrian art, including Nineveh itself. It has crenellated curtain walls, projecting square towers, gates, and so forth. The soldiers involved in the siege are portrayed in stock style and in stock positions: slingers whirling their slings, archers crouching and firing, spearmen cowering for cover behind huge wicker siege shields. And the siege engines likewise are in stock positions against the wall. More worryingly, only one ramp was found at the site, while two appear in the reliefs, converging from opposite sides of the gatehouse. Despite the towers on the reliefs, there is no evidence for projecting towers at the site of Lachish itself.

All in all, in my view, rather than striving for rigorous accuracy, it seems much more likely that the Assyrian sculptors worked off a stock set of images that denoted "Us Besieging a City," and then tweaked those images, possibly by gleaning details from eye-witnesses, or court records, or even, as suggested, from field artists. In this way, they could customize their stable of familiar stock images to suit a particular locale. This would readily explain why certain details fit but others do not.

The reliefs are unsparing in showing the aftermath of the siege. Emerging from the gatehouse are women and children carrying their belongings. This scene and the siege operations are shown in the same frame, but they must have occurred in sequence; civilians would not tramp dejectedly through a raging battle. Soldiers are shown taking loot to Sennacherib, who sits in state outside his royal lodge in front of the Assyrian camp; but the camp as well is very, very closely and carefully shown: crossroads in the middle and projecting towers and so on. Jewish envoys beg and plead and prostrate themselves at Sennacherib's feet. Elsewhere, less fortunate prisoners are impaled on stakes, have their throats cut, or are staked out in preparation for flaying alive.

In a remarkable scene, deportees, on carts and camels, the small children and the adolescents carefully depicted, are led away to captivity. These are some of the 200,150 unfortunates Sennacherib boasts of deporting from the region. Deportation, by the way, was a policy favored by the Assyrians, since it mingled conquered populations and, as a consequence, undermined their solidarity and so their ability to resist. The task of dominating them was made all the more easy by this act.

The Lachish reliefs, and others, show that the Assyrians had no qualms about showing the drastic human costs of this policy. The scenes of deportees are often marked by what we might call small, human moments: a mother giving her child a drink under guard; or starved-looking oxen, their ribs protruding, pulling a cart with toddlers and teenagers sitting atop their meager belongings.

The ultimate fate of at least a portion of the deportees from Lachish does not appear to have been an easy one. Another relief sequence from Sennacherib's palace at Nineveh depicts the carving and transportation of a colossal stone winged bull, from quarry to palace. Hauling away at the ropes, while being ordered about and cudgeled by overseers, are a party of workers wearing precisely the same headgear as the defenders and deportees from Lachish. Just as the Assyrian reliefs distinguish between different ethnic units in their army by these means, so do they also among their captives. Hard labor for the King of the four corners of the universe was the destiny of many.

The siege of Jerusalem is known mostly from Sennacherib's account and from that in the Bible. Sennacherib's account is interestingly disingenuous. It gives the impression of subjecting Jerusalem to his power but, clearly, he did not take the city. As the Records have it: "As for Hezekiah, the Jew, like a caged bird I shut him up in Jerusalem, his royal city. Earthworks I threw up against him— anyone coming out of his city gate, I turned back to his misery." There is then talk of other cities subdued in the region. And then we read, "As for Hezekiah, the terrifying splendor of my majesty overcame him, and the Urbi and his mercenary troops, which he had brought in to strengthen Jerusalem, his royal city, deserted him." Then we hear that Hezekiah offers tribute of 30 talents of gold, 800 of silver, various other valuables, his daughters, harem, and court musicians, all of whom are then taken to Nineveh. And Sennacherib ends his account with saying, "To pay tribute and to accept servitude he dispatched his messengers."

Sennacherib, then, never claims to have taken Jerusalem by assault, the way he does the 46 strong, walled cities elsewhere. He does say that he subjected Jerusalem to a blockade and shut up Hezekiah inside. By shifting focus at crucial moments in the account and emphasizing what appears to have been a buy-out by Hezekiah at the end, Sennacherib leaves the impression of success for what was obviously an abandoned siege.

Now the Biblical account of these events is rather different. It also gives a terrific insight into an otherwise loosely aspect of Assyrian siege-craft: psychological warfare.

The fullest account is in 2 Kings 18,19. The narrative, like Sennacherib's Royal Records, describes Sennacherib's descent into Judah, and his taking many cities there. Hezekiah sends an apology and an offer to buy Sennacherib's withdrawal. Hezekiah then sends much loot to Sennacherib, who is stated to be at Lachish. The amount of gold in this shipment, 30 talents, exactly matches that in the Assyrian account. But the amount of silver in the Bible, 300 talents, is less than half the 800 recorded in Sennacherib's version; and there is no mention in the Biblical version of Hezekiah's daughters, harem, and court musicians going off to Nineveh. I suppose we couldn't really expect that, given the context.

Two points are worth stressing at this point. First, the Biblical account locates Sennacherib at Lachish when Hezekiah's offer is made. This corroborates the reliefs from Nineveh, a pleasing and very rare instance where separate strands of ancient evidence confirm each other independently. Clearly, Lachish was the most important siege of this campaign, as the king supervised it personally, and chose it as the subject worthy of permanent commemoration in his royal palace.

Second, in contrast to Sennacherib's account, Hezekiah hands over the loot before the siege of Jerusalem even begins. In the Bible, this is not a buy-out that settles the dispute at the end and sends Sennacherib away, and that's how it is presented in the Assyrian version. Rather, in the Bible, it's an example of Sennacherib's perfidy. Having taken the loot, he then sends an army against Jerusalem anyway, under the generals identified as the Tartan, the Rabsaris, and the Rabshakeh. This army camps outside Jerusalem.

This is where things get really interesting. The Rabshakeh addresses the defenders, and does so in Hebrew. He asks them what exactly they think they're doing. What makes them think they can win? Do they trust Egypt, "that broken reed of a staff, which will pierce the hand of any man who leans on it," as the Bible says? Or, goes on the Rabshakeh, are they relying on their god? But hasn't Hezekiah removed the altars and high places in the country to leave only the temple of Jerusalem as the place of worship? Hezekiah is weak, states the Rabshakeh, who can't even field 2,000 cavalrymen without Egyptian help. In any case, the Assyrians are the instruments of the Jewish god, sent by him to destroy Jerusalem.

Hezekiah's courtiers, standing on the wall, interrupt at this point and ask would the Rabshakeh mind speaking in Aramaic, which they, as educated men, can understand; the Hebrew is comprehensible to the common defenders. This request suggests that the Rabshakeh's propaganda was having an effect. The Assyrian response is not terribly encouraging: "Has my master sent me to speak these words to your master and to you, and not to the men sitting on the wall, who are doomed with you to eat their own dung and to drink their own urine?" He then appeals directly to the defenders to abandon Hezekiah, for he has deceived them. They cannot stand against Assyria. "Come out," he says, "and you'll enjoy a comfortable resettlement in a land like your own. They ought not to trust in your god to save them. What use were their gods to those already crushed underfoot by Sennacherib?" At this point, Hezekiah's representatives, in great distress and with their clothes rent, report the Assyrian's words to the Jewish king. More clothes are rent and a general despair descends.

This is astonishing stuff. The level of sophistication in psychological warfare displayed by the Assyrians in this fascinating passage is just remarkable: they have senior officers who speak the local language; in mentioning Hezekiah's suppression of rural high places, they appear to have specific intelligence about local politics; and they make use of both the carrot and the stick in their communications with the defenders: come out to a comfortable deportation—of course, there's no mention of hauling huge stone bulls around—or resist and eat dung.

If Sennacherib's account is believed, it may have been at this point that some of Hezekiah's hired or else allied defenders deserted him. But if so, it finds no mention of 2 Kings, which is, again, hardly surprising. But the Bible is unequivocal that the Rabshakeh's words had a very disheartening effect on Hezekiah and his court, and probably on the common defenders. Amid the renting of clothes and the wearing of sackcloth, we read: "Thus says Hezekiah: This day is a day of distress, of rebuke, and of disgrace; children have come to the birth, and there is no strength to bring them forth."

What follows in this darkest of hours, of course, is a well-timed divine intervention. Through the prophet Isaiah, God assures Hezekiah that deliverance is at hand and that Sennacherib will die violently, as indeed he did twenty years later, but he was murdered in a palace coup. After a threatening letter arrives from Sennacherib, who has now said to have moved on from Lachish to a place called Libnah, Hezekiah prays to God and his prayer is answered, as follows:

Therefore thus says the Lord concerning the king of Assyria, 'He shall not come into this city or shoot an arrow there, or come before it with a shield or cast up a siege mound against it. By the way that he came, by the same he shall return, and he shall not come into this city, says the Lord. For I will defend this city to save it, for my own sake and for the sake of my servant David.' And that night the angel of the Lord went forth, and slew a 185,000 in the camp of the Assyrians; and when men arose early in the morning, behold, these were all dead bodies. Then Sennacherib king of Assyria departed, and went home, and dwelt at Nineveh.

Now, one can take that account as read if one wishes, but there are several more reasonable possibilities to explain what happened. Elsewhere God says of Sennacherib through Isaiah: "Behold, I will put a spirit in him, so that he shall hear a rumor and return to his own land." This seems rather more plausible than the angel of the Lord and 185,000 corpses. Perhaps Sennacherib heard of unrest at home, and broke off his campaign prematurely. Certainly internal unrest was a perennial problem for the Assyrian state.

Another possibility is that a plague struck the Assyrians, who had to withdraw as a result. The plague was the angel of the Lord, since the ancients often interpreted epidemics in divine terms. Or perhaps there was a buy-out; the two accounts agree that this happened, but diverge on the crucial issue of timing. In the end, what really induced the Assyrians to withdraw, we shall probably never know. But both accounts are in perfect accord on one essential matter: Sennacherib, indeed, did not set foot in Jerusalem.

From all this detailed evidence, we are in a position now to piece together a composite picture of Assyrian siege techniques. The army arrived and set up an organized camp, with palisades, projecting towers, gates, and internal roadways. The camp would lie within sight of the targeted city. Next, envoys threatened and cajoled the defenders, preferably in their own language, to give up. Passive siege techniques were used to restrict the defenders to the zone of operations. When circumstances were right, active methods came into play. In this regard, the Assyrians owned an impressive toolbox, with a broad array of special assault methods and equipment at their disposal. Slingers and archers protected by massive wicker shields covered the assault teams. Sappers worked on the lower walls or mined underground, while siege engines, sometimes prefabricated, worked away at the gates and towers. It was an all-out effort. The Assyrians came over, under, and through the walls of their enemies, apparently all at once.

It is fair to say that the Assyrians achieved a degree of mastery in siege warfare that was to be unparalleled until Hellenistic and Roman times. Armed with these methods, and given the complexity of their military system overall, it is little wonder that they conquered the entire Near East and, for the first time, united it under a single ruler.

At about the same time that Sennacherib was busy in Judah, the art of warfare in the Balkan Peninsula was taking an unusual turn. So it is to Greece, and the peculiarities of hoplite battle, that we next turn our attention.

Lecture Nine
A Peculiar Institution? Hoplite Warfare

Scope:

The Greek *hoplite* was a heavily armed and armored infantryman who fought in a formation called the *phalanx* and who dominated the battlefields of the ancient world for almost four centuries (c. 700–338 B.C.). Two controversies swirl around hoplite warfare: (1) its origins or, indeed, whether it had origins at all and (2) the nature of the fighting in phalanx battles. The first two parts of the lecture, therefore, lay out the various positions of scholars on these two controversial topics. In the final section, we examine the notion of a peculiarly "Western way of war" that had evolved in Greece prior to the Persian Wars (490, 480–79 B.C.), which were to demonstrate the effectiveness of hoplites against the armed forces of the most powerful nation on earth at the time. In particular, the standard view about the peculiar nature of hoplite warfare is assessed.

Outline

I. The question of a "hoplite reform" in Archaic Greece has been hotly debated for decades and remains so today.

    A. Older views deduced that a revolution in Greek fighting techniques had occurred in the decades around 700 B.C., and debate focused on its nature and sociopolitical ramifications.

        1. The hoplite's panoply was centered on a large round shield; he also wore a bronze helmet and breastplate and carried a thrusting spear and short sword.

        2. Hoplites fought in a tight formation called a *phalanx*, arrayed into ranks and files, usually eight deep.

        3. Two views prevailed about how this new system of fighting emerged: sudden change and gradual change.

        4. Both agreed that the system had a major sociopolitical impact on Greeks.

        5. Arguments about the hoplite shield are emblematic of this controversy.

        6. The sociopolitical consequences of this change in fighting were also debated.

B. Recent opinion is more diverse; there is no consensus on all sorts of issues.

    1. An influential view today is that a hoplite phalanx is identifiable in Homer; thus, given that we have Homeric hoplites, there was no hoplite revolution at all.

    2. Another view revitalizes and extends the gradualist position, disengages hoplite equipment from the phalanx, and redates Homer to the 7th century B.C.

    3. A third view revives the sudden change position and recouples the connection between hoplite equipment and the phalanx; the process was over by 675 B.C.

    4. In all this, the sociopolitical consequences of hoplite battle have been reconsidered.

    5. All in all, the issue of the hoplite reform remains largely unsettled. In some quarters, it was a sudden process; in others, a slow process; and in the opinion of others, it never took place at all.

II. Whatever its origins, the hoplite phalanx appears to have been the predominant form of fighting in Greece by 600 B.C. (perhaps somewhat earlier, depending on one's point of view). What was hoplite battle like?

    A. The standard view stresses the ritualized nature and physical intensity of hoplite warfare.

        1. Warfare was another arena for conducting the *agon* ("struggle") among Greek males. Hoplite warfare was heavily ritualized.

        2. Their form of warfare seems to fit this agonistic pattern, only on an interstate rather than an interpersonal level.

        3. The course of the actual fighting, in this view, was marked by intense, close-ordered combat and by the mass push (*othismos*) to force the enemy to yield.

    B. The standard view has its critics, and their objections are not slight.

        1. The arguments are technical and detailed; two are outlined as exemplars.

            a. The very notion of a mass physical push is inherently implausible; othismos can refer to various types of fighting.

        b. Greek hoplites engaged in weapons play; their battles were not affairs of dense, scrimmage-like shoving between packed masses of men.

    2. The critics offer their own versions of hoplite battle, not all of them mutually compatible.

III. Greek warfare in the Archaic and Classical periods is widely held to have been the sole preserve of hoplite infantry armies, a peculiar institution that can be designated as a truly unique "Western way of war." Some serious questions hang over the details of this view, however.

  A. The standard view insists on several unique features of Greek battle.

    1. There was an exclusive reliance on heavy infantry.

    2. Hoplite warfare placed a premium on direct frontal assault. This limited the damage done by war but created fearsome contests on the battlefield.

    3. From this raw material, the Greeks constructed a model of warfare that, for the first time in history, made the pitched battle the only valued form of engagement.

    4. These features are unique to Greece and are not found in other cultures' modes of fighting.

    5. Finally, this Greek way of war is a legacy we are living with in today's military culture in the West.

    6. This view, therefore, represents hoplite warfare as a peculiar institution, a unique development of Greek conditions that casts its shadow down to the present.

  B. Despite its attractive simplicity, the standard model has some severe weaknesses.

    1. Some of the main problems we shall review at the end of the course; here, it is sufficient to note the issue of evidence.

    2. The standard model is undermined by a very serious problem: the lack of contemporary sources for Archaic battles.

    3. Some of the main sources cited to support the standard model are ambiguous in their applicability.

    4. These difficulties with the evidence make the standard model much more questionable than it is often presented.

Essential Reading:

Hanson, *The Western Way of War*.

Sage, *Warfare in Ancient Greece*, pp. 18–35 for some (but by no means all) ancient literary evidence.

Van Wees, *Greek Warfare*, pp. 115–197.

Supplemental Reading:

Goldsworthy, "The *Othismos*, Myths and Heresies."

Van Wees, *War and Violence in Ancient Greece*, especially pp. 125–232.

Questions to Consider:

1. If forced to choose, which of the various positions on the hoplite reform would you nominate as the most convincing? Why? What particular pieces of evidence are decisive in determining your decision?

2. Is the standard model of the Western way of war as invented by the Greeks convincing? If so, why? If not, why not?

Lecture Nine—Transcript
A Peculiar Institution? Hoplite Warfare

For this and the next seven lectures we turn our attention to what has been a growth area in ancient military studies in recent decades: Greek warfare. Many clashes are ongoing in this dynamic scholarly battlefield, but three concern us in this lecture: first, the transition to hoplite mode of warfare in the 8th and 7th centuries B.C.; then, the mechanics of hoplite battle; and finally, the proposition that classical Greek warfare displays unique characteristics that stand at the root of a peculiarly western way of war.

We saw in Lecture Six that the Homeric epics are thought in many quarters to portray a distinct style of combat that was practiced up to about 700 B.C. After that date a new warrior appeared on the Greek battlefield. He was called *hoplites*—"hoplite" in English—after the Greek word *hopla*, which means "equipment" or "tools." So "hoplite" denotes something like "the man in gear," or "the equipped man."

The defining feature of the hoplite's equipment was his shield. It was termed an *aspis*, rather than a *hoplon*, as is sometimes wrongly asserted in books. The hoplite shield was round and concave, usually about one-meter in diameter, and was made of heavy wood, rimmed and sometimes faced with bronze, and it was carried in a very special way. Earlier shields, such as those carried by Homer's heroes, had a central handgrip or were slung over the shoulder with straps. The hoplite, however, put his arm through a hoop at the shield's center, called the *porpax,* and gripped a handle at the rim, called the *antilabe*. So the shield's weight, up to 20 pounds if it was faced entirely in bronze, was borne by the forearm, rather than by the wrist or by the shoulders.

Hoplites wore bronze helmets, the most popular being the fearsome-looking "Corinthian" type, which completely enclosed the head, and allowed sight and breathing only through a narrow T-shaped opening on the front. A man wearing such a helmet had his hearing and peripheral vision greatly impaired. Bronze or, later, linen corselets encased the hoplite's chest, back, and abdomen, and greaves protected his shins below the knee.

Other pieces of armor could be applied to the forearms, ankles, and feet, and sometimes a leather blanket was suspended from the shield

But these were optional features, since the hoplite really provided his own equipment, and so much depended on how much he could afford to buy.

The hoplite's main offensive weapon was a stabbing spear, about eight feet long and equipped with an iron head at the business end, if you like, and a bronze spike at the other end. A short sword was carried as a secondary weapon.

Hoplites fought in a tight formation called a *phalanx*, which seems derived from the Greek for "log." In the phalanx, the men were arrayed in ranks that ran laterally down the length of the phalanx, and files, which ran from front-to-back. The phalanx was normally eight ranks deep, but the number of files would depend on how many men were available for muster.

It is immediately obvious that a phalanx of heavy infantrymen stands in stark contrast to the sort of open-order fighting characteristic of the Homer battlefield, or that's shown on the Dipylon pots from Athens, dated to about 750 to 725 B.C. The Dipylon warriors, it will be remembered, were armed with javelins, spears, swords, and bows, and used chariots, from which they apparently dismounted to fight on foot. Their distinctive shields resemble apple cores in silhouette and bear no resemblance to the heavy, concave, and round hoplite shield. Models of Dipylon shields show that they were carried with a central handgrip, or were strapped over the shoulders. Indeed, the equipment of the Dipylon warriors is largely consonant with a supposed "Homeric" mode of combat, marked by high mobility and plenty of missile action.

Yet by 650 B.C., a pot in the Corinthian style, the so-called Chigi Vase found in an Etruscan burial in Italy, shows hoplite warriors, with their distinctive double-grip shields, bronze breastplates, greaves, and head-encasing helmets. They seem arrayed in the tight phalanx, at least so far as a pot-painter can depict such a formation. Clearly, Greek combat methods had changed between the Dipylon pots and the Chigi vase. How had this happened? And why?

Until quite recently, two views dominated the debate. The first was the "gradualist" position. It saw hoplite equipment adopted piecemeal over a protracted period. There was evidence of a transitional stage between full Homeric and full hoplite warfare. Thus, for instance, the Spartan poet Tyrtaios, writing around 650 to

625 B.C., mentions archers and stone throwers intermingled with armor warriors in tight formation, a thing unheard of in the fully developed hoplite phalanx. Archaeology offered clues as well. A panoply from a burial at Argos, dated to about 720 B.C., comprised a bronze breastplate and a rather Assyrian-looking conical helmet. Unfortunately, no shield was found to clinch the identification of the warrior as a hoplite; the equipment could equally be that of a bronze-clad Homeric *promachos*, or "fighter up front."

Other finds of armor, unfortunately, are less useful. It was customary to dedicate suits of armor to the gods at sanctuaries like the one at Olympia. These dedications could so clutter the place that they were occasionally gathered up and dumped. But while useful in preserving much Greek armor, such deposits present us with a jumble of elements from different eras, all thrown together into a single pit. This limits the conclusions that can be drawn from them about warfare in particular periods. Nevertheless, the physical evidence, claimed the people who support the gradual view, generally supported a piecemeal transition to hoplites spanning perhaps 150 years or more, and ending by about 600 B.C.

The second view took precisely the opposite tack: the emergence of hoplites was sudden, spanning perhaps 50 or, at most, 75 years, between about 725 and 650 B.C. The first date represents the last depictions of Dipylon warriors, and the second represents the appearance of hoplites on the Chigi Vase. Once the hoplite phalanx made its appearance, goes this line of argument, everyone either had to adopt the new techniques rapidly or face defeat on the field of battle. Therefore, this form of fighting appeared and spread quickly throughout mainland Greece, with formation and equipment arriving more or less concurrently.

Arguments about the double-grip of the hoplite shield are emblematic of how this debate played out. The proponents of a "sudden change" pointed out that this shield—heavy, difficult to maneuver, lacking a shoulder strap, and gripped in such a way that its left half offered little or no protection to its wielder—such a shield was not suited to the hit-and-run tactics of the Homeric or Dipylon open-cast battlefield. Hoplites, in fact, jettisoned their shields when taking flight, since it was such an encumbrance. So why would a Homeric-style fighter pay for an expensive piece of equipment if it could get him killed or had to be thrown away when he decided to retreat from the front? No, the hoplite shield was inherently linked to the massed formation of the phalanx, since the apparently useless left half would cover the right side of the neighboring hoplite in the phalanx. All this implies that shield and phalanx showed up more or less at once, and that we are dealing with a sudden revolution in military methods, not a gradual transition.

The "gradualists" responded that the hoplite shield was far more maneuverable than the limited imaginations of the "sudden-changers" allowed. They pointed out that routed soldiers are not in the same situation as soldiers moving about in an open-order form of combat, and, they also said, similar double-grips are found in some Roman and Medieval shields, where they did not require a phalanx to be useful. There was therefore no inherent link between the double-grip shield and the phalanx, and the transition therefore did not have to be a sudden one.

In general, major sociopolitical changes were also ongoing in Greek city-states at this same period, between about 750 and 650 B.C. For instance, there was a shift away from monarchies to oligarchies, or ruled by a few, backed by popular assemblies of adult male citizens. And in some places, revolutions brought forth strongmen termed "tyrants," who seized power by force. We would call them, I suppose, "military dictators" today. Scholars have long wondered whether there was a connection between these sorts of developments and the contemporary transformation of Greek military techniques. Everyone was agreed that the phalanx implied a greater general wealth among the Greeks, since now small farmers could afford the sort of expensive equipment that had previously been the preserve of the Homeric *promachoi*.

One suggestion was that the appearance of tyrants at this time was directly tied to the emergence of the new "hoplite class," so called, here exercising their political muscle at the expense of formerly dominant aristocrats. Marxist historians offered a very different view. Hoplite warfare was nothing other than a grand scheme by an expanding elite to exclude those who could not afford the expensive hoplite equipment from the prestige and influence of military service. The adoption of hoplite warfare was thus a form of class warfare, aimed not at undermining aristocratic privilege, but at protecting it in times of change. And so the debate rolled on—detailed, technical, wide-ranging, and multifaceted.

Recent opinion however is much more diverse. As we saw in Lecture Six, an influential view today is that massed-rank warfare is already identifiable in Homer. In fact, goes this argument, Homeric massed-rank combat is nothing other than the hoplite phalanx. So there was no hoplite reform as such, since there was no definite Homeric style of combat to reform in the first place. And naturally, there can have been no sociopolitical consequences for something that did not happen.

The greatest weakness of this position we have already seen in Lecture Six. Namely, it generalizes massed-rank action depicted by Homer as occasional rallies of hard-pressed troops into the standard hoplite formation of the phalanx, which was adopted on entering battle and sustained throughout the fighting. This is not at all how Homeric battles actually play out.

Another position, championed by Hans van Wees, agrees that hoplites are identifiable in Homer, but only up to a point. Homeric warriors are not fully developed hoplites, but transitional prototypes. There is no mention, for instance, in Homer, of the double-grip shield in Homer. The Chigi Vase portrays not a full a hoplite phalanx, but a transitional one. The warriors carry javelins, for instance, as well as a stabbing spear, and that fully developed hoplite did not use javelins. This echoes other 7th century evidence, such as Tyrtaios who, as we just saw, has archers and stone throwers mingled into the ranks. So the process of transition to the fully-fledged phalanx was not complete even by mid-to-late 7th century B.C.

Since Homer's battle descriptions are consistent with so much 7th century evidence, Van Wees then takes the next logical step and redates Homer himself to the 7th century. Accepting this view allows a hoplite reform of sorts, but now the nature of pre-hoplite warfare becomes very indistinct, since a later Homer already describes a transitional form of hoplite battle.

Victor Davis Hanson takes a different position still. He insists that the sudden-change view is more or less correct, and that on the basis of military considerations, the shield and other elements of the hoplite equipment require the existence of a phalanx. On this model, proto-phalanxes in Homer were elaborated into full phalanxes in the period around 750 to 675 B.C., as more and more small farmers became prosperous enough to join the battle line. The full hoplite panoply rapidly appeared to fit this new tactical situation.

In all of this, the sociopolitical consequences of the changeover to hoplite battle have been radically reconsidered. A common view today, in fact, is that the appearance of hoplites reflected rather than caused the political and social changes that were already underway in Greek states for entirely non-military reasons, perhaps linked, for instance, to changing patterns of land ownership.

In sum, then, the issue of the "Hoplite Reform," despite decades of scholarly debate, remains today very unsettled. Some hold it to have been a sudden process, others a slow process, and some question whether it ever took place at all. What is clear, however, is that by 600 B.C., a phalanx of heavily armored hoplites was the standard mode of land combat across mainland Greece. The nature of such engagements is the next topic for our consideration.

What was hoplite battle like? The dominant view today stresses the ritualized nature and physical intensity of hoplite warfare. To an extent, all battle is ritualized, in the sense that rules, spoken or unspoken, give cultural structure and meaning to battles. These rules will usually be gleaned from the wider context within which soldiers live, as well as fight and die.

In the case of the Greeks, battle has been tied to the culture of competition that prevailed among Greek males, and is often termed the *agon*, or the "struggle" or "competition." The *agon* is most clearly found in the periodic athletic competitions at places like Olympia, Nemea, and Delphi, to which all Greek states sent representatives. These festivals usually superseded warfare. Truces were declared to allow champions, who were also often impressive warriors as well, to pass through hostile territory unharmed en route to the festival. The *agon* pervaded the Greek male ethos, and warfare ranks alongside the athletic festival, popular assembly, or the courts as just another arena for its prosecution.

This approach shapes the views or the interpretations of what actually happened when phalanxes collided. The Greek sources, it must be said, are laconic on these details, presumably because they assume most of the readers would know what happened in a phalanx battle, as many of them would have experienced it. Now, about the fullest account of hoplite combat that we get is from Xenophon and his description of the battle of Coronea in 394 B.C. between the Spartans and the Thebans. The Spartans, writes Xenophon, "crashed into the Theban army head-on, and as they threw shield against shield they pushed, they fought, they killed, they died." Other sources speak of a huge noise and spears shattering, and men exhorted to stand their ground and not yield an inch. The emphasis is on holding the line, keeping cohesion, and pushing.

Now, the standard view of hoplite battle mechanics takes such statements as literally descriptive. Greek hoplites advanced shoulder-to-shoulder in close-ordered formation and crashed into each other head-on in this same formation. Then they sought, quite literally, to shove their opponents off the field, all the while stabbing with their spears. Since hoplites were well armored and carried large shields, most wounds were incurred in the throat or in the groin; that is to say, above the shield or under it. Victory was achieved by a push, termed *othismos* in Greek, which saw the opposing phalanxes heaving against each other, trying to shove the enemy backwards. When one side succumbed to the intense pressure of shoving and ran, the battle was over.

This model neatly explains why phalanxes were eight ranks or more deep. The rear ranks added their weight—literally their physical weight—to the push of the *othismos*, shoving with their shields into the backs of the men in front of them. Further, as the winning phalanx rolled over fallen enemy hoplites, the rear ranks would stab downward with the bronze butt-spikes of their spears to finish off the wounded, hence the reason for the butt-spikes.

These unusual battle conditions are also invoked to explain why Greek hoplite values shunned individual displays of bravery and emphasized collective effort, steadfastness, and maintaining formation. This model is immensely popular today, and is now often cited as established fact in general works on ancient warfare.

But it has its critics. The arguments are technical and detailed, and I outline a few here as exemplars. Eight ranks of men, standing shoulder-to-shoulder and pushing with all their might against an opposing eight ranks of men, who are also pushing with all their might, is, to put it mildly, a little implausible. How could the front ranks retain their footing, let alone use their weapons in such a scenario? Would not the front ranks be pushed upwards, into a sort of human pyramid?

References to such things as the clash of shields, the shattering of spears, the great noise of impact, or the closeness of opponents do not require mass scrimmaging of the type required by the standard view. These things will occur quite naturally when large bodies of armored men collide on the battlefield. Such allusions also have the advantage of echoing Homer, the Greek warrior's holy bible.

Further, the appearance of the word *othismos* in ancient Greek battle narratives does not necessitate a physical mass shove by opposing ranks of densely packed hoplites. It may denote individual acts of pushing with shields to topple opponents over, rather than a mass joint shove; and we know that the word *othismos* was used figuratively in Greek, as it is today, in the sense of "to push the enemy back" or "the big push is coming." Greek authors use *othismos* in reference to the cut and thrust of rhetorical argument, where clearly a mass physical shove is out of the question.

Ancient depictions of hoplites in battle, mostly in painted parts, do not support the standard view. We do not see mass shoving or densely packed men. What we do see are men fighting with spears and swords, their shields held out at an angle in front of them. Further, most Greek battle narratives are noticeably vague in their terminology, and cannot be used to support the singular picture of Greek warfare proffered by the standard view.

A classic example is Thucydides' comment that a phalanx moving into battle generally edges to the right, since each man thinks, as one modern translation has it, "that the more closely the shields are locked together, the safer he will be." So as the man on the extreme right shies his exposed side away from the enemy, he drags the whole phalanx with him.

This comment seems to offer unequivocal support for the standard view: we have shields locked together for protection and density of formation. But problems emerge under closer scrutiny. First, Thucydides says that this formation was adopted on the advance, not necessarily when battle was actually joined. Indeed, things usually get very unclear once the fighting starts, and we can expect formations to begin to fall apart rather rapidly as the confusion of battle spreads. Second, Thucydides' wording is actually much vaguer than the translation cited above suggests. Translated literally, the phrase says, "that the men edge to the right," "thinking that the denser their closeness is, the better protected they are." There is no mention of locked shields in the Greek at all. Other questions then arise from this wording. What is meant exactly by "the denser their closeness is?" What did "close" mean to the Greek hoplite, anyway? We can't say, since Thucydides assumes a basic knowledge of hoplite battle conditions that we do not possess.

As I say, these are only some examples of the sort of objections to the standard view, but there are many others that seriously undermine the notion of agonistic, ritualized, massed-shoving of densely packed ranks. In its stead, critics offer their own versions of hoplite battle, not all of them mutually compatible. Some favor phases: that is to say a close-ordered advance and impact; then open-order weapons play; then, once more, close-ordered shoving at the end to end the contest. But how were such phases orchestrated? How did the hoplites know when to open up and when to close up again? Greek sources are consistent in stressing the indispensability of maintaining cohesion in the face of the enemy. Would not a mistimed opening of the ranks invite instant defeat? On the basis of considerations like these, the phased battle model has very few supporters.

Another suggestion is that hoplite battle was generally more open-ordered than is usually envisioned, though less so than the supposed Homeric style of warfare. Hoplites did not stand shoulder-to-shoulder literally, but rather up to six feet apart, as later Roman legionaries were to do. This allowed the wielding of weapons for which we know Greek hoplites trained individually. Other features of hoplite engagements, such as the shift from an over arm to an underarm spear grip, the removal of dead and wounded comrades from the front, can be accommodated in this model, but they do not fit neatly within the standard view of the tightly-packed shove. In tight spots, the formation might indeed close up, but this was not a predetermined phase; it was a reaction to immediate threats.

On this model, the object of hoplite battle was not to push the enemy off the field with a mass shove, but rather to fight one's way into the opposing formation and break it up. The function of the rearward ranks then was not to shove, but to stiffen resistance against such attempted infiltration. The greater the number of ranks an opponent had to fight his way through, the greater psychological disadvantage he fought at. Contrary to widespread opinion, individual hoplites were praised for displays of bravery. The battle narratives of Herodotus, for instance, consistently end by naming men who had earned particular kudos for their battlefield exploits. Although to be fair, the Greeks, in this instance, were fighting non-hoplite Persian armies.

To be sure, open-order battle is the minority view among Greek military historians today. But, it seems to me, it has a lot more going for it, and is a lot more plausible, and is supported by the ancient evidence better than the strange business of ritualized shoving proposed by the standard scenario.

Finally, we turn to the equally widespread notion that the Greeks invented a peculiarly western way of war, the main features of which were as follows. First, with hoplites, the Greeks relied exclusively on heavy infantry to decide their battles. Down to the Peloponnesian War, fought between 431 and 404 B.C., they disdained light-armed infantry, cavalry, chariots, archers, and other missile troops. They relied wholly on a clash of hoplites to get a result.

Next, hoplite warfare was conducted face-to-face, at close quarters and "openly," insofar as deceit, ambushes, ruses, and the like were eschewed. The fight had to be as clean as it was brutal for a genuine winner to emerge. This is consonant with the wider Greek ethos of the *agon*. That hoplites were small farmers who did not want to be away from their land for long periods meant everyone involved had a vested interest in reaching a decision as quickly as possible. So there emerged a unique emphasis on the quick, decisive engagement in the open field. Hoplite warfare was limited to these brief periods of intense brutality. Rather than aiming at wholesale conquest, or the subjugation and incorporation of the losers' territory, warfare was merely a way of settling a dispute.

From this raw material, goes the argument, the Greeks developed a model of warfare that, for the first time in history, made the decisive, pitched battle the only valued form of engagement. This view insists that decisive battle was not a major concern among Egyptians or among Near Easterners, who laid greater emphasis on deceit, ambush, outflanking and encircling maneuvers, and winning without a fight. Near Eastern armies were also made up of conscript peasantry serving a despot, very unlike the Greek hoplite, who was a free smallholder, a citizen with a stake in his polity, and a voluntary member of a citizen militia. Greek hoplite-citizens voted themselves into battle; Asiatic peasant-conscripts were whipped to the front on the orders of a despot.

This peculiar institution of hoplite battle is held to stand at the root of a western way of war that continues down to this day. Westerners seek out the enemy and want to defeat him in an honest fight where the maximum force is brought to bear in a decisive, brutal engagement. Other cultures often seek to avoid battle altogether, or place a premium on ambushes or ruses in their military practice, such is the view.

This model however, which is immensely popular today, has, in my opinion, very severe deficiencies. In the first place, we've seen that decisive battles were prized, even sought after, by Egyptians, Asiatics, Hittites, and Assyrians. Settling disputes in full-on engagements was not a Greek invention. More troubling still is the matter of the evidence used to support the "western way of war" model.

The Greek devotion to hoplite-only battles is said to pertain to the Archaic era of Greek history, that stretching roughly from 700 to 500 B.C. Yet most of our evidence for what Greek battles were like comes from the later Classical period, from writers like Thucydides writing in the 5th century, or Xenophon in the fourth, or from even later writers, such as Polybius, writing in the 2nd century B.C. In these later eras, the use of archers, missile troops, light-armed infantry, and cavalry units was standard practice in Greek warfare. For the supposedly hoplite-only period prior to the 5th century, we have only scraps and allusions, and not a single complete description of a contemporary battle.

This is a huge problem for the standard model, since it is forced then to operate, essentially, in an evidence vacuum which it fills in with bits and pieces of later testimony, derived from ages which, on the whole, do not conform to the hoplite-only model. It is therefore a worrisome degree of selectivity in the presentation of the standard model.

Let me illustrate the point. Two passages are often cited in support of the standard model for Archaic Greek warfare. One is a passage in Herodotus, where the Persian general Mardonios informs his king, Xerxes:

Besides, from all I hear, the Greeks usually wage war in an extremely stupid fashion, because they're ignorant and incompetent. When they declare war on one another, they seek out the best, most level piece of land, and that's where they go and fight. The upshot is that the victors leave the battlefield with massive losses, not to mention the losers, who are completely wiped out. What they should do, since they all speak the same language, is make use of heralds and messengers to settle their differences, since anything would be preferable to fighting. If they had absolutely no choice but to go to war, they should find a battleground where it is particularly hard for either side to defeat the other and fight it out there.

This passage offers apparently terrific support for the standard model, from the agonistic mode of Greek warfare right down to the Eastern aversion to head-on battle and seeking victory without a fight. But context is vital here. This is not Herodotus laying out the raw facts. Rather, this is an opinion voiced by a leading Persian courtier on the eve of the great Persian invasion of Greece in 480 B.C.

Now Mardonius was to command the Persian forces at the Battle of Plataea at the end of that invasion, as we shall see in Lecture Twelve. Given that Mardonius lost both the fight and his life at Plataea, there must be a suspicion of irony, perhaps even parody in the presentation of his opinion here: Mardonius is going to be defeated and, indeed, killed by the very system of warfare he is here denigrating, and which, it seems to me, he grossly distorts. He goes on to say, "the Greeks go about things in the wrong way." I, for one, can imagine Herodotus' Greek audience laughing at the barbarian's foolish judgment, a judgment they knew would cost him his life at the hands of a mode of combat he clearly did not understand.

As if that weren't enough, Herodotus has another Persian courtier, named Artabanus, speak immediately after Mardonius. Artabanus warns the king not to underestimate the Greeks. He specifically brands Mardonius' portrayal of Greek warfare foolish and misleading. Given this context, it seems to me highly dubious to invoke Mardonius' opinion as hard evidence for hundreds of years of Greek military practice.

Another passage, this time in Polybius, writing in the 2nd century B.C., has also had much heavy lifting asked of it. Writes Polybius:

> The ancients chose not to conquer their enemies by deception, regarding no success as brilliant or secure unless they crushed their adversaries' spirit in open battle. For this reason they agreed with each other not to use hidden missiles or those discharged from a distance against each other, and they considered only a hand-to-hand, pitched battle to be truly decisive. Therefore they declared wars and battles in advance, announcing when and where they were going to deploy. But now they say only a poor general does anything openly in war.

Once more, this seems to offer corroboration for the standard model. There is a rejection of deception and the use of missile troops on principle, and a commitment to open, pitched battles at close quarters as the only valued mode of engagement.

But, once again, can we take the passage at face value? Does it not have a distinct whiff of nostalgia about it? Would we accept uncritically other statements about how much more honorable things were in the good old days? In any case, precisely who were "the ancients" to Polybius' way of thinking? When were they around? Do we know for sure that he had the mainland Greeks of the Archaic Age in mind when he wrote those words? The standard model is really far more problematic than it is often presented.

Having acquainted ourselves then with these generalities, it is now time to turn to specific engagements. We begin with an imperiled Athens, fighting for her life against the largest empire the world had seen to date.

Lecture Ten
The Battle of Marathon

Scope:

Our first task is to establish the context of this historic and important confrontation. The rise of the Persian Empire, the Ionian revolt (499–494 B.C.), and the determination of Darius, Great King of Persia, to punish the Athenian involvement in the revolt form the backdrop to the battle. These events are briefly surveyed, as are the intentions of the Persians in striking against Athens: Were they aiming at a surgical, punitive strike, or did they want to establish a permanent foothold in Greece? Next, the ancient accounts of the battle, the main source being Herodotus, are summarized and their numerous interpretive difficulties outlined. Despite these problems, the importance of the battle is in no way diminished. Marathon saw Athens defended in the first major confrontation between Greek and Persian on the Hellenic mainland, and the forces of the Persian superpower were vanquished. Despite producing such a decisive result, the battle actually decided little in the geopolitical sphere and merely set the stage for the second, far more serious clash of Greek and Persian arms a decade later, which we will discuss in our next lecture.

Outline

I. Persian expansion to the shores of the Aegean provides the broad context for the Battle of Marathon, and the Ionian revolt of 499–494 B.C. is the immediate background to it.

    A. The collapse of the Assyrian Empire in the late 7th century allowed the Persians to forge the largest land empire yet seen.

        1. The Persians have left us very little written information; most of their history has to be reconstructed from archaeology and the evidence of their enemies, the Greeks.

        2. The Assyrians had been laid low by a league of enemies, among them the Medes, one of whose vassal states was Persia.

3. The Persians overthrew their Media masters, and Cyrus the Great (r. c. 559–530 B.C.) became the king of Persia and Media.

4. Cyrus and his successors expanded the Persian realm in all directions, forging the largest land empire yet seen.

5. The conquered Greek city-states in what is called Ionia were controlled by the installation of pro-Persian tyrants, answerable to a Persian governor.

6. The Persian Empire was a huge, unified polity under the command of the Great King. The Persian army was an efficient and formidable fighting machine.

7. It is not exactly clear how this army functioned tactically in the field.

B. In 499 B.C., the Ionian Greeks rebelled against Persian rule. Only two mainland Greek states answered the Ionian call for help—and with grave consequences for themselves.

1. The causes and course of the Ionian revolt need not delay us.

2. As help, Athens sent 20 ships and Eretria sent 5. The Athenians participated in the burning of the Persian satrapal seat at Sardis.

3. After five major battles, four of which were won by the Persians, the revolt ended in defeat for the Ionians in 494 B.C.

4. In 490 B.C., Darius sent an expedition against Athens and Eretria; whether his motives were entirely punitive or whether he entertained wider ambitions of conquest is unclear.

5. The Persian force sailed across the Aegean, destroyed Eretria, and headed to Athens.

II. After destroying Eretria, the Persians landed in Attica at Marathon, where they were opposed by a force of Athenian hoplites. Stunningly, the outnumbered Athenians won.

A. The sources for the battle are confused, but the outline of its course is clear enough.

1. Our main source is Herodotus, but he can be supplemented by some other writers.

2. When Eretria fell and the Persians were moving to Marathon, the Athenians sent for help to Sparta but received only cold comfort.
3. At Athens, the hoplite army under Miltiades marched out to meet the Persians, who had landed at Marathon.
4. The Athenians took up station at a sanctuary (*temenos*) of Herakles and were there joined by a small contingent of hoplites from the allied town of Plataea.
5. There followed a stand-off while the Athenian generals debated what to do.
6. Under Miltiades's command, the Athenians charged the Persian force and battle was joined.
   B. The problems with this account are many.
   1. Herodotus is perfunctory with details.
   2. Topographical details are unclear.
   3. Aspects of our ancient accounts are confusing or contradictory.
   4. There are puzzling aspects to both Persian and Athenian behavior as reported, such as why the Persians waited for the Athenians to attack, why the Athenians did not attack sooner, and why, during combat, the Persian breakthrough in the center did not secure a Persian victory.

III. None of these problems diminishes the importance of Marathon in the history of Greece. Yet the battle itself was strategically indecisive in that it left Persians with unfinished business in the Greek peninsula.

A. The aftermath of the battle saw the withdrawal of the Persians.
1. After a lackluster attempt to take the city of Athens by stealth, the defeated Persians withdrew.
2. The Spartans arrived.
3. The Athenian dead were cremated and entombed on the battlefield, a signal honor in Greek times.
4. Miltiades became a hero, but his success was short-lived.
5. The battle took on legendary proportions within decades.

B. The importance of Marathon has to be seen in the right perspective.

1. It demonstrated, in shocking fashion, the effectiveness of hoplite phalanxes against Persian arms.
2. In terms of tactical decision, the outcome was nothing less than sensational.
3. Too much should not be made of how this great victory was achieved, however.
4. If we take a historical long view, the battle's outcome was of immense importance.
5. Strategically, however, Marathon decided very little.

Essential Reading:

Herodotus, *The Histories*, Book 6.

Nepos, *Miltiades*.

Pausanias, *Guide to Greece*, 1.32.

Green, *The Greco-Persian Wars*, pp. 3–40.

Lazenby, *The Defence of Greece*, pp. 1–80.

Lloyd, *Marathon: The Crucial Battle That Created Western Democracy.*

Supplemental Reading:

Gabriel and Boose, *The Great Battles of Antiquity*, pp. 138–150.

Hammond, "The Campaign and Battle of Marathon."

Raaflaub and Rosenstein, *War and Society*, pp. 105–128.

Questions to Consider:

1. Was the clash of Greek and Persian arms on the Greek mainland inevitable? If so, why?
2. Do the problems with the sources make incomprehensible this battle's course? Outline the five most likely outcomes that, in your view, would have followed a Persian victory.

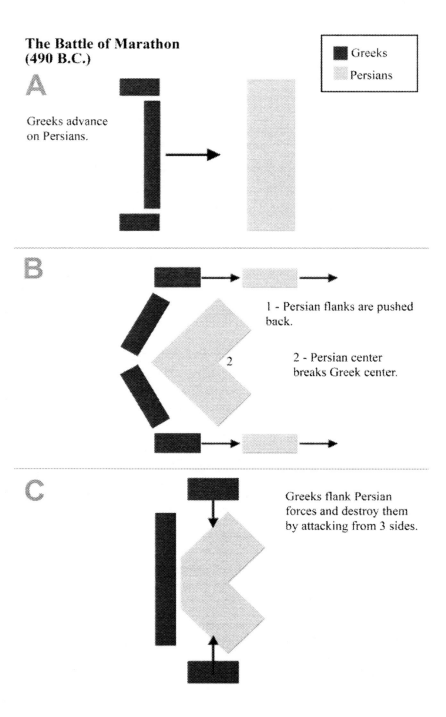

The Battle of Marathon (490 B.C.)

A — Greeks advance on Persians.

Legend: Greeks, Persians

B
1 - Persian flanks are pushed back.
2 - Persian center breaks Greek center.

C
Greeks flank Persian forces and destroy them by attacking from 3 sides.

Lecture Ten—Transcript
The Battle of Marathon

Now that we are familiar with the broad shape of hoplite warfare and the scholarly debates that swirl around it, we turn to consider the hoplite in action. The occasion is the first Persian expedition to Greece, for which some background on the Persian Empire and the reason for the expedition will be necessary.

The Persians have left us very little written information, so most of their history has to be reconstructed from archaeology and the testimony of their enemies, the Greeks. Around 700 B.C., the Persians had formed a kingdom in Iran under king Achaemenes. This Achaemenid kingdom, as it's often called, joined with their neighbors, the Medes, to lay the Assyrians low in 612 B.C. But when the Medes became embroiled in a conflict with Babylon, the Persians saw an opportunity.

Under King Cyrus, who ruled from 559 to 530 B.C., they struck out on their own and built an empire. Note that our Greek sources used the term "Medes" and "Persians" interchangeably, so closely were the two peoples associated in at least the Greek imagination.

Cyrus and his successors expanded the Persian realm in all directions, forging the largest land empire yet seen, embracing the Near East and Egypt, and abutting the Russian steppe and the plains of northern India. Cyrus also incorporated many Greek city-states and islands along the Aegean coast of Asia Minor, in the area that's generally called "Ionia." We are told that when the Spartans sent a delegation to reprimand Cyrus for this, Cyrus asked, "Who on earth are the Spartans?" His successors would soon find out.

The Persian philosophy of governance was to use local systems that best served their interests. In Ionia, the Persians established tyrannies favorable to themselves in the Greek city-states, who were then accountable to a Persian governor, termed a *satrap*, stationed in the royal city of Sardis in western Turkey. Vassal kingdoms acknowledged Persian overlordship by offering symbols of submission: earth and water.

The Persian Empire represents the pinnacle of ancient Near Eastern political sophistication, the inheritor of millennia of established practice that centered on the absolute rule of the Great King. Given the immensity of the empire, the Persian royal army was suitably gargantuan. While Greek sources speak exaggeratedly of armies in the region of 800,000 or more, royal musters of over 100,000 are not implausible for so vast a realm.

Persian armies were levied locally under orders from the king and organized around *myriads*, or units of 1,000. We read of contingents of 10,000, and subdivisions at the level of 100 and of 10. Persian infantry was light and largely unarmored, equipped with a wicker shield, a composite bow, a spear, and a short sword. Cavalry units derived from the richer Persian classes and also used bows, javelins, spears, and, it seems, wore impressively ornate clothing. Chariots were largely obsolete by now and don't appear to have been a mainstay of Persian arms, though they did survive in one strange form that we look at a bit later.

Elite units were centered on the king, such as the royal guardsmen called "The Immortals", who were always maintained at a full strength of 10,000; and several cavalry units organized as *myriads* of 1,000 each who were termed "the Kinsmen", meaning the kinsmen of the king.

A variety of ethnic groups also contributed units, dressed and equipped in their own peculiar fashion. The Persians continued then the Assyrian practice in this respect, and were similarly excellent besiegers, a fact that also reflects also a strength in engineering. The only armament lacking was heavy infantry. This deficit was to prove costly on the plain of Marathon in 490 B.C.

The dearth of Persian sources makes deducing the tactical system of this army difficult. Working from rather vague Greek accounts of their behavior in battle, and from what we know of their equipment, a plausible model can be constructed more or less as follows. As the enemy advanced or stood some way off, they found themselves showered by arrows shot from the Persian infantry, who were arrayed behind a wall of large wicker shields called *spara*.

As casualties mounted and the enemy formations wavered or broke, the infantry, predominantly Persians, teamed up with fearsome fighters from modern Turkmenistan called the Sacae, closed with spear and sword. Meanwhile, the Persian cavalry, stationed on the flanks of the infantry line, attempted encirclement around the enemy's flanks. The cavalry was also used then to chase down broken and fleeing foes.

Up to Marathon, Persian armies had been immensely successful in quite varied types of terrain and against diverse foes, including the Ionian Greeks, who, in 499 B.C., rose in revolt against their Persian overlords. This event marks the immediate backdrop for the battle of Marathon.

The causes and course of the Ionian revolt need not delay us. What matters is that, as the revolt spread, an appeal was sent to the Greek mainland for assistance against the "barbarian." For ancient Greeks, by the way, anyone who was not a Greek was a *barbaros*, since foreign languages sounded so crude in comparison to the lilting mellifluence of Greek. Greeks heard foreign languages as sounding like "bar, bar, bar, bar."

This aid, when it arrived for the rebels, was not terribly impressive. Only two city-states responded: Athens sent twenty ships, and Eretria five. The Athenian contingent joined the rebels in a drive against the satrapal seat at Sardis, which was sacked and burned. The temple of the Great Mother Goddess, Cybele, was destroyed in this action.

After five major battles, four of them won by the Persians. The revolt ended in defeat for the Ionians in 494 B.C. It is important to note that the Persians had little difficulty winning against Greek armies in pitched battles during this revolt, and their only defeat, in fact, was an ambush at night. In one of these battles, the Athenian contingent was wiped out, after which Athens refused any further aid to the rebels. But the damage had been done. The Persian king, Darius, was enraged at mainland involvement in the revolt. It is reported that he enlisted a slave to remind him three times at every dinner, "Master, remember the Athenians."

Darius' rage is not unfathomable. Earlier, in 513 B.C., Athenian ambassadors had been sent to Sardis to seek Persian aid in the face of a threat from Sparta. In an unfortunate move, these ambassadors had, on their own initiative, pledged to yield earth and water. The Persians would have interpreted this as a pledge of submission, even if the promised earth and water never actually showed up. Yet now, Darius learnt, these same Athenians had helped burn his Royal provincial capital at Sardis, and with it, a temple to a major goddess.

As we saw with the Assyrians in previous lectures, Near Easterners took a dim view of oath-breakers and breeches of fealty. So the Persian expedition to Greece in 490 B.C. was probably punitive in intent and purpose, very much as Herodotus presents it. Then again, in strategic terms, it might have been desirable to conquer the Greek mainland entirely, since full security among Persia's Ionian subjects could not be assured while the Balkan Peninsula remained outside Persian control. In 492 B.C., a Persian expedition to Macedon had floundered and withdrawn, and in 491 envoys were sent around Greece demanding earth and water. Some scholars insist from these facts that a full-fledged invasion was now afoot.

While the dominant intent of Darius' expedition is thus a little clear, the motives of punishment and conquest, it seems to me, are not at all mutually exclusive. A chastened Athens could also serve as a useful beachhead for future operations in Greece. I would not rule out both motives as underlying Persian designs in 490 B.C.

Under their generals Datis and Artaphrenes, the Persians, numbering perhaps 24,000 foot and 1,000 or more horse, set out for Greece directly across the Aegean. Many Greek states, terrified, capitulated without argument or, to use the Greek term, they "medized," a Greek verb meaning, "to go Mede." The Athenians, however, killed the Persian envoys sent to them by hurling them into a place ominously called "The Pit," while the Spartans flung their Persians down a well, saying they would find plenty of earth and water at the bottom. These actions mark the seed of a crucial cooperation between Athens and Sparta, who were normally rivals, against the Persian incursions.

By now the Persian expeditionary force had arrived. It headed straight for Eretria. And within a week, the city was betrayed and destroyed. I note in passing that the Persian force's small size, about 25,000, and its first action surely secure punishment as at least one of the main Persian objectives of this expedition.

After destroying Eretria, the Persians moved on to Athens and landed at Marathon on the north coast of Attica. The future of Athens hung in the balance.

Our main source for what happened at Marathon is Herodotus, the first Greek historian. But he can be supplemented by some other writers, such as Diodorus Siculus, a Greek Sicilian writing during the reign of the emperor Augustus; Cornelius Nepos, a minor Latin author of the 1st century B.C., who composed short lives of historical figures, among whom was *Miltiades*, the Athenian commander at Marathon; and a Byzantine lexicon of about A.D. 1000 called the *Souda,* which includes an account of the battle. The second-century A.D. traveler Pausanias visited the battlefield, and saw and described pictures of Marathon that were set up in a public building called the Painted Stoa in the Athenian market place, about 30 years after the fact. There are also scattered references in other sources. From this mélange of material, the general outline of the battle is clear enough.

After the fall of Eretria, and when the Persians were moving toward Marathon, the Athenians sent to Sparta for help. The expert runner Philippides, sometimes named wrongly Pheidippides, ran to Sparta baring this appeal. This represents a distance of some 140 miles, yet Herodotus tells us that Philippides ran it overnight. Many regarded this as an exaggeration typical of this author, until the same route was covered on foot in 34 and 35 hours respectively by two RAF pilots in 1982. An experienced ancient Greek athlete could surely have done no worse.

At Sparta, Philippides pleaded that the Spartans not allow an ancient city of Greece fall under the yoke of foreigners. He was told the good news first: the Spartans would assist. Then came the bad. It would be some days before they could depart, since religious scruple dictated that Spartan armies could only set out during this particular month—it was August or September—under a full moon. This was no cop-out on the Spartan part, since to disrespect the gods at the outset of a military adventure was to invite catastrophe. And when the full moon did finally shine, 2,000 Spartan hoplites marched with lightening rapidity to arrive at Athens in only three days.

Meanwhile at Athens, there was undoubtedly debate about the proper course of action—defend the city or go out and meet the Persian threat in the field. The Athenian army was commanded by a board of 10 generals called the Sertagoy, among them the nobleman, Miltiades, the scion of a prominent Athenian family. He was to emerge in tradition as the hero of Marathon.

The decision was made, and a force of Athenian hoplites marched out and took up station at a sanctuary of Herakles, on the slopes of a hill overlooking the Persians' landing spot at the edge of the plain at Marathon. The precise location of this sanctuary is one of the problems that dogs this battle, but wherever it was, it just over a mile from the Persian position.

While camped here, the Athenians were joined by 1,000 hoplites from the town of Plataea, a tiny place in Boeotia, which had put itself under Athenian protection some decades earlier and now felt obliged to help its protectors in their hour of need. The entire military force of Plataea showed up that day.

Remarkably, Herodotus does not provide a figure for the size of the Athenian force, one of the many failings of his narrative. But several other sources record the Athenian strength as either 10,000 hoplites, with the Plataeans added for a total of 11,000 or 10,000 hoplites including the Plataeans. Since either figure approximates the strength of both cities' contingents at the later battle of Plataea in 479 B.C. given by Herodotus as 8,000 and 600 respectively, neither is inherently implausible.

Once in position, there was a standoff while the Athenian board of ten generals debated what to do. The committee was split on whether to fight it out or withdraw. The deciding vote was cast by an eleventh official, called the polemarch—an ancient Athenian office traditionally charged with overseeing military matters—and he, having been persuaded by Miltiades, voted to fight. The holding of this council, after the army had set out and was now within range of the enemy, suggests that the mere sight of the Persian force, its size and appearance terrifying, caused the hearts of some to quail.

In a fashion consistent with Athens' democratic institutions, the command of the army rotated on a daily basis through the board of ten generals, and we are told that everyone waited for Miltiades' day to come around before doing anything. The standoff therefore appears to have been of several days' duration.

On Miltiades' day of command, the Athenians marched out to join battle. The Plataeans were stationed at the extreme left, the Athenian polemarch Callimachus on the right. In the center, the phalanx had to be stretched to match the length of the Persian line, since the Athenians were inferior in numbers. The result, says Herodotus, was that the center was thinned and stood "at only a few ranks deep." Now remember that eight ranks appears to have been the normal depth for the classical hoplite phalanx. This meant that the Athenian wings were deeper relative to the center.

The battle was preceded by the usual rituals of sacrifice and the reading of omens. Nepos comments that the pictures of Marathon in the Painted Stoa in Athens showed Miltiades haranguing his troops; but Herodotus, for whatever reason, makes no mention of this customary pre-battle event.

Then the Athenians advanced. Herodotus says that they charged the roughly one-mile gap between the armies at the double; a feat that many have justifiably doubted was possible for men of about 150 pounds encumbered with between 40 and 70 pounds of equipment. Experiments conducted at Penn State in 1973 and 1974, with Phys. Ed. majors wearing weighted jackets and carrying mock nine-pound shields, showed the difficulty of a mile-long run so encumbered. Only one of these trained athletes completed the course, and he was utterly exhausted afterward and not in a position to fight 24,000 Persians.

Far more likely is that the Athenians charged only across the last 200 or so yards toward the Persian line, to limit the casualties from their bows. Herodotus notes that this was the first time he knew of where a phalanx ran into battle.

The Persians, thinking the Athenians mad to be attacking without cavalry or archers, prepared to receive them. As the armies joined battle Herodotus' account becomes very laconic, and is limited to a single, if rather long, sentence; although in English, translation is broken up into several sentences. But really in the Greek, it's one single sentence. And here's what it says:

> The fighting at Marathon was long and drawn out. In the center, where the Greeks were faced with the Persians themselves and the Sacae, they were beaten; the invaders got the better of the Greeks at this point, and broke their lines and pursued them inland. However, the Athenians and the Plataeans on the respective wings were victorious. They left the Persians they had routed to flee the battlefield and concentrated into a single fighting unit—and the Athenians won.

That's the whole extent of Herodotus' account of the undecided combat at Marathon. While certainly offering more than Egyptian or Assyrian battle narratives, it's still rather thin on details.

The Persians were driven into the sea and seven of their ships captured. By way of casualties, we are told that the Persians lost 6,400 men, and the Athenians 192, including Callimachus the Polemarch.

The problems with this battle are many. Herodotus, for instance, is perfunctory with details. He does not give the numbers of troops arrayed on each side, which is a very basic fact in most normal battle narratives. Other authors provide impressive Persian hordes of half a million, in the case of Plato, or 90,000, in the case of Simonides, a contemporary poet. But these are clearly too large, given that the expedition was a seaborne one. If the Persian dead numbered 6,400, and if we take that to represent a little over a third of the fighting force, such a casualty rate being not unusual for the age, we arrive a figure of around 24,000 or so Persians at the battle. There are other omissions also in the account of Herodotus: Miltiades' pre-battle speech, or there is no mention of the Ionian contingents who undoubtedly fought with the Persians. And the actual fighting, as we've seen, is covered in a single sentence.

Topographical details are also unclear. Two examples are emblematic. One is the location of the sanctuary of Herakles, near which the Athenians camped. The other problem is the marsh that stood near the Persian position. Herodotus makes no mention of it, but Pausanias says that the pursuit and slaughter of the Persians in this marsh was a significant enough feature of the battle to warrant depiction in the Painted Stoa. So why is Herodotus apparently unaware of the marsh? We can't be sure.

Stated details are no less confusing or contradictory. Herodotus says that the Persians landed at Marathon to give their cavalry free rein, but the cavalry make no appearance in the battle narrative. As a result, a long and windy scholarly debate has taken place about whether or not the Persian cavalry even took part in the fight. We'll look at it in a minute.

Nepos reports that the Persians attacked at Marathon, with 100,000 infantry and 10,000 cavalry. This contradicts the Herodotean portrayal in a crucial detail—the Persians charged, not the Athenians. Pausanias says that he saw a monument to Athenian slaves who fought at Marathon alongside their masters. These slaves go entirely unmentioned in any of the ancient literary accounts of the battle, so that their numbers and role in the fighting are a complete mysteries to us.

Finally, there are puzzling aspects to both Persian and Athenian behavior, as reported in our sources. We take three examples and propose solutions for each.

Problem one: Why was there a standoff for several days, and why did the Persians not attack the Athenians, instead of waiting passively for the Athenians to take the initiative? Possible answers here are that the Persians were tired after the week of exertions at the site of Eretria, or that they were waiting for local defectors or some other aid to come to them from Athens. They had in train a certain Hippias, who had been tyrant at Athens until expelled 20 years earlier. Perhaps he was filling their ears with false hopes of treachery or aid from inside Athens—so they were waiting.

Problem two: On the Athenian side, even despite the debate among the generals, once the decision was made to fight, why did the Athenians not attack sooner rather than later? Why wait several days and let the Persians gather strength and get well rested before attacking them? And, above all, why charge a force that actually outnumbers you more than 3 to 1? A possible and simple solution here is that the Athenians were waiting for the Spartans to arrive. And since the Persians were on the offensive and they were the ones who had an objective to meet, it is not at all unlikely that they made some sort of move on the final day of the battle that prompted the Athenian charge. Herodotus reports that the Athenians stretched their line to match that of the Persians, implying that the Persians were already deployed in line of battle when the Athenians moved. If so, Nepos' claim that the Persians charged is a simple misunderstanding of what actually transpired. The Persians made a strategic move of some sort that triggered an unexpectedly aggressive Athenian response. In this way, the accounts of Nepos and of Herodotus can be reconciled.

Another possibility, which is widely held, is that the Athenians heard or noticed that a large part of the Persian cavalry was absent from the field, which would also explain the curious absence of cavalry from the battle narrative. So they chose to attack at an opportune moment when the enemy was weakened.

Now, the only solid piece of evidence that the Persian cavalry was absent from Marathon is a cryptic comment in the Byzantine lexicon, the *Souda*, which just states, "the cavalry were away,"—*chwris hippies* in the Greek, whatever that means—and that Miltiades then attacked on hearing this. So modern scholars have concluded that the Persian cavalry had re-embarked on their ships and taken off, for whatever reason. But why the Persian cavalry being AWOL is not mentioned in any other source is a serious problem for this theory, despite its popularity. Herodotus reports that the Persians thought the Athenians mad to be attacking without archers or cavalry, which implies the presence of the Persian cavalry. Nepos says that Miltiades moved his men down to a position with scattered trees around about to prevent encirclement by the Persian cavalry; and Pausanias reports the local ghost story that at night one can hear men fighting and horses neighing at Marathon. The preponderance of evidence therefore is that the Persian cavalry were present.

The only reasonable conclusion has to be that the Persian cavalry was there, but somehow neutralized or, at least, that it played no significant role in the fighting. Why this should have been so remains yet another great mystery of the battle of Marathon.

Problem three: In the combat phase, why did the victorious Persian center, having driven off the Greeks, not wheel and attack the flanks or rear of the Greek wings? Why, instead, did they allow the Greek wings to wheel and attack them? The chaos and confusion of ancient battle must be taken into account here. Fighters in one area of the field would have no idea what was going on elsewhere. So the Persians, having broken the Greek center, simply set off in pursuit of those running away in front of them, unaware that their wings were faring badly. Crucially, it was the Greeks who showed greater discipline and command-and-control at the unit level. The officers on the victorious wings let the defeated Persians flee before them, and turned their troops to the business of taking on the Persian center, whose formation would now, in any case, be in some disarray as it was pursuing the fleeing Athenians.

These three problems are emblematic of the sort of theorizing that surrounds many aspects of this battle, but all devolve ultimately into confronting inherently defective source material. So the battle of Marathon will have to remain opaque in its details, even if the outline is more or less discernible.

Defeated at Marathon, the Persians withdrew to their ships and sailed around Attica, with a view to taking Athens itself. There were rumors of planned treachery by some Athenian dissidents inside the city. And remember that the city of Eretria had fallen also by treachery. While the Persians were underway, the victorious army at Marathon marched back to the city and took up position on the shore. On seeing them there, the Persians declined a further confrontation and sailed back to Asia. This march of the victorious Athenians, by the way, or perhaps the dash of the runner who announced the victory in the city, is the origin of the modern Marathon foot race.

Meanwhile, the Spartan contingent finally arrived, some days later. It can only be imagined what carnage these crack troops would have wrought had they arrived in time for the fight. As it was, they requested to view the Persian dead, presumably to make an assessment of their equipment in the full knowledge that more confrontations with the foreigner were inevitable. Having seen the Persians and having praised the Athenian achievement, they went home.

The Athenian dead were cremated and entombed on the battlefield, a signal honor in Greek armies. Their burial mound, called the *Soros*, can bee seen to this day, and Pausanias records that all 192 names of the fallen were listed on the tombstone. The veterans were honored ever afterward as the *Marathonomachoi* or the *Marathon Fighters.* Some physical evidence of the battle is traceable. Excavations have yielded Persian arrowheads, and two helmets were found in the arms dumps in the sanctuary of Zeus at Olympia, which we talked about in the last lecture. One, a conical-looking Assyrian-style helmet, bears an inscription that it was taken by the Athenians from the Medes, which must mean that it came from Marathon. And the other, a Corinthian-style Greek helmet, bears the name of Miltiades himself.

In 1884, a German officer visiting Marathon reported that a local farmer had found a mass of bones, a claim he verified with some digging of his own. It has been suggested that these bones are the remains of the Persians who perished in the Great Marsh, as depicted in the Painted Stoa in Athens. If so, then the Persian dead of Marathon were given no honorable burial. Certainly, Pausanias reports seeing no graves or markers for them at the site. It is a melancholy thought indeed that young men from central Asia could travel thousands of miles at the behest of a despot, only to end up drowning in the mud of Marathon's marsh or transfixed by heavily armored Greek spearmen, and then be left unmourned and also unburied as carrion.

Miltiades was hailed as a hero in Athens. But his prominence spawned many opponents, and following a failed attack against the island of Paros in 489 B.C., they orchestrated his censure. He was fined, but died of a wound incurred on Paros a few days later. His son paid the fine.

Marathon quickly became legendary. This is most obviously indicated by the stories of divine intervention included in the account of Herodotus', such apparitions of ghostly warriors and Athenian heroes appearing to slay Persians. So within decades of being fought, Marathon took on the mantle of a Homeric encounter.

Marathon demonstrated, in shocking fashion, the effectiveness of hoplite phalanxes against Persian arms. Do note, however, that this point is to emphasize specifically the superiority of Greek arms over Persian, and not to suggest some generalized inferiority of Persian armies as a whole.

As a decisive battle, the outcome was nothing less than sensational. The Persian superpower had met an unexpected defeat at the hands of a numerically inferior force in a corner of the world that, by Persian standards, was a complete backwater.

But too much should not be made about how this great victory was achieved. The details of the fighting are far too vague in our sources to make distinct judgments about tactical Athenian genius, as some have thought to do. In all likelihood, events during the combat phase evolved rather haphazardly and opportunistically. There is little evidence of detailed tactical planning by the Athenians beforehand; and citizen militias of early classical Greece—Sparta excepted—lacked the intense training needed to be adept at grand maneuvers in the face of the enemy. Rather, the decision rested on the immense courage and determination of the Athenian hoplite fighting in defense of his house and kin.

On the long view, the outcome of Marathon was of huge importance. Taking the fate of Eretria as a blueprint, a Persian victory at Marathon would have resulted in the capture and destruction of

Athens. Two further outcomes then present themselves in this counterfactual scenario: (a) The Persians establish some sort of suzerainty over Attica, and use it as a basis for future attempts on the Greek heartland; or (b) the Athenian survivors are transported to Susa and brought before the great king Darius, just as the Eretrians were.

On either scenario, Athenian history would have ended after the battle of Marathon. The cultural achievements of Athens, all of which occurred subsequently, would never have come about. We would read no tragedies of Aeschylus, Sophocles, or Euripides; laugh at no comedies of Aristophanes or Menander; be enlightened by no histories of Herodotus or Thucydides; we would gaze in wonder at no acropolis and no Parthenon; we would not contemplate the philosophy of Socrates, Plato, or Aristotle; and, of course, there would be no democracy. The landscape of European history would have looked very different had the Athenians succumbed that day at Marathon.

Despite its tactical decisiveness, strategically, the battle decided very little. The Persians had lost a battle. Their resolve to settle their ongoing account with Athens only deepened. They would be back.

Lecture Eleven
The Battle of Thermopylae

Scope:

The events leading up to this dramatic confrontation are reviewed and the battle itself is examined. Xerxes, son of Darius I, had launched a full-scale land-and-sea invasion of the Greek mainland with an army so large that it dismayed the Greeks. The advent of this Persian host forced most Greek states in its path to surrender, or *medize*, given that none could seriously contemplate standing up to it. Yet a handful of Greek *poleis* in central Greece and the Peloponnese, led by Athens and Sparta, did just that. Facing insurmountable odds, a Spartan contingent of 300 warriors led by one of their two kings, along with allied troops, was charged with stopping the Persian invader at the narrow pass of Thermopylae, while the Greek armies mustered in the rear. The battle ended in a Greek defeat, following betrayal by a local with topographical knowledge. The Battle of Thermopylae can be viewed as the first in a great cultural tradition: the *Glorious Defeat*. The essence of this tradition is that a military defeat be converted into a moral victory, most commonly by claims that it manifests admirable national, cultural, or ethnic qualities.

Outline

I. In the period between the two Persian assaults on the Greek mainland (490–480 B.C.), two events are particularly noteworthy.

   A. At Athens, the leader Themistocles grew in prominence and oversaw the construction of a formidable Athenian navy.

   1. Themistocles, one of the 10 generals at Marathon, emerged as a man of energy and vision following the death of Miltiades.

   2. He had been instrumental in convincing the Athenians to make providential use of metal deposits at Laurium.

   3. Athens became the major naval power in Greece in the decade between the wars, equipped with a fleet of the most modern ships.

4. Otherwise, so far as our poor evidence allows us to see, life in Greece continued as it always had done in the decade between the Persian invasions.

B. In 486 B.C., Darius died and the Persian crown passed to his son, Xerxes. He began preparing for a major assault on Greece to avenge Marathon.

    1. Darius had prepared to invade Greece again, but preparations were not complete when he died.

    2. Xerxes's preparations for the invasion of Greece were delayed by his subjection of Egypt.

    3. Herodotus presents the Persian force as ethnically diverse in composition and immense in scale.

    4. Messengers and mighty works preceded the Great King's arrival in Greece.

    5. Two shocking incidents illustrate the despotic nature of Xerxes's character and what Greece could expect from their new master, should he win.

II. The resisting Greeks decided to make an effort to stop the Persians before they reached central Greece and the Peloponnese. Thermopylae was selected as the site of the stand. After a three-day battle, the Persians emerged victorious.

    A. Many Greek states medized (went over to the Persians). After consulting oracles, the defiant Greek states held a congress and settled on blocking the Persian advance at Thermopylae.

        1. The size of the Persian host ensured that Xerxes's messengers demanding submission met with great success.

        2. An oracle from Delphi offered cold comfort to Athens until Themistocles came up with a brighter interpretation of its meaning.

        3. In the face of the threat, internal truces were agreed upon and messengers dispatched to unaligned Greek states.

        4. A congress was held at the Isthmus of Corinth, and an important strategic decision was made.

        5. After the Greeks had taken up position at Thermopylae, with their fleet at Artemisium, they awaited the arrival of the invasion force.

B. The fight at Thermopylae was intense and lasted three days; it ended in betrayal and death for all remaining Greek defenders.

1. Herodotus provides more detail for this battle than for Marathon.
2. The charge of the small force under the Spartan king Leonidas is not immediately obvious.
3. Xerxes drew near, camped outside the pass, and scouted the Greek position.
4. With Xerxes watching from a throne set up on the heights over the pass, the battle commenced and raged for two full days without result for the Persians.
5. The details of the combat are passed over in relative silence by Herodotus, but it must have been ferocious.
6. Xerxes got his break when a local betrayed to him a mountain path that led down behind the Greek position.
7. Despite fighting like madmen, the Greeks finally succumbed.
8. Meanwhile, off Cape Artemisium, the Greek fleet fought three indecisive engagements with the Persian.

III. Thermopylae, though a blow to the Greek war effort, stands as the first in a great cultural tradition of the Glorious Defeat.

A. Thermopylae was a serious blow to the Greek war effort; for the Athenians, it marked the certainty of their city's demise.

1. The fall of Thermopylae allowed the Persians free rein in central Greece, which lay open to the invader.
2. Athens was evacuated, in all likelihood before and during the Thermopylae campaign.
3. With an uncertain future, with Athens abandoned to the barbarian, the Greeks awaited the Persian arrival on their doorstep.

B. Once the war had been won, Thermopylae was quickly transformed into a Glorious Defeat, the first in a long tradition of romanticized military disasters.

1. The Glorious Defeat reinterprets what is really an abject military disaster into something noble and valuable.
2. There are several elements of a Glorious Defeat narrative, some of them optional.

3. In this way, the actual circumstances of a Glorious Defeat are transformed into a moral victory that shows up the nobility of the defeated over the baseness of the supposed winners.

4. The main elements of the Glorious Defeat were established in the Battle of Thermopylae.

Essential Reading:

Diodorus Siculus, *Library of History*, 11.1–11.

Herodotus, *The Histories*, Book 7.

Green, *The Greco-Persian Wars*, pp. 109–149.

Lazenby, *The Defence of Greece*, pp. 81–150.

Supplemental Reading:

Cartledge, *The Spartans*.

Clough, "Loyalty and Liberty."

Pressfield, *Gates of Fire* (a novel).

Strauss, *The Battle of Salamis*, pp. 11–89.

Questions to Consider:

1. What were the major differences between Xerxes's and Darius's assaults on Greece? Was the intent of each manifestly different? On what evidence do you rest your assessment?

2. Reanalyze the Battle of Thermopylae in light of the Glorious Defeat tradition. What other examples of the tradition, not mentioned in the lecture, can you think of? What elements of the tradition are present or absent in the examples you have chosen, and how do you account for these differences?

Lecture Eleven—Transcript
The Battle of Thermopylae

The Athenian victory at Marathon, the subject of our last lecture, was only the beginning of Greco-Persian antagonism. In this lecture we review the start of the second round of the contest for the Greek mainland, and focus on a significant Greek defeat that has had an interesting cultural afterlife. We begin with the decade between the Persian onslaughts, 490 to 480 B.C.

One of the ten generals at Marathon was a man named Themistocles. After the death of Miltiades in 489 B.C., Themistocles emerged as a leader of energy and vision. The Athenians ran state mines at in southeastern Attica that had produced silver and lead for many centuries. In the 480s B.C., the mines generated a huge surplus, which the citizenry was inclined to distribute as a per-capita cash handout. Themistocles, instead, convinced the assembly to invest the extra money in building new warships. At the time, Athens was engaged in a war with the nearby island of Aegina, so their need for ships was immediate. Athens already had a navy, but now it perhaps doubled in size to 200 warships.

Thucydides praises Themistocles for his foresight; so it may be that Themistocles took this action with a view to a future Persian invasion, and used the war with Aegina as a cover. Such manipulation was wholly in character for him, as we shall see. But the result was unquestionable. Athens now became the preeminent naval power in Greece, fitted out with a fleet of the most modern war ships. The impact of this Athenian fleet on the Persian invasion of 480 B.C. was to be decisive, and it also provided the basis for Athenian domination in the Aegean for much of the century.

Otherwise, so far as our evidence allows us to see, life in Greece continued as it always had done in the decade between the Persian invasions. States quarreled, competed, and fought.

In 486 B.C., Darius died, and the Persian crown passed to his son, Xerxes. A revolt in Egypt diverted Darius from Greece, who died without avenging Marathon. Xerxes took up the torch, but had to first re-conquer Egypt, an effort that actually added no new lands to the empire. Since all previous Great Kings of Persia had extended the realm, he could not be seen to fall short. So Xerxes' intentions on Greece, as stated in Herodotus, was both to punish Athens and to subdue all of Greece, thereby avenging his father's defeat and expanding the empire with one stroke. "Thus those who have wronged us will bear the yoke of slavery, as will those who have not," announces the vainglorious and vindictive Xerxes of Herodotus' account.

The Persian force was comprised of both a land and naval force of massive size and, typically, it was ethnically diverse. Land and sea forces would move in tandem along the north coast of the Aegean and descend into the Greek peninsula hand-in-hand. Stopping it would require a coordinated naval and land defense of a sort the divided and puny Greek city-states seemed most unlikely to organize. Hopes must have run high in the Persian command.

Two reviews of the army were held en route to Greece: at a place called Abydos, and another at Doriscus. The second review occasions Herodotus to survey the composition of the Persian forces, and he describes their equipment in detail. In all, he documents no less than 61 nationalities representing 17 or 18 different types of troops. Among them are Ionian and Dorian Greeks from the Persian realms, equipped in the Greek fashion.

These reviews have been used to identify a great weakness at the heart of the Persian host. So many different peoples, equipped differently, and probably speaking different languages, practically ensured tactical incoherence on the battlefield. This argument, however, displays a deep ignorance of Near Eastern military practice, particularly among the Assyrians. Further, in accounts of the actual fighting to come, it was the Persians, the Medes, and the Sacae from Iran who took part in the main combat. The more exotic contingents were probably window-dressing that impressed on the locals the size of the Persian realm.

This enormous host, according to Herodotus, ate all the grain and livestock in the lands it passed through and drank entire rivers dry. He later estimates its size at 5,283,220, with the combat troops alone numbering 2,641,610. Clearly, these are preposterous figures. By way of comparison, note that Nazi Germany launched 3 million troops into Russia in 1941, in what is the largest land operation in recorded history. Other ancient sources are a little bit more reasonable, but still quite incredible; 800,000 or 700,000 troops are the sorts of figures we encounter.

But at even ten percent of Herodotus' total, the entire Persian force of perhaps 300,000 to half a million, which would include rowers, logistical support, and other camp followers, would not be entirely impossible. And of this, perhaps 100,000 would be fighting men, a force comparable in size to the Persian armies that later confronted Alexander. One Hundred Thousand combat troops still represented an order of magnitude greater than anything even the most populous Greek city-state could put into the field—compare the 10,000 Athenians at Marathon.

As to the Persian fleet, Herodotus gives a figure of 1,207 warships and 3,000 other vessels. This too seems probably too large, but we have no way of being able to estimate its actual size. Whatever the details, the entire Persian force was enormous, and the exaggerated Greek estimates of its numbers only reflect the utter dismay the Greek mind felt in the face of such odds.

Xerxes had ordered, some years earlier, that the Hellespont be bridged, and a canal be dug through the peninsula of Athos in Northern Greece, which was a region then under Persian control. Aside from their practical purpose, these monumental engineering efforts were designed to impress the locals with Persian capabilities, and so strike fear into any who were contemplating resistance. In 481 B.C., Xerxes moved his royal army to Sardis, the jumping off point for his invasion. Once more, envoys were dispatched to Greece demanding earth and water. Pointedly, no such messengers were sent to Athens or Sparta. The army then advanced in three columns across Northern Greece.

Two incidents during these months illustrate the character of Xerxes, and what Greece could expect from their new master, should he prevail. The first attempt to bridge the Hellespont was thwarted by a storm. Xerxes ordered the men in charge beheaded, and the sea whipped and scolded for defying his will. This last action ranks, alongside Nero's fiddling while Rome burned, as the *locus classicus* of despotic hubris in antiquity. It also says much about the Great King's personality.

The second incident shows what Xerxes expected of his subjects. Pythius the Lydian was the richest man in the empire after the king himself. He had approached Xerxes and offered his whole disposable wealth to help fund the war. Xerxes graciously refused and honored

Pythius with, of all things, a gift of money. Later Pythius came to Xerxes again and asked the king a favor in return: of his five sons, all of whom were enrolled in the king's army, would Xerxes spare Pythius his eldest, to look after him in his old age?

The King interpreted this request as insolence from a slave he had previously honored, as well as a vote of no confidence in his Greek adventure. He became angry. So he granted Pythius four of his sons, but the eldest and favorite he had cut in two and the halves impaled on either side of the royal road along which the army was marching. Such was the man whose rule the Greeks could look forward to.

Meanwhile, in Greece, Xerxes' envoys were meeting with great success, probably as a result of the expedition's enormous size. The vast majority of mainland Greek states either medized or stayed neutral. Out of several hundred polities, only three powerful city-states, Athens, Sparta, and Corinth, resisted the Persian invader. The commemorative monument later erected by the Greeks at Delphi listed 31 Greek participants in the war, led by the big three. That represents about five percent of known Greek city-states. In effect, all of Greece down to the borders of Attica had surrendered without a fight. Things were looking bleak.

The mood was not improved by ambivalent words from the Delphic oracle. It was standard Greek practice among both private persons and states to consult the famous oracle of Apollo at Delphi before embarking on any important endeavor. Word came back that Athens should trust in her wooden walls, and there were ominous allusions to death at Salamis, an island off the Attic coast.

The meaning of the oracle was not immediately clear and has been debated ever since, but Themistocles insisted that the fleet was the city's wooden walls, and that it was the Persians, not the Athenians, who would meet death at Salamis. Convinced and heartened, the Athenian resolve to fight was strengthened by Themistocles' clever interpretation.

In the face of the emergency, ongoing internal squabbles were halted and a meeting held. The allies, termed *symmachoi*—literally, "those who fight together"—took oath to cement their alliance. The command on both land and sea was probably decided, and it went to the Spartans, the Greek military experts. Spies were sent to Sardis, and calls for help issued to non-aligned Greek states.

The spies were apprehended at Sardis, but on Xerxes' command, they were sent home unharmed to report the size of army to the Greeks. The Persian, like the Assyrian, appreciated the value of psychological warfare.

The calls for help ended in failure. For many Greeks, local rivalries trumped the national crisis. The people of Argos, for instance, could not overcome their longstanding hatred of the Spartans and now fight alongside them. The allied ambassadors were given until sunset to vacate Argive territory. Envoys arrived at Syracuse on Sicily, arguably the strongest Greek city-state in the whole Greek world. Gelon, its tyrant, promised a massive reinforcement, but on condition that he either command the whole allied force or its naval contingent. The envoys retorted, "We came here not for a commander, but for an army," to which Gelon replied, "Then you'll have plenty of commanders, but you won't have many men for them to command." No help there, nor indeed from any of the states approached.

These diplomatic efforts would have occupied the winter of 481 to 480. As spring came around, and Xerxes' horde departed Sardis, the defiant states knew they were on their own.

A congress was held at the Isthmus of Corinth and an important strategic decision was made. The Greeks would confront the Persians in the north, before they got into the heartland of central Greece. A large force of 10,000 hoplites and 250 warships was sent north to the coastal pass at Tempe, in Thessaly near Mt. Olympus. The Greek trust in this force was as touching as it was callow. It illustrates their inexperience in dealing with major campaigns. Their wars were border disputes between small city-states. They simply could not conceive of what was coming against them, a force probably four times bigger than that faced by the Athenians at Marathon. Ten thousand hoplites were not very likely to stop it.

As it turned out, Tempe had to be abandoned when it became clear that the Greek position could be readily outflanked. The people of Thessaly, their homeland now fully exposed to the Persians, medized.

After the Tempe debacle, a new congress was held, but the original strategy retained. A land army would hold the narrow pass at Thermopylae—which means "hot gates"—a natural bottleneck that narrowed to only 50 feet across, and had high mountains on one side and the sea on the other. An ancient wall across this pass was rebuilt as a further obstacle.

To Thermopylae was sent a Spartan King named Leonidas with a corps of 300 handpicked Spartan hoplites and various allies. With the Greek fleet stationed nearby off Cape Artimesium to block a Persian landing in their rear, the Greek army at Thermopylae awaited the arrival of the invader. It was sometime in August 480 B.C.

Herodotus provides more detail for this battle than he does for Marathon. The Greek force is enumerated at 300 Spartans—apparently, all men with sons—and about 5,900 others, including 400 Thebans. Now, the position of the Thebans in the alliance is most unclear, and Herodotus is unusually hostile toward them, perhaps reflecting bias among his informants. He presents the 400 Thebans as virtual hostages to the allies. Each contingent had its own general, but all of them deferred to Leonidas as the commander in chief.

Leonidas' force, smaller even than that sent to Tempe, seems risible. But it was supposed to be an advanced guard, charged with holding the pass until reinforcements arrived. So what was the delay? Why weren't large forces sent up there immediately?

Well, the Spartans were yet again delayed by religious commitments, and the rest of the Greeks were celebrating the Olympic games. It may seem absurd to us today to put an athletic festival in front of national survival, but recall that the ancient Olympic games honored Zeus, the Father of Gods and Men. It would not bode well for allied military efforts if Zeus were not properly honored at one of his chief festivals. To the Greek mind, national survival in fact depended on the festival proceeding. The good will of the gods was critical to any endeavor.

Herodotus therefore is quite clear that the defense of Thermopylae was no suicide mission. His interpretation has been challenged by modern scholars, who think it rather illogical. Leonidas' tiny army is the main cause for their concern. The promise of reinforcements is described by one author as, "dust blown in the eyes of the extra-Peloponnesian allies." There was a vacuous promise. Or perhaps Leonidas' mandate was to delay the Persians on land while the fleet at Artemisium did damage to the Persian armada. If so, this was a holding action, not a definitive stand. These are possibilities, to be sure, but Herodotus is very clear that the Greek alliance planned to stop the entire Persian invasion at Thermopylae.

Xerxes approached. A Persian scout was sent ahead to count the Greek numbers and assess their dispositions. Amazed at the tiny force, the scout reported back to the king an even more bizarre detail: the Spartans were all standing about combing their hair and exercising. Were these men really preparing to fight it out with the royal host?

At this point Herodotus inserts an exchange between Xerxes and the exiled Spartan King Demaratus, who had put himself at the service of the Persian court, where he was honored, and received some Ionian cities to govern. Demaratus is occasionally trotted out by Herodotus to hold imaginary conversations with Xerxes, whenever some contrast between Greek and Persian customs requires dramatic emphasis. This is one such occasion.

Demaratus had warned Xerxes on a prior occasion not to underestimate the sort of men he was going up against if he attacked Greece. So now Xerxes asks Demaratus whether he was really serious about how dangerous these preening dandies were. Most certainly, replies Demaratus, they were just doing what their custom dictates before risking their lives. In any case, the outcome would show whether he was lying or not. Another tradition has it that Xerxes sent notes to Leonidas demanding that the Spartans give up their arms, to which Leonidas replied, "Come and get them!"

After four days of waiting, Xerxes enthroned himself on a good vantage point and ordered his core troops, Kissians and Medes, to assault the Greek position at Thermopylae. They were butchered ferociously in the narrow path in a fight that lasted most of the first day. Toward the end of the day, Xerxes withdrew the Medes and sent in his crack troops, the Immortals. They too suffered grievously at the hands of the Greek defenders, who fought a little in front of the wall, at the mouth of the narrows.

It is noteworthy here that the Greeks used deception on the Persians. They would feign flight and then, as the Persians chased them and lost cohesion, the Greeks would suddenly wheel and attack. Xerxes leapt from his throne on three occasions during this phase of the fighting, so intense was the engagement.

On the second day, the Persians faired no better. The Greeks fought in sequence, each ethnic contingent facing the Persians in turn, so some system of ordered retirement was employed.

The details of the combat are passed over in relative silence by Herodotus, but it must have been horrendous. The confined space of these confrontations, where the Persians were channeled onto the narrow Greek front, can only have ensured unimaginable and horrific scenes of butchery in front of the Greek lines. There was no escape for the Persians forced onto the phalanx; they could not flee right or left or to their rear. At the point of contact, the combat would have been purely for survival. This would have made it particularly harrowing and desperate.

An excellent evocation of its undoubted hideousness can be gained from Steven Pressfield's 1998 novel, *Gates of Fire*. Pressfield powerfully, if imaginatively, portrays the churning crush of the battle, with its cacophony of noise and screams, its welter of spurting blood, spilled intestines, and excrement discharged in terror. It makes for rough reading. Herodotus provides a detail that illustrates the combat's viciousness. At the end, he reports, men were fighting with their fists and their teeth.

After two days of this, the Persian situation did not look good. Many hundreds, perhaps thousands, of the king's men had been slaughtered and the Greeks were still holding their position. What to do?

Betrayal saved Xerxes. The traitor was Ephialtes of Malis, who was later reviled by his compatriots and came to a bad end. Ephialtes showed Xerxes a mountain path that circumvented the strong Greek position. It could be flanked. Now the Greeks knew of this path and had set a contingent of 1,000 Phocians to guard it. The Persian Immortals, however, set out at night and, coming upon the Phocians, assailed them and drove them in confusion up the heights, and so out of the action. The Immortals then pressed on their way.

The Greeks were made aware of the Persian turning maneuver, but how so is not made clear—perhaps Persian deserters or Persian prisoners—and they held a council to discuss what to do. Leonidas and the Spartans insisted on staying and doing their duty to the end. The others either went home or were sent home. The reason for the Spartan decision to stay is not obvious. Herodotus says Leonidas stayed in response to an oracle promising either the destruction of

Sparta or the death of one of its kings. This is very convenient and smacks of later, justificatory composition.

The later Spartan reputation for not abandoning their posts stems from this very action at Thermopylae, so it can't have been the reason for Leonidas' decision now. Perhaps the Spartans stayed to give their escaping allies maximum time to get away. Whatever their reasons, the Spartans were joined by the Thespians. The Thebans, says Herodotus, were forced to stay. This seems highly unlikely. Why make a bad situation worse by having to rely on potentially disloyal confederates? Why waste needed manpower guarding them? In all likelihood, the Thebans in fact chose to stay.

The third day at Thermopylae ranks as one of the most famous conflicts in the annals of military history, up there with Pickett's charge at Gettysburg or the battle of Waterloo. The reputation is well earned. Herodotus probably enjoyed access to Greek survivors, perhaps also Ionian Greek witnesses on the Persian side for what happened next. So we need not be so skeptical as to think his whole account was made up.

On this final day Leonidas led the remainder of his tiny force out to a wider spot in front of the narrows. He is likely to have done so because he believed that this position afforded a better opportunity for killing Persians in large numbers than had the confines of the pass. And so it transpired. I note in passing that this tactical detail perhaps supports the open-order model of hoplite combat over the standard model of tight-packed scrimmaging, as we discussed in Lecture Nine. In order to do maximum damage, Leonidas needed more space. As the Spartans occupied this forward position, someone said to Dieneces, the man that Herodotus deemed the bravest of the Spartans at Thermopylae, that the Persians were so numerous their arrows would block out the sun, to which Dieneces replied, "Fine, we'll fight in the shade."

The fighting started at about 10 AM. Xerxes once more launched a frontal assault, this time knowing that the Greek rear would soon be attacked. The scene of carnage at the mouth of the narrows was again frightful. Persians troops were whipped into battle, trampled each other, and some pitched off the cliffs into the sea.

The Greeks, certain of death, fought like madmen. Leonidas fell, and a fierce struggle developed over his body. I note, by the way, that

Herodotus denotes this fight as an *othismos pollos*. Clearly in this context, *othismos* cannot mean a physical shoving of phalanx against phalanx, but something vaguer like "a major struggle" or "a serious fight." Later, at Plataea by the way, he also makes mention of an *othismos* between the Persians and the Greeks; and the latter, of course, did not fight in a phalanx. So *othismos* can mean something other than massed physical shove.

By now the Persians who had taken the path were coming up from the rear, so the Spartans and allies who were left retired to a hillock and there fought to the last man. It was now that some of them, having lost their weapons, used their fists and teeth.

Calculating casualties is a difficult matter. Herodotus says that 20,000 Persians fell at Thermopylae, which seems excessive. He also says that Xerxes concealed these dire losses from the rest of his army by secretly burying all but 1,000 of the corpses, and that he heaped up 4,000 Greek dead to be viewed by the Persian sailors, summoned from Artimesium. Even if precision proves elusive, we may reasonably imagine several thousand Greek dead and, given the nature of the fighting and the terrain on which it took place, significantly greater losses on the Persian side: 8,000 to 10,000 would not be an impossible guess; but it is a guess, and among them were several brothers of Xerxes.

Given the size of the Persian force, the victory here cannot be described as Pyrrhic, but it was certainly very costly.

While all this was underway on land, off Cape Artemisium the Greek fleet fought three indecisive engagements with the Persian forces. We shall say a little more about this facet of the Thermopylae campaign in the next lecture, when we discuss naval warfare in slightly more detail. But we do note that the Persian sailors, principally Phoenicians and Egyptians, were proving more of a match for the Greeks than their counterparts in the land army. When news of the fall of Thermopylae arrived, the Greek fleet withdrew south.

The defeat at Thermopylae was a serious blow to the Greek war effort. Persian forces now enjoyed free rein in central Greece. Athens lay open to the invader, whose expertise in siegecraft ensured the city would fall, even if it were defended. In the event, the city was evacuated. From Thermopylae, the Persian army could make it to the border of Attica within about a week. This was far too short a timeframe for the transport of perhaps 250,000 men, women, and children from Athens to safe havens in the Peloponnese or on the island of Salamis, especially when so many Athenian ships and rowers were with the fleet at Artemisium. So the evacuation had probably been initiated as a precaution before Thermopylae took place.

With their future uncertain, the Athenians abandoned their city to the barbarian, and the Greek alliance awaited the Persians' arrival on its doorstep. Once the war had been won, the events at Thermopylae were reinterpreted into a Glorious Defeat, the first in a long tradition of romanticized military reverses.

The Glorious Defeat is a phenomenon whereby what is really an abject military disaster is transformed into something noble and valuable. The genre has several elements, which can be mixed and matched as needed. Usually, the Gloriously Defeated are underdogs who find themselves in a tough position. This is true of the Spartans at Thermopylae; the besieged Jewish rebels at Masada in A.D. 73, who we'll be looking at in Lecture Twenty; the defenders of the Alamo in 1836; or the surrounded British at Dunkirk in 1940. "Desperate straits" is the essential element of the Glorious Defeat here.

Usually, the enemy are the aggressors and the Glorious Defeat is a defensive action. Not all narratives in the genre display this feature. The Battle of Little Bighorn, for instance, in 1876—formerly Custer's Last Stand, until recent re-interpretation removed it from the ledger of Glorious Defeats entirely—was actually an act of aggression. Custer was seeking out the Lakota to exterminate them. Similarly, at the time of the Battle of Gettysburg in 1863, which is a totemic example of the Glorious Defeat, Lee was invading the North. In both cases, of course, a defensive veneer can be glossed onto the action. Custer was seeking to protect white settlers from Indian attacks, or Lee was defending a way of life that had been attacked in 1861. These dubious arguments emphasize that usually the Gloriously Defeated are defenders.

It adds great luster to a Glorious Defeat if the underdogs have the option to save themselves, but choose the nobler path—that is, dying, to a man. The preferred mode is for the Gloriously Defeated to go down taking as many of the enemy with them as possible. Again, not all Glorious Defeat narratives have this feature of choice, but there can be little doubt that the power of the story is enhanced by the underdogs rejecting safety in favor of staying the course and going down swinging. Also, most Glorious Defeats are inscribed in the annals of the eventual victor in the wider struggles that they are part of.

The true power of the Glorious Defeat genre lies in what the events are believed to reveal about valued group characteristics. Invariably, the Defeat celebrates honored traits: commitment to valued goals, such as honor or national identity; a willingness to sacrifice the self for the collective goal; valor, steadfastness, and courage in the face of overwhelming odds; and ancillary traits such as skill at arms, perseverance, discipline, and devotion to duty. This is how the real circumstances of a Glorious Defeat are transformed into no defeat at all and become instead a moral victory.

The main elements of the Glorious Defeat narrative were established by the battle of Thermopylae. The process of reinterpretation started almost immediately, with the battle's commemoration by the Greeks themselves. The epitaph of the 300 Spartans at Thermopylae, composed by the poet Simonides, who lived between 556 and 468 B.C., heralds the key elements in the fully developed tradition. And the epitaph is, "Go tell the Spartans, traveler, that here we lie, obedient to their orders."

The Spartan ethos is now defined primarily as staying at one's post at all costs. All—or all but one, as we shall see—chose to do so. The epitaph thus puts widely admired national characteristics of the Spartans at center stage—namely, strict obedience and devotion to duty—and celebrates their display in the context of what was really a pretty catastrophic reverse. Herodotus' account of the battle closes with some anecdotes that further illuminate how the events at Thermopylae were reinterpreted shortly after they had occurred.

Two Spartans, Eurytus and Aristodemus, were off the line due to eye infections. On the last day, Eurytus armed himself and joined the last stand, helped to his place in the ranks by a servant. Aristodemus, in contrast, stayed outside the combat zone and later returned safe and sound to Sparta. There, Eurytus was celebrated, and Aristodemus, in his lifetime, shunned by his compatriots.

My favorite moment, however, is when Herodotus once more wheels out Demaratus. Xerxes first commends Demaratus for having told him the truth about Spartan military prowess in their earlier conversation. The king then asks, "Tell me, how many more are there like the ones who fell here? And how may I go about defeating them?" These questions say it all. They show that Xerxes, for all his external power and majesty, is inwardly afraid. His moral vacuity is stressed when a few sections later, he orders Leonidas' head to be cut off and stuck on a pole. Herodotus expressly comments that this act went against the Persian custom of honoring valiant adversaries. What else can the reader think than that Xerxes is a moral midget, who cannot abide even by his own people's sense of decency?

A defeat at the hands of such a man is no defeat at all.

Lecture Twelve
Naval Warfare and the Battle of Salamis

Scope:

Thus far, we have focused exclusively on land warfare. However, at least since the later Bronze Age, naval operations had also been a part of ancient military practice in the Mediterranean. We briefly survey naval developments in the region up to the emergence of the *trireme* in the late 6th century B.C. The vital statistics of that unique and successful ship are then examined, with particular attention paid to the disposition of the oarsmen and the classic maneuvers of the *diekplous* and *periplous*. After a brief consideration of the imputed connection between naval power and democracy at Athens, we return to the course of the Persian Wars and the Battle of Salamis (September 480 B.C.). The various sources for these major engagements are examined, and problems of interpretation are outlined. We then address some of the difficulties surrounding the Battle of Salamis, survey the events of the battle, and assess its importance. The lecture ends with a short account of the Battle of Plataea (479 B.C.), the land engagement that finally denied any hope of Persian victory against Greece.

Outline

I.   Naval warfare had been a part of military operations from early in the history of the Mediterranean basin.

    A. Egyptians conducted naval operations, though not on a huge scale.

        1. The Old Kingdom tomb of Weni records a joint land-sea assault against Sand-Dwellers.

        2. Ramesses III's great fights with the Sea Peoples occurred partly on the sea.

        3. So far as we can tell, Egyptian naval capabilities were very limited.

    B. In the Near East, naval warfare was minimally practiced, but the Phoenicians were regarded as the masters of the art.

        1. The Assyrians used boats and ships in campaigns up and down rivers, in marsh lands, and across rivers.

2. Yet the Assyrian palaces do provide an early depiction of a warship with a ramming beak.
3. The Persians employed the Phoenicians and Ionian Greeks more aggressively.

C. The Greeks were a maritime people, long accustomed to naval warfare.
1. Minoan wall paintings show ships and, apparently, a sea battle.
2. According to the Greek traditions of the Trojan War, Bronze Age Greece could muster large fleets.
3. Dipylon pots show naval actions.
4. Sometime toward the end of the 6th century, a new form of ship emerged, the *trireme*.
5. Among Archaic and Classical Greek states, Athens emerged as the foremost naval power in the years following the first Persian attack.

II. The adoption of naval warfare in Athens has been linked to the appearance there of radical democracy in the 5th century B.C. We briefly examine this issue.

A. Aside from foreign-policy matters, the adoption of naval power has been argued to have had major effects on domestic politics in Athens.
1. The need for rowers lent to the poorest members of Athenian society an importance they had previously lacked. They gained power in the citizen-assembly as a result.
2. This is the view of the "Old Oligarch," an anonymous pamphlet highly critical of Athenian democracy and dated to the late 5th century B.C.
3. The model, then, proposes that naval power and democracy were inherently linked at Athens, with the former undergirding the latter.

B. As always, this model is not without its problems.
1. First, it requires taking a critic of the democracy at Athens at his word.
2. Study of how the Athenian navy was crewed and who rowed the ships does not support the model.
3. Any inherent connection between naval power and democracy is belied by other powerful Greek naval

states (Syracuse, Corinth, or Corcyra), which were not democratic in nature.

III. After Thermopylae, the Persians continued their advance and met the allied Greek fleet at Salamis. The engagement decided the fate of Greece.

    A. The Greek position after Thermopylae was not good. It was not helped by sharp strategic differences within the Greek high command.

        1. Athens was evacuated, and the city was taken, plundered, and burned by the Persians. The allied fleet gathered at Salamis.

        2. Strategic divisions emerged between the Peloponnesians and the Athenians.

        3. Themistocles orchestrated a fight with the Persians by stubborn diplomacy and a ruse.

        4. It is clear that this account of the prebattle situation in Herodotus, particularly the debates, is deeply flawed.

    B. The Battle of Salamis took place in late September 480 B.C. and was a decisive Greek victory.

        1. The details in our sources are sparse, and the battle's course is hard to reconstruct.

        2. One of the major problems is the deployment of the fleets in the straits.

        3. The key to the Greek success was confusion in the Persian fleet.

        4. The fighting itself must have been horrendous.

        5. The victory was a huge moral blow to the Persians, but its importance can be easily overstated.

        6. A recent interpretation of the battle as illustrative of Greek cultural superiority over the Persians is questionable.

IV. The defeat at Salamis was not the end of the Persian effort. The land army was still unbeaten and remained in Greece under the command of Mardonius until spring 479 B.C.

    A. Mardonius remained with hand-picked troops in Boeotia over the winter of 480–479 B.C. The final battle took place at Plataea.

        1. Persian strategy was to seek a decisive engagement.

2. The Persian host moved into the flatlands of Boeotia and awaited the Greeks there.
3. The Greek army arrived and a standoff ensued.
4. After some confused maneuvering by the Greeks, battle was joined and the Persians were crushed.

B. On the same day as Plataea, an allied Greek army defeated the Persians at Mycale in Ionia. The Persian designs on Greece were at an end; they were now on the defensive.

Essential Reading:

Aeschylus, *The Persians*.

Diodorus Siculus, *Library of History*, 11.11–37.

Herodotus, *The Histories*, Books 8–9.

Plutarch, *Life of Themistocles, Life of Aristides*.

Lazenby, *The Defence of Greece*, pp. 198–261.

Strauss, *The Battle of Salamis*, pp. 93–252.

Van Wees, *Greek Warfare*, pp. 199–231.

Supplemental Reading:

Green, *The Greco-Persian Wars*, pp. 153–287.

Hanson, *Carnage and Culture*, pp. 27–59.

McGrail, *Boats of the World*.

Questions to Consider:

1. What relationship, if any, do you see between the development of land and naval warfare in the period prior to the 5th century B.C.?

2. Which battle, Salamis or Plataea, do you regard as the most important in determining Greek victory in the Persian Wars? Why?

Lecture Twelve—Transcript
Naval Warfare and the Battle of Salamis

Our focus thus far has been exclusively on land warfare. Now it is time to broaden our horizons to include naval operations. We first survey early developments, then examine the revolution initiated by the introduction of the ship called the trireme, and then turn our attention to the Battle of Salamis, the next big clash in Xerxes' invasion of Greece.

The naval warfare had been a part of military operations from early in the history of the Mediterranean Basin. The Egyptians conducted naval operations, though not on a huge scale. The Old Kingdom inscriptions in the Tomb of Weni, which we examined in Lecture Four, record a joint land-sea assault on the Asiatic "Sand-Dwellers," so called: "I crossed over in transports with these troops. I made a landing at the rear of the heights of the mountain range on the north of the land of the Sand-Dwellers." But it appears that the ships here were deployed as adjuncts to a land campaign, rather than that fighting at sea.

Similarly, Ramesses III's great fights with the Sea Peoples early in the 12th century B.C. occurred in the Nile Delta and took place partly on land, partly on the river, and partly at sea. Reliefs show curved boats, which if shown to scale, are rather small and carry both missile troops and shielded spearmen. The fighting seems to be limited to combat on deck; ramming is not depicted. So far as we can tell then, Egyptian naval capabilities were fairly limited. The Egyptians are not known to have launched major naval or seaborne campaigns at any time in their independent history. Ships, therefore, appear to have played mainly a delivery and support role in land operations.

The situation was similar in the Near East until the Iron Age. Naval warfare was only minimally practiced, but after about 1000 B.C., the Phoenicians, inhabitants of modern-day Lebanon, were regarded as the regional masters of the art. The Assyrians used boats and ships in campaigns in river lands and in marshy regions. Reliefs show fighting from reed boats in marshes, the transportation of chariots across rivers in what looked like coracles, and Assyrian troops crossing rivers by swimming on inflated animal skins. As with Egypt, these are all support actions for land operations.

Yet the palace of Sennacherib at Nineveh has yielded a relief, of about 700 B.C. in date, which depicts what is probably a Phoenician warship. It has a rowing crew on two levels—so it's a so-called "bireme,"—who are shown inside the ship. A top deck has round shields, as sort of a wall around the edge, and is manned by a crew armed with bows and arrows. Only two of these can be seen since the relief is broken and the rest are lost. Most importantly, however, it has a ramming beak at the front.

The addition of ramming beaks to ships changed them from mere fighting platforms into weapons unto themselves. Use of rams required the proper training of crews, demanded more sophisticated maneuvering capabilities, and led to the development of "set piece" maneuvers. How all this was used by the Assyrians is not obvious. Their transmarine imperial holdings appear limited to the arm of Cyprus, and that is more likely a claimed suzerainty than any reality. So despite their access to Phoenician ships, the Assyrians did not develop their naval capabilities to any great extent, and remained a land power.

The Persians reversed this tendency. They deployed Phoenician and Egyptian and Ionian Greek fleets in the Aegean and used them to attack Greek islands and, as we saw in Lecture Ten, to deliver an invasion force across the Aegean to mainland Greece in 490 B.C. In 480 B.C., during Xerxes' invasion, their fleet acquitted itself quite well against the Greeks off the coast of Artimesium during the Thermopylae campaign. Their greatest test however was yet to come.

The Greeks themselves were a maritime people and were long accustomed to naval warfare. Wall paintings from the Bronze-Age Cretan culture dubbed Minoan show ships and, apparently, a sea battle. A frieze from the so-called West House on Thera, dated to around 1500 B.C., shows oared ships fitted out with bunting, perhaps involved in a regatta of some sort. One scene seems to show disembarked warriors attacking a coastal town and, perhaps, a naval engagement proper, with sailors pitched into the sea. But this, must be admitted, may also just be a storm wrecking the ships.

It is largely agreed by scholars that the Mycenaeans from mainland Greece conquered Crete, or parts of it, around 1450 B.C. If so, they must have arrived as seaborne invaders. And, of course, remember that the traditions of the Trojan War have a large naval expedition to

Asia at its core, even if naval engagements themselves, or even if there were any, are not specifically described. The Homeric poems, possibly reflecting here the situation in the 8th century B.C., do refer to sea-fights and the extra-large pikes used in them, even if no engagements are, again, specifically described.

But raiding and piracy are part and parcel of the Homeric world, an accepted and acceptable mode of making a living. At one point, for instance, a host in the *Odyssey* asks his newly-arrived visitors, "Where did you sail from, over the running sea-lanes? Out on some trading spree or roving the waves like pirates, sea-wolves raiding at will, who risk their lives to plunder other men?" Nearly contemporary "Dipylon" vases show beaked ships, which include scenes of disembarking warriors and, in one case, a sword fight underway on deck. What these scenes commemorate—actual events from real life, or scenes inspired by the Homeric tradition—well, that's another matter.

Toward the end of the 6th century, a new form of ship emerged that was to revolutionize naval warfare in the Mediterranean basin. This was the trireme. Up to this point the ship of choice, among the Greeks anyway, had been the pentekonter, a fifty-oared ship with a crew the same size. The trireme carried four times as many men. It was more than 120 feet long and a little under 20 feet wide. The 170 crewmembers toiled on three banks of oars to propel the vessel at speeds of up to nine knots, as was established by sea trials conducted on the replica trireme, called the *Olympius* in the 1980s and 1990s.

The ship could cover 130 sea-miles in a single day. It appears to have been invented by the Persians, or probably the Phoenicians, but was enthusiastically adopted by the Greeks. And by 500 B.C., it was already ubiquitous in Greek lands.

As a warship, the trireme combined speed, maneuverability, and strength. Its on-deck armaments were minimal: usually a contingent of 4 archers and 10 hoplite marines. The focus, rather, was on ramming with bronze beaks, sometimes fitted with several blades. A fine example of one, by the way, and has been found off the coast of Israel, at a place called Athlit, in 1980, and can be seen today in the Museum at Haifa, and dates to the Hellenistic era. The Greeks developed, or at least adopted from the Persians, several maneuvers that optimized the trireme's advantages. The *diekplous*, meaning a "sailing through and out," saw attacking triremes pass between enemy ships and then wheel around and ram them from the sides or from the rear.

The *periplous*, meaning a "sailing around," may have been a phase of the *diekplous*, or some sort of encircling maneuver in its own right. A defensive posture against both moves was the *kyklos*, or the circle, with the prows all facing outwards. The Greeks in fact, we are told, adopted this formation when fighting the Persians off the cape at Artemisium. The trireme, then, revolutionized naval combat, which became much more sophisticated, and was conducted on a far larger scale than the raids of the "sea-wolves" referred to in Homer.

The deployment of a substantial Persian Royal Navy in the Aegean, as well as ongoing local Greek rivalries, forced many Greek city-states with maritime interests to look to their ships in the late 6th and early 5th centuries B.C. None did so more than Athens. As we saw last time how Themistocles persuaded the Athenians to double their navy's size between 490 and 480 B.C. As a result, Athens commanded the largest and most modern fleet in Greek lands, followed by Corinth, and then behind them, Corcyra, which is the modern island of Corfu. After the Persian wars, the Athenians used their fleet to exert undue influence over the affairs of the Greek islands and the Aegean coastal regions. Naval power had come to define the *polis* or city-state of Athens.

It is often argued that the turn to naval power had major ramifications on the domestic front inside Athens. Rowers were drawn from the lower orders, the ones usually excluded from the muster since they could not afford the expense of hoplite equipment. But the manpower requirements of the trireme—40,000 alone for Athens' 200 triremes, if fully crewed and all in service at once—meant that these poor Athenians now played a vital military role and so enjoyed unprecedented political leverage in the democratic assembly. This, in any case, is the view of the pamphleteer called the "Old Oligarch," who is judged to have lived sometime towards the end of the 5th century B.C., and is a strong critic of the Athenian democracy, hence his name, the Old Oligarch. We don't actually know what his name was, but that's the name given to him by modern scholars. His views, by the way, are echoed in the 4th century by Aristotle, who was no friend of democracy. The Old Oligarch's critique has been used to argue that naval power and democracy were inherently linked at Athens, the former undergirding the latter.

207

This suggestion is not without its problems. First, it requires taking critics of Athenian democracy at their word. Study of how the Athenian navy was actually crewed and who rowed the ships does not support the proposal. So great was Athens' need for rowers that demand far outstripped supply. Many rowers were hired from abroad, drawn from the non-citizen resident population of Athens, or they were slaves. None of these groups, of course, enjoyed political rights in Athens. The percentage of lower-class Athenian citizens, then, who consistently served in the navy, may well have been rather small. Without naval service, their alleged political clout dissipates. In any event, other powerful Greek naval states—Syracuse, Corinth or Corcyra—were not democracies. The supposed inherent connection between naval power and democracy in Athens may well be a figment of the Old Oligarch's polemic.

With the background duly filled in, let's return to the desperate situation facing the Greek alliance after Thermopylae.

Athens, as we have seen, had been evacuated. The city was then captured by the Persians, plundered, and burned. Only some die-hards held out on the Acropolis, convinced that the "wooden-wall" mentioned in a Delphic oracle was to be taken literally. So they barricaded themselves in behind a wooden wall on the Acropolis, which was promptly burned down by the Persians.

Meanwhile, the allied fleet gathered in the strait of Salamis, off the south coast of Attica. It numbered between 320 triremes, depending on which source one reads. Of these 180 were Athenian ships. The size of the Persian fleet is harder to estimate, but it must have been huge. Aeschylus, in his play, *The Persians*, which was composed within a decade of the battle of Salamis, puts it an even 1,000 ships—surely a poetically handy figure. Herodotus has 1,207 Persian ships before Artemisium, as we saw last time, and with a few hundred lost to the fighting at Artemisium, and some severe storms right before Salamis, we may imagine somewhat less than that. Modern estimates vary wildly and depend on the degree of the scholar's trust in the ancient authors. But the Greeks insisted that they were vastly outnumbered at Salamis, so a figure of 600 to 800 Persian warships, each with crew of about 200, would not be impossible.

In the crisis, strategic fault lines yawned open between the Peloponnesians and the Athenians. The Peloponnesians wished to build a wall across the Isthmus of Corinth and defend their peninsula by land, while the fleet anchored off the coast. To be fair, the three naval engagements at Artemisium during the Thermopylae campaign did not offer much cause for hope; the sea-fights had all been stalemates. Further, should the naval battle at Salamis go badly, the Peloponnesian coast would be virtually defenseless. The mood was therefore for withdrawal.

Themistocles was convinced that, should the fleet move to the Isthmus, it would disperse, as each contingent looked to its own interests. They must stay and fight in the strait at Salamis. He prevailed on Eurybiades, the Spartan commander-in-chief, to hold another meeting. First he tried arguments based on strategy: the heavier Greek ships would have an advantage over the more numerous and lighter Persian vessels in the strait, he argued. But the Peloponnesians, chiefly led by the Corinthians, were not convinced. So Themistocles threatened a unilateral Athenian withdrawal from the entire war: they would make a new home for themselves in Italy. This worked. Eurybiades agreed to stay at Salamis.

Themistocles, however, had no faith in his compatriots' constancy, so he sent a false message over to Xerxes. He reported that the Greeks were intent on escaping out the other end of the strait, and that Xerxes should act to prevent them from doing so. Xerxes took the bait and sent some 200 ships from Egypt around the island of Salamis to block the northern entrance of the strait. The Greeks were now trapped and had no choice but to fight. Themistocles, by threats and deceit, had manufactured a confrontation in the strait at Salamis.

This whole account, as we have it in Herodotus, is seriously flawed. We have to accept the following: the Greek command at Salamis started debating whether to fight or to cut and run before the Persians even reached Athens. They were still debating this issue when word was brought that the Acropolis had fallen. But Herodotus elsewhere reports that the Acropolis held out for some time—the debate seems unduly protracted. Next, another assembly was called on the following day, to discuss the same issue again: stay and fight, or withdraw to the Isthmus? It is during this debate that Themistocles sends his false message to Xerxes. On the third day, when the Greeks were informed that they had been blocked into the strait, they are still in assembly, and still debating the same issue. The account borders on the incoherent.

There can be little doubt that strategic and tactical debates took place on both sides before so vital an engagement, but we can't accept Herodotus' illogical account of their content without serious caution. In all likelihood, he jerry-rigged his version from diverse sources, who provided different anecdotes and details that he tried to string together into a coherent narrative. He failed.

The defective and patchy source material make tracing the battle's course equally difficult. The Persian fleet was made up of Phoenician and Ionian Greek ships and, having bottled the Greeks up in the strait, it approached from the wider southeastern end. Herodotus says that the Greeks were dismayed at the armada's size and, on its approach, began to backwater until one ship, claimed by both Athens and the island of Aegina, charged the Persian line, changed the course of the fighting, and led to the defeat of the Persians. This incident is suspiciously dramatic. After this, Herodotus' account devolves into a catalogue of individual exploits and stories, which makes a tactical assessment of the fighting all but impossible. Other sources provide some additional details, but little by way of a wider perspective on the engagement.

One of the major problems is the initial deployment of the fleets in the strait. Herodotus envisioned the fleets lined up parallel to the shores on either side of the strait: the Persians lined up parallel to the Attic coast, with the Phoenicians on their right "toward Eleusis," as he has it, and the Ionians ships on the left. The Greeks would then be opposite, parallel to the shore of Salamis. Now, such a disposition makes no sense. How could one fleet file past the other in column, its ship's sides exposed to ramming, without risking disaster? Much more likely is that the Greek fleet spanned the strait, facing southeast, and the Persians entered from the southeast, the fleet splitting to pass around the Nile at the narrows' entrance. The engagement then took place in the middle of the strait and on this island, as the Greek's wrested it from Persian control.

Although the tactical phases of the battle are lost to us, it emerges clearly that the Persian defeat was due to their numbers and the confusion in their ranks as their armada became compressed in the strait, while the Greeks kept their order. Despite several modern attempts to identify complex tactical maneuvers during the battle, there is no solid evidence to suggest that they actually took place. The Greeks won by keeping their cool and making the most of the confusion among their enemy. Such is a perennial recipe for success in battle.

The human cost of Salamis was huge. Ancient naval warfare, with its combination of ramming, missile exchanges, deck fighting, and the threat of drowning, was particularly lethal. For the rowers in the immediate vicinity of an enemy ram crashing into their ship, death would come by mashing or splinter wounds. If a ship sank, there would be a panicked scramble to reach the deck, where missiles or enemy soldiers were waiting. Herodotus says that the Persian crews could not swim, so most were doomed as soon as their ships were holed. Even for those who survived a sinking, it was standard practice to shoot at survivors and hit them with oars and weapons, in the scene. If any Persian survivors washed up onto the shores of the island of Salamis, Athenian ground troops awaited them; and likewise for any Greeks who made it to the Persian-occupied mainland, where Persian ground troops would have killed them all.

All in all, the scene in the strait of Salamis by battle's end would have been one of horrific carnage, wreckage, and corpses littering the narrow patch of contested sea. The scene is vividly evoked by Aeschylus in his play *The Persians*, as a Persian messenger brings word of Salamis to the court back home:

> The hulls of our vessels rolled over and the sea was hidden from our sight, strewn as it was with wrecks and slaughtered men. The shores and reefs were crowded with our dead. But, as if our men were tunnies or a haul of fish, the foe kept striking and hacking them with broken oars and fragments of wrecked ships, and groans and shrieks together filled the open sea until the face of sable night hid the scene.

Curiously, Herodotus does not record losses. Diodorus Siculus says that the Greeks lost 40 ships, the Persians 200, not including those captured. If these figures are right, then the Persians lost between 25% and 30% of their naval fighting force that day. It was a crushing defeat. Since, as we've seen, Herodotus states that the Persian crews could not swim, we may be looking at up to 40,000 men floundering the strait, a good proportion of whom would have perished.

Xerxes, who had watched proceedings from a throne set up on a nearby hill, was shaken. Our Greek sources think of him as fleeing home in a panic, but he had good reason to return to Asia. A victorious Greek fleet could have sailed to the Hellespont and, by smashing the pontoon bridge there, cut him off from home. This course of action was actually proposed, but rejected by the Greek command. Also a Persian king defeated in distant lands was, by Persian standards, a fruit ripe for the plucking. Ambitions lurking in the hearts of royal relatives might be stirred by such news. Xerxes had to get back to Asia.

The importance of Salamis is not to be doubted, but it has been overstated in certain quarters. Victor Davis Hanson, in his account of the battle in the book *Carnage and Culture*, credits the outcome of Salamis to the Greek devotion to freedom, a concept absent from Persian political culture. The Greeks fought more ferociously at Salamis because they were free men; the Persians were the slaves of a despot. In particular, he singles out the importance of free speech in the Greek pre-battle debates, of which he writes: "The freedom to explore different strategies, debate tactics, and listen to the complaints of the sailors was raucous and not pretty, but when the battle itself got underway, the Greeks, not the Persians, had at last discovered the best way to fight in the strait of Salamis."

This interpretation, while cleverly argued and certainly appealing, does not jibe particularly well with the known facts, as far as I'm concerned. There is no compelling evidence, from Salamis or indeed anywhere else, that free people fight harder and more determinedly than conscripts in the service of autocrats. Some of the most feared and effective fighting forces in world history have been the Mongols, the Ottoman Janissaries, the Nazi panzer divisions, and the Red Army of the Second World War—all serving systems not notable for their devotion to individual liberty. As military historian, John Lazenby, succinctly puts it: "war puts no premium on freedom."

Also, as we saw earlier, Herodotus' account of the Greek debates before the battle borders on the incoherent. Even as presented, they were dominated by only one issue: do we stay or do we go? There is no indication of prolonged discussion of specific tactical approaches for fighting in the strait, outside of how such considerations impinged on that overarching question. In the end, the Greeks were threatened and tricked into fighting at Salamis by Themistocles. This is hardly a banner example of discovery through debate.

As to the fighting at Salamis, we simply do not have enough detailed information to declare that the Greeks fought better because they were free men. Herodotus in fact, documents two episodes of courage on the Persian side and two on the Greek. He also records the cowardice of the Corinthians on the Greek side, but recounts no corresponding example of cowardess on the Persian side. So if anything, perhaps the edge goes to the Persians for having fought ferociously, even if they lost.

On the surface, then, both sides fought equally hard at Salamis. But the Persians did so at a huge tactical disadvantage, with a much larger fleet compressed into the small strait. This latter fact, rather than the degree of freedom enjoyed by the combatants, is what determined the outcome at Salamis.

As to the historical importance of Salamis, one assessment reads as follows: "We would live under a much different tradition today—one where writers are under death sentences, women secluded and veiled, free speech curtailed, government in the hands of the autocrats' extended family, universities mere centers of religious zealotry, and the thought police in our living rooms and bedrooms—had Themistocles and his sailors failed"

This sort of thing strikes me as rather overstated, even a little confused. It equates a rather tolerant ancient Persian Zoroastrianism with a less forgiving modern Islamic extremism. No doubt, had the Greeks lost at Salamis, western history would have been very different, but how different is impossible to say. Greeks were well ensconced in South Italy and Sicily; survivors could have found refuges there and continued their traditions. Remember, Themistocles had said that if the fleet would not stay at Salamis, he would take the Athenians off to Italy. Well, survivors could have done that. So I really see no good reason to think that defeat at Salamis would have heralded "the end of Western civilization," although certainly, that civilization would have looked rather different.

In the context of the war in 480 B.C., Salamis was definitely the decisive turning point. But there was more work to be done. A huge Persian land force was still on Greek soil. And it yet might secure the conquest of Greece for the Great King.

Despite Salamis, the Persians still entertained high hopes for victory. They were not unfounded. The enormous army under Mardonius wintered in Central Greece over 480 into 479 B.C. It was comprised of hand-picked troops: Persians, Medes, Sacae, and Ionian Greek hoplites. Herodotus numbers the host at 300,000 Persians and 50,000 Ionians. The numbers are, as usual, seriously exaggerated, but an army of even one-third the size would still be around 100,000 strong, and not untypical for Persian Royal host. And if you imagine the initial invading force has been about 100,000 combatants and having lost maybe 8,000 to 10,000 at Thermopylae, we're still looking at maybe 90,000 to 100,000.

Using diplomacy and money to undermine Greek resistance was discussed by the Persian high command, but Mardonius rejected this softly-softly approach. He wanted to settle the issue in battle. So the Persians moved into the open plains of Boeotia, where their cavalry could be cut loose, and set up camp on the Asopus River near Plataea. Mardonius had chosen his ground well.

An allied Greek army was assembled, numbered by Herodotus at 110,000, drawn from 23 states. Of this force, 40,500 were hoplites, the rest light-armed. This was the largest hoplite army ever mustered. The most important Greek contingents were 10,000 Spartan hoplites under their king, Pausanias, and 8,000 Athenian hoplites under a guy called Aristides the Wise. The other Greek contingents, some as few as 200 strong, had their own commanders, but everyone recognized, of course, Pausanias the Spartan as the ranking officer.

The Greek force occupied positions on the low hills and ridges facing the Persians across the Asopus. Some skirmishes ensued. According to Herodotus, in these engagements, the Persian cavalry charged the Greeks in squadrons, wheeled and turned. This makes it clear that the Persian cavalry relied first and foremost on missile weapons, and that they were not heavy cavalry, designed to charge en masse and break enemy ranks. The main bodies, however, occupying positions favorable to themselves and reluctant to surrender the advantage, did not engage for many days.

The Greek army, in three main contingents, with the Athenians on the left, the Spartans on the right, and everybody else in the middle, moved about on its ridges. In the course of these maneuvers, the center, nearly 20,000 men strong, got lost in the dark and ended up almost four kilometers behind the front. Dawn broke on the Athenians and the Spartans widely separated. Seeing an opportunity, Mardonius pounced.

The main brunt of the assault fell on the Spartans and their allies, probably numbering about 20,000 strong, both light armed and hoplites. But the Persians lost cohesion in their advance, rather like the Athenians at Marathon; the Spartans charged the Persian lines, smashed through their wall of wicker shields, and came to grips with the lightly armored Persian infantry. Marathon quickly repeated itself: the Persians fought tenaciously but under the huge disadvantage of lack of armor and shorter spears. They also engaged the Spartans in small groups rather than en masse, and so effectively negated their numerical advantage. Not even breaking the Spartan spears gave them an edge. In this sort of messy, close-quarter combat the Persians were no match for the Spartan hoplite, for whom this sort of thing was the norm. The fight was intense and protracted, and this is a testament to the fighting spirit of the Persian troops. They tried their best, but were outclassed.

Mardonius and his cavalry faired no better than the infantry did, as is the case whenever cavalry confront infantry who maintain their good order. Not long into the fight, Mardonius was killed. Leaderless, Persian resistance disintegrated, and the battle phased into the slaughter of desperate and fleeing men.

Meanwhile, the Athenians had set out to assist the Spartans in their crisis. But they were intercepted en route by the Ionian Greeks and endured a tough fight of their own, in which they eventually prevailed. The Greek center, far to the rear, tried to get in on the action, but it was caught in the open by Persian cavalry and suffered 600 casualties.

Herodotus numbers the Greek casualties as 91 Spartans, 17 Tegeans, and 52 Athenians as opposed to 257,000 Persians. These figures are, of course, nonsensical, and make no mention of the 600 losses from the Greek center. Other sources, no less confused, speak of anywhere from 1,300 to 10,000 Greek dead. We will never know the exact figures, but ancient battles usually transmogrified into massacres once one side turned its back to flee. So a disproportion of casualties on the losing side is to be expected, though hardly on the scale stated in the figures given for Plataea.

The Battle of Plataea cemented the victory at Salamis the previous year, and freed Greece from the threat of Persian rule. On the same day as Plataea, a Greek army and fleet confronted the remnants of the Persian fleet from Salamis on a shore-side battle on the peninsula of Mycale, on the Turkish coast. Here, too, the Persians were routed. What was different about this fight, of course, was that it took place on Persian—not on Greek—soil. The Greeks were taking the fight to the enemy.

But in a great historical irony, the allied Greek assault on the Persians and those Greeks who had medized during the Persian invasions, ultimately led to a vast intra-Greek conflict, a conflict that was to break the back of Greek power and see Athens, the hero of Marathon and Salamis, laid low. The turning point in this, the Peloponnesian War, is the subject of our next lecture.

Timeline

1 million–c. 10,000 B.C.	Paleolithic (Old Stone Age). Humans evolve. Sporadic conflicts take place amid low population density.
35,000–10,000 B.C.	Upper Paleolithic. *Homo sapiens* are fully evolved, but population density is low; sporadic conflicts are ongoing.
10,000–8,000 B.C.	Mesolithic (Middle Stone Age). Beginnings of agriculture take place.
12,000–10,000 B.C.	Jebel Sahaba burials in Sudan.
8,000–3,000 B.C.	Neolithic (New Stone Age). Agriculture and settled communities appear. Population increases, and chiefdoms and proto-states appear.
c. 7000 B.C.	Jericho (Israel) is equipped with large stone walls and tower.
c. 6500 B.C.	Çatal Hüyük settlement in Turkey shows signs of defensive thinking.
c. 6000–4000 B.C.	Cave paintings from Spain show warrior bands, "execution," and "army of four versus army of three."
c. 5350 B.C.	"Skull nests" arranged in cave at Ofnet, Germany.
3500–2700 B.C.	Predynastic periods in Mesopotamia and Egypt. Egypt is unified into a monarchic state c. 2900 B.C., and Sumer sees appearance of city-states (Uruk, Ur, and others).
c. 3100 B.C.	Fortress Palette in Egypt shows possible attacks on walled towns.

3000–2900 B.C.	Narmer Palette in Egypt shows the pharaoh smiting enemies and headless corpses.
c. 3000–2350 B.C.	Early Dynastic period of Sumer, usually divided into three subphases: Early Dynastic I (c. 3000–2750 B.C.), II (2750–2600 B.C.), and III (2600-2350 B.C.). Rulers compete for the august title "King of Kish."
c. 2700–2180 B.C.	Old Kingdom Egypt. Exclusivist state ideology evolves, and sieges are depicted in tombs.
c. 2600 B.C.	Umma-Lagash border dispute starts. Relief from Girsu shows "POW execution."
c. 2500 B.C.	Royal Standard of Ur depicts uniformly equipped infantry, war carts, combat, ruler, officers, and POWs.
c. 2450 B.C.	Eanatum, king of Lagash, battles Umma. Vulture Stela depicts war carts and massed infantry, and text records open-field battles.
2350–2100 B.C.	Akkadian (Sargonid) Empire.
c. 2350 B.C.	Sargon of Akkad conquers all of Mesopotamia. Wars with Asiatics are attested in biography of Weni (Uni) in Egypt.
c. 2250 B.C.	Naram-Sin, grandson of Sargon, ruler of Akkadian Empire, is deified.
2180–2040 B.C.	First Intermediate Period in Egypt; much intra-Egyptian warfare.
c. 2000–1650 B.C.	Middle Kingdom Egypt. Weapons inventory increases. Sophisticated

	fortifications are attested (for example, "Wall of the Ruler" and Buhen).
1960 B.C.	The *Story of Sinuhe* tells of Egyptian-Asiatic relations.
1880 B.C.	Stela of Khu-Sebek implies standing army and royal guard.
c. 1800–1200 B.C.	Hittite state/empire in Anatolia.
c. 1660–1570 B.C.	Second Intermediate Period in Egypt (a.k.a. Hyksos Invasion).
c. 1600–1100 B.C.	Height of Mycenaean civilization on mainland Greece.
c. 1570–1070 B.C.	New Kingdom Egypt. This is an aggressive, militaristic state with pharaoh as war leader, a state army of infantry, and chariotry used extensively.
c. 1479/68 B.C.	Battle of Megiddo (April or May): The Egyptians defeat the Asiatic coalition. The first example of battle narrative appears.
c. 1350–1100 B.C.	First Assyrian Empire (a.k.a. Middle Assyrian Period).
c. 1285/75 B.C.	Battle of Kadesh (May): Egyptians and Hittites fight to a stalemate.
c. 1200 B.C.	Trojan War.
c. 1100–800 B.C.	Dark Age in Greece.
c. 900–612 B.C.	The Neo-Assyrian Empire dominates the Near East.
853 B.C.	Battle of Karkar (Assyrians versus Syrians).
753 B.C.	Traditional date for the foundation of Rome.

c. 750–700 B.C.	Accepted date range for composition of Homer's *Iliad* and *Odyssey*.
714 B.C.	Sargon II's eighth campaign in Urartu.
701 B.C.	Sieges of Lachish and Jerusalem by Sennacherib.
c. 650 B.C.	Chigi Vase depicts warriors in hoplite equipment.
521–486 B.C.	Darius I, king of Persia.
499–494 B.C.	Ionian revolt against Persia.
490 B.C.	Battle of Marathon (September): Athenians defeat Persians.
486–465 B.C.	Xerxes, king of Persia.
480 B.C.	Battle of Thermopylae (August/September): The Persians defeat the Greeks, thus establishing the great cultural tradition of the Glorious Defeat. Battle of Salamis (September/October): The Greek fleet defeats the Persian fleet.
479 B.C.	Battle of Plataea (early summer): The Greeks defeat the Persians.
478–431 B.C.	Athenian dominance grows in the Aegean.
431–404 B.C.	Peloponnesian War between the Spartans and Athenians.
421 B.C.	The Peace of Nicias is signed: A ceasefire is called in the Peloponnesian War.
415–413 B.C.	The Athenian expedition to Sicily.
414 B.C.	The arrival of the Spartan Gylippus energizes Syracusan resistance.

413 B.C. ....The second Athenian expedition arrives: The entire Athenian force on Sicily is annihilated.

406–367 B.C. ....Dionysius I, tyrant of Syracuse, makes great strides in the development of siege warfare.

404–338 B.C. ....Period of great instability in mainland Greece. Experimentation with traditional hoplite phalanx continues.

401–399 B.C. ....Cyrus's "march up-country" and the March of the Ten Thousand.

401 B.C. ....Battle of Cunaxa (September): Artaxerxes wards off a challenge to his throne by Cyrus.

399–398 B.C. ....Siege artillery (catapults) invented at Syracuse.

c. 380–304 B.C. ....Romans adopt manipular formations sometime during this period.

371 B.C. ....Battle of Leuctra: Epaminondas of Thebes experiments with hoplite phalanx and defeats the Spartans.

362 B.C. ....(Second) Battle of Mantinea: Epaminondas of Thebes defeats Spartans and allies.

359–338 B.C. ....Reign of Philip II, growth of Macedonian power.

356 B.C. ....Birth of Alexander the Great (late July or October).

338 B.C. ....Battle of Chaeronea: The era of the independent Greek city-state ends, and Greece is made subordinate to Macedonian interests.

336 B.C. ....Philip II assassinated; Alexander succeeds to the Macedonian throne.

334 B.C.	Alexander invades Asia. Battle of the Granicus (summer): Alexander defeats the Persians.
333 B.C.	Battle of Issus: Alexander defeats the Persians, led by Darius III.
332 B.C.	Siege of Tyre: Alexander captures the city after a seven-month siege.
331 B.C.	Battle of Gaugamela (1 October): Alexander defeats the Persians, led by Darius III.
323 B.C.	Alexander dies in Babylon (10 June).
305–304 B.C.	Unprecedented complexity is displayed in the siege of Rhodes by Demetrius Poliorketes.
280–274 B.C.	Pyrrhic War in Italy and Sicily.
280 B.C.	Battle of Heraclea: Pyrrhus defeats Romans but suffers huge casualties.
279 B.C.	Battle of Asculum: The result is unclear.
275 B.C.	Battle of Beneventum: The Romans defeat Pyrrhus.
264–241 B.C.	First Punic War.
218–202 B.C.	Second Punic (Hannibalic) War.
218 B.C.	Battle of Trebia (December): The Carthaginians defeat the Romans.
217 B.C.	Battle of Lake Trasimene (June): The Carthaginians defeat the Romans.
216 B.C.	Battle of Cannae (2 August): The Carthaginians defeat the Romans.
215–204 B.C.	Hannibal is ineffective in Italy.
213–211 B.C.	Siege of Syracuse by the Romans.

208 B.C. ....Battle of Baecula (Spain): Scipio defeats the Carthaginians.

206 B.C. ....Battle of Ilipa (Spain): Scipio defeats the Carthaginians and ends the Punic Empire in Spain.

202 B.C. ....Battle of Zama (October?): Scipio defeats Hannibal.

197 B.C. ....Battle of Cynoscephalae (April/May): The Romans defeat the Macedonians.

190 B.C. ....Battle of Magnesia-ad-Sipylum (December): The Romans defeat the Seleucids.

168 B.C. ....Battle of Pydna (22 June): The Romans defeat the Macedonians.

133 B.C. ....The Romans take the Spanish stronghold of Numantia.

107–100 B.C. ....Period of so-called Marian reforms in the Roman army. They probably extended before and after Marius's era of prominence. The process of professionalization begins.

102–101 B.C. ....Battles of Aquae Sextiae (102 B.C.) and Vercellae (101 B.C.): The Romans defeat the German invaders in the first major clash of German and Roman arms.

55 and 53 B.C. ....Caesar takes Roman arms across the Rhine into Germany for the first time.

52 B.C. ....Siege of Alesia (July–October?): Caesar captures the Gallic stronghold and ends the revolt of Vercingetorix.

49–45 B.C. ....Caesar's civil wars.

48 B.C.	Siege of Dyrrhachium (January–July): Caesar is forced to withdraw from besieging Pompey's forces.
48 B.C.	Battle of Pharsalus (9 August): Caesar defeats Pompey in Greece.
47 B.C.	Battle of Zela (2 August): Caesar defeats the Pontic pretender Pharnaces in Turkey.
46 B.C.	Battle of Thapsus (6 April): Caesar defeats the Pompeians in North Africa.
45 B.C.	Battle of Munda (17 March): Caesar defeats the Pompeians in Spain.
27 B.C.–A.D. 14	Augustus reforms the Roman army into a standing force of volunteers. The process of professionalization is completed.
12 B.C.–A.D. 9	Roman efforts to conquer German territory between the Rhine and Elbe Rivers.
A.D. 9	Battle of the Teutoburg Forest (September): Three Roman legions are ambushed and massacred by Germans under Arminius.
A.D. 66–70	Great Jewish revolt in Judea.
A.D. 72–73	Siege of Masada (November?–16 April): The Romans capture the last holdout of Jewish rebels on the shores of the Dead Sea.
A.D. 235–280 B.C.	"Third-century crisis" in the Roman Empire marries internal instability with increased pressure on the frontiers.

A.D. 251 .... Battle of Abrittus (1 July): The Goths defeat the Romans; Emperor Decius is killed on the field.

A.D. 255–257 .... The Goths cross the Danube and ravage the Balkans.

A.D. 262–269 .... The Goths cross the Black Sea and ravage Asia Minor and Greece.

A.D. 306–337 .... Constantine, building on earlier developments, divides the Roman army into field troops (*comitatenses*) and border-garrison troops (*limitanei*).

A.D. 376 .... Tervingi and Greuthungi Goths cross into Roman Thrace.

A.D. 376–382 .... The Gothic War in Thrace.

A.D. 378 .... Battle of Adrianople (9 August): The Goths defeat the Romans and kill Emperor Valens.

Glossary

Achaemenid: Title of dynasty that ruled the Persian Empire from Cyrus the Great (r. c. 559–530 B.C.) to Darius III (336–330 B.C.).

Acies triplex (tripartite battle formation): The set formation of the Roman Republican army in battle; employed throughout most of Roman history, though with variations.

Agema: Royal guard in the Macedonian army, usually handpicked from among the *hypaspists*.

Alans: Originally a steppe culture of the horse, the Alans settled along the north coast of the Black Sea. In the 4th and 5th centuries A.D., they joined the Huns in visiting depredations on the Roman Empire.

Allies (*socii*): Nonlegionary troops, either Italian or foreign, who fought with Republican-era Roman legions. Commanded by their own leaders (if foreign) or Roman prefects (if Italian).

Antilabe: The rim-grip of a hoplite's shield.

Asiatics: Contemptuous label applied by Egyptians to their northern opponents, no matter what their ethnicity.

Assur: Chief city and deity of the Assyrian state.

Assyrian Royal Records/Archives: Inscriptions carved on clay and stone objects glorifying the king's annual campaigns.

Auxiliaries: Noncitizen troops in the Roman imperial army. They served 25 years and were granted citizenship and a pension on discharge. Organized into cohorts of 500 or 1,000, they were often commanded by their own leaders or Roman prefects.

Barbarization: Term for the growing presence and prominence of Germanic peoples in the western Roman Empire during the Late Empire, particularly in the army.

Casus belli (lit. "occasion for war"): Latin phrase for a reason for going to war.

Cataphract: A type of heavily armored cavalryman developed in the east. The fully developed cataphract and his mount were encased in mail, but earlier versions may have been less comprehensively protected.

Center: The central portion of an ancient battle line.

Century: A subunit of the Roman legion that was nominally 100 strong but actually comprised anywhere from 30 to 80 men. Their commanders were called *centurions*.

Chariot: Popular horse-drawn war vehicle in the Bronze Age Near East and Egypt. War carts drawn by donkeys are attested as early as 2500 B.C. at Ur in Sumeria, but true chariots appeared only in the 18th century B.C. Adopted by the New Kingdom Egyptians, the chariot became one of the twin pillars of the Egyptian army, the other being infantry. Uncertainty prevails as to how the chariot was used tactically, but its horses and light frame argue strongly against shock impacts. It was principally used as a mobile firing platform. Its popularity declined in the Assyrian Period, but it was retained as a prestige, if ineffectual, arm of Eastern armies into the 1st century B.C. Caesar faced chariots at Zela in 47 B.C.

Circumvallation/contravallation: Processes in passive siege warfare whereby a besieged location is walled in to prevent the inhabitants from escaping or from gaining access to food and other resources from without. Technically, *contravallation* refers to siege works facing the besieged place and *circumvallation*, to siege works facing in the opposite direction, to block relief forces.

Cohort: Administrative, then tactical unit in the Roman army. Italian allies were organized into cohorts in the republic, and after Marius's reforms, the cohort of 480 men replaced the maniple as the legion's principal tactical unit.

Comitatenses (sing. *comitatensis*, "escort"): Field-army soldiers of the Later Empire, often commanded by emperors in person. Formerly, they were thought to be predominantly cavalry troops, but in reality, they were a mixture of both cavalry and infantry units. Field armies were stationed in the hinterland to address successful barbarian incursions, bring relief to besieged fortifications, and act as a block on internal unrest. The name derives from the *comitatus*, the Late-Imperial court and, thus, means "Soldiers of the Court."

Companions: Term used to denote favored units in the Macedonian army. There were Companion cavalry about 2,000 strong around the king, and the phalangites, 10,000 or more strong, were termed Foot Companions.

Consul: Chief annually elected magistrate in Republican Rome. Two were elected each year and held top powers in the political, judicial, and military spheres. They had the greatest *imperium* in the state.

Contubernium (pl. *contubernia*): A group of eight tent mates in the Roman legion.

Dictator: Extraordinary Roman magistracy instituted in crises, often, but not exclusively, military in nature.

Diekplous: Meaning "sailing through and out," this was a Greek naval maneuver with triremes in which the attackers sailed through an enemy formation between ships, then wheeled around to ram from the rear or the side.

Dominate (< *dominus*, "master"): The term sometimes applied to the autocratic system of rule founded by Diocletian and to the period of its operation (A.D. 284–476). The term is used chiefly to distinguish it from the Principate, as established by Augustus.

Early Dynastic Period: Name assigned to the early period of Sumerian history, c. 3000–2350 B.C. It was marked by independent city-states in competition, often of a military nature. It is usually divided into three subphases: Early Dynastic I, II, and III.

Equites: Roman term for cavalry and for a social class parallel to, but larger than, the senatorial order.

Glacis: The sloping lower section of a fortification wall, designed to deter sapping and battering.

Hastati (sing. *hastatus*, "spearman"): Along with *principes* and *triarii*, these troops made up the heavy infantry of the pre-Marian Roman legion. Deployed as 10 maniples, they fought in the first line of the *acies triplex*. Armed with a large shield (*scutum*), helmet, mail shirt or pectoral plate, and greaves, they carried a short Spanish sword and two javelins (*pila*).

Hegemon ("leader"): The position aspired to by large Greek city-states, such as Athens, Thebes, Sparta, or Corinth. The struggle for hegemony helped generate the Peloponnesian War and the subsequent instability in the 4th century.

Hellenistic Period/Kingdoms: Name given to the period after Alexander the Great's death in 323 B.C.; it ended in 30 B.C., the year when Ptolemaic Egypt fell to Rome. The kingdoms into which

Alexander's eastern empire divided and that existed in this period are termed *Hellenistic*.

Homeric warfare: Disputed style of combat portrayed in the Homeric poems, particularly the *Iliad*. Scholars disagree over its nature or even if the poems reflect a genuine style of warfare at all.

Hoplite: The Classical Greek warrior, emergent in 700-600 B.C. and dominant from c. 600–338 B.C. The hoplite was armed with a large, round shield; breastplate; bronze helmet with crest; and greaves. His offensive armament was an eight-foot spear and short sword. The word derives from *hopla*, which means "equipment"; the hoplite was an "equipped man."

Hyksos: Asiatic rulers of Lower Egypt (that is, the Nile Delta) in the Second Intermediate Period. They were formerly thought to have introduced the chariot to Egyptian warfare but are no longer held to have done so.

Hypaspists: Elite unit of Macedonian infantry, usually 3,000 strong, that could fight in various styles, either with the Macedonian *sarissa*, as regular hoplites, or even as light-armed. They were usually stationed on the right flank of the main body of the phalanx.

Immortals: Elite unit of Persian royal guard that was always maintained at its strength of 10,000 and, hence, given its special name.

Imperial Period: Habitual designation for the period of Roman history from Augustus to the "fall" in the 5th century, thus covering the period 31 B.C.–A.D. 476.

Imperium: Originally, this term meant the "power of command" in a military context and was conferred on kings and, later, on consuls and praetors (and dictators). It was also used to denote the area over which the Romans had the power of command and, hence, came to mean "empire" in a territorial sense.

Invest: Term used to describe the process of laying siege to a place, as in "Caesar invested Alesia."

Kardaka (**or** *cardaces*): Form of Persian infantry introduced in the mid-4th century, prior to Alexander's invasion in 334 B.C. The equipment and fighting technique of the *kardaka* are disputed; some see them as a Persian version of hoplites; others as a sort of *peltast*; others as a purely Persian form of light infantry.

King of Kish: Ancient honorific title, of uncertain origin, that Sumerian rulers competed for in the Early Dynastic Period. It seems that it was earned by achieving a recognized military dominance in the region.

Komarch: Headman of a village (*kome*) in the Persian Empire.

Legate (*legatus*, pl. *legati*): Roman term for a man sent (< *legare*, "to send, commission") to represent someone, either an individual or a community. In military terms, it could denote (as *legatus*) a commander of an Imperial-era legion or (as *legatus pro praetore*) a governor or commander of a larger body of troops, who was sent out as a representative of the emperor's *imperium*.

Legion: The basic infantry unit of the Roman army. It varied in size over time, starting out at about 4,200 strong, raised to over 5,000 under the emperors, then reduced to 1,000 in the Later Empire.

Light-armed: Refers to any sort of unit (infantry or cavalry) that was lightly armored, if at all. Good examples are the Persian infantry, who were almost wholly unarmored, lacking helmets and carrying only wicker shields. Light-armed were often used as skirmishers, scouts, and support troops for cavalry.

Limitanei (sing. *limitaneus*, "that at the border"): Garrison troops of the Late Roman Empire (contrast with *comitatenses*) who occupied fixed, often fortified positions. They were less prestigious than the field armies.

Lugal: Sumerian word for a ruler, often rendered as "king" but originally meaning something like "boss man."

Macedonian phalanx: Variation on the Classical Greek hoplite phalanx developed by Philip II, father of Alexander the Great. The Macedonian phalanx was deeper than the traditional version, with files 16 men deep. Phalangites were armed with huge pikes (*sarissae*) so long that the points of the first five ranks projected out in front.

Maniple: Basic tactical unit of the pre-Marian Roman legion. It was comprised of two centuries of 60 men each, commanded by the centurion of the "front/first maniple" (*manipulus prior*).

Marduk: Patron god of Babylon, adopted by the Assyrians as one of the main divine protectors of their empire.

Medize: Greek verb used to denote the decision by some Greek city-states in the early 5th century to submit to Persian rule rather than to fight the Persian invader. In Greek parlance, "Mede" = "Persia," so "medize" = "to go Persian."

Military horizon: A concept developed by anthropologist H. H. Turney-High to demarcate primitive war from genuine war. The military horizon is a matter of social organization rather than weapons development.

Mycenaean Greece: The Bronze Age period of mainland Greek history, from the late third millennium B.C. to the end of the second. The Mycenaeans were discovered by Heinrich Schliemann in the 1870s and 1880s. Their relationship to the Homeric corpus is debated.

Nome: An administrative district in ancient Egypt, headed by a *nomarch*.

Ostraca: Potsherds with writing on them commonly used in ancient times for casting ballots.

Othismos: The "push" in hoplite warfare. It is variously interpreted as a mass shove of close-ordered hoplites against their opponents (rather like a rugby scrum), individual pushes by hoplites fighting in a more open-cast formation, or a figurative term for the to-and-fro of combat.

Paean: Greek religious song, often to Apollo, that was usually sung as armies advanced.

Panoply: A collective term for all the armored elements worn by a warrior (helmet, body armor, shield, and so on).

Peltast: A form of light-armed Greek soldier named after the light, scalloped shield (*pelte*) he carried. Offensive weaponry was comprised of javelins and a short sword. The *peltast*, possibly adapted from Thrace, became prominent in the Peloponnesian War and remained popular for several centuries afterward.

Pentekonter: An older form of Greek warship rowed by 50 men.

Periplous: Meaning "sailing around," this was a Greek naval maneuver, ill-understood, in which the attacker sailed around enemy ships to seek advantageous ramming opportunities.

Phalangite: The term for a member of the Macedonian phalanx. He was armed with a small, round shield; helmet; breastplate; and possibly greaves. He carried an 18- to 20-foot pike called the *sarissa* and was deployed in units of 250 men arrayed 16 deep.

Phalanx: The mass formation adopted by Greek hoplites. In Classical times, it was usually eight ranks deep and as wide as the army could afford. Men stood close together, although how close is debated. Later, attempts were made to deepen sections of the phalanx. Ultimately, it was transformed in the Macedonian phalanx.

Pilum (pl. *pila*): The lethal javelin of the Roman legionary, about six to seven feet long. The upper third was a long iron-barbed spike for greatest penetration. Two types are attested, a heavy and a light version. Legionaries probably launched them in volleys for maximum effect.

Porpax: The central armband of the hoplite shield through which the carrier thrust his forearm to grip the *antilabe* on the rim. In this way, the substantial weight of the hoplite shield (perhaps 20 pounds) was distributed along the warrior's forearm.

Praetor: Second-highest annually elected magistracy in Republican Rome. Originally assistants to the consuls, six were elected each year by 150 B.C., with two more added by Sulla. They carried out judicial, political, and military functions. They had *imperium* and, thus, could command troops.

Praetorian Guard: Originally a special detachment of soldiers who guarded the commanding officer's tent (*praetorium*) in a Roman army's camp, the term was adopted for the imperial guard of the emperor in Rome. Formed by Augustus and discreetly billeted in towns around Rome, they were barracked in a single camp on the outskirts of the city by Tiberius before A.D. 23. They numbered from 9,000–16,000 men, depending on the emperor's inclination. They played some role in imperial politics, although it has often been exaggerated, killing some emperors (such as Gaius [Caligula]) and elevating others (including Claudius, Otho, and Didius Julianus). Their commander, a prefect of equestrian status, could be a person of great influence, as was the case with Sejanus under Tiberius or

Macrinus, who himself became emperor in A.D. 217–218. They were disbanded by Constantine in A.D. 312.

Prefect (< *praeficere* "to put in charge"): Roman term for a military officer of equestrian status, usually appointed to command allied or, later, auxiliary troops.

Primitive war: Term applied to war fought by simpler social orders (clans, bands, tribes, and chiefdoms). It is marked by low-intensity conflicts, indecisive engagements, and a lack of clear-cut objectives.

Principate (< *princeps*, "first citizen"): Term used to describe both the imperial system established by the Roman emperor Augustus and the period of its operation. Its start can be variously dated to anytime between the Battle of Actium (September of 31 B.C.), which saw Octavian established as the undisputed master of the Roman world, and the First Constitutional Settlement (13 January 27 B.C.), which saw Octavian installed as Augustus, the first emperor.

Principes (sing. *princeps*, "front ranker"): Along with *hastati* and *triarii*, these troops made up the heavy infantry of the pre-Marian Roman legion. Deployed as 10 maniples, they fought in the second line of the *acies triplex* and were armed identically to a *hastatus*.

Promachoi (sing. *promachos*): A Greek term, found in Homer, for "fighters in front." Its application in Homer is disputed: Does it denote a socially superior class of bronze-clad warriors, or just anyone who happens to be at the front when the poet's eye shifts its focus in that direction? Later, it was used to describe the front ranks of the hoplite phalanx.

Quincunx: Latin designation for the five-side of a die. The term is applied by modern scholars to the deployment of the manipular legion in three lines of 10 maniples each, with the gaps between the maniples of each line covered by the maniples behind. Note, however, that it has no ancient attestation in this sense.

Regal Period: The period when kings ruled Rome, traditionally dated 753–509 B.C.

Republican Period: Traditionally dated 509–31 B.C., this period of oligarchic rule by senate and magistrates is often subdivided into the Early Republic (down to 264 B.C. and the First Punic War), Middle

Republic (264–133 B.C.), and Late Republic (corresponding to the Roman Revolution, 133–31 B.C.).

Romanization: Modern historians' term for the process of making previously uncivilized regions into Roman ones, although it can also be applied to the adaptation of urbanized cultures to the Roman way.

Sacred band: An elite unit of Theban hoplites, 300 strong (allegedly 150 pairs of homosexual lovers), who occasionally intruded in battle narratives of the 4th century, notably Leuctra (371 B.C.) and Chaeronea (338 B.C.). They were slaughtered by Philip at Chaeronea, and 254 of them probably lay buried under the enigmatic Lion of Chaeronea monument.

Sapping: In siege warfare, the process of undermining a fortification by tunneling underneath it or attacking the lower regions of its walls or towers.

Sarissa: The Macedonian pike, 18 to 20 feet long with a long iron head and heavy counterweight at the butt end. It was possibly first developed exclusively for cavalry but then used by infantry in the mass formation of the Macedonian phalanx. Some *sarissae* came in two halves that, like a pool cue, could be joined together with a metal sheath in the middle.

Satrap: governors of provinces (satrapies) in the Persian Empire. They were remarkably independent of the Great King.

Scutum (pl. *scuta*): A large Roman legionary shield, sharply curved and held in the middle by a single handle. Originally oval in shape, the *scutum* became rectangular under the empire and reverted to an oval, though flat, shape in the Late Empire.

Servian reform: A military-political reform traditionally attributed to King Servius Tullius in the 6th century B.C. but of unclear date. It ascribed citizens to different classes and types of military equipment according to relative wealth.

Spanish sword (*gladius Hispaniensis*): A short cut-and-thrust weapon about three feet long adopted by Roman troops, probably during the First Punic War (264–241 B.C.). It was a lethal weapon that inflicted horrible penetrating and slashing wounds.

Spara: Large wicker shields used by Persians. They appear to have been set up as a wall in front of infantry formations.

Stela (pl. stelae or stele): A freestanding stone monument of no fixed dimensions inscribed with images and/or text. Stelae can mark graves or boundaries or commemorate particular persons or events.

Tartanu: An Assyrian term for field marshals, the highest military officers below the king himself.

Triarii (sing. *triarius*, "third-liner"): Along with *hastati* and *principes*, these troops made up the heavy infantry of the pre-Marian Roman legion. Deployed as 10 maniples, they fought in the third line of the *acies triplex*. They were armed like a *hastatus* or *princeps*, only with a spear (*hasta*) instead of the *pilum*.

Tribune of the Soldiers, a.k.a. Military Tribune (*tribunus militum*): A mid-level legionary staff officer in the Roman army of the republic (when tribunes were elected) and empire (when they were appointed). In the Late Imperial army, *tribune* denotes a more senior officer, of both cavalry and infantry units.

Trireme: A warship of uncertain origin (possibly Phoenician), developed in the 6th century B.C. and adopted by the Greeks. It was propelled by three banks of rowers and carried a crew of 200.

Turma (pl. *turmae*): A 30-strong squadron of cavalry attached to a legion.

Velites (sing. *veles*, "quick"): The light-armed skirmishers assigned to the pre-Marian Roman legion. They were not organized into maniples but screened the formation of the Roman battle line and harassed the enemy with javelins.

War elephants: Introduced to the West after Alexander encountered them in India, they became a favorite weapon of the Hellenistic armies. The Romans used them briefly in the 2nd century B.C. The elephants could be armored and fitted with a tower on their backs, from which missile troops rained javelins and arrows down on the enemy. But despite their fearsome appearance, they rarely proved effective on the field.

Wings: The two portions of an ancient battle line on either side of the center, usually referred to as the "left wing" and "right wing," from the perspective of soldiers in the line.

Biographical Notes

These notes are divided into two groups: (1) ancient authors and (2) historical figures. Note that these two categories are *not* mutually exclusive.

All names are listed by the form used in common English currency (for example, Pompey for Pompeius) and by whatever name they are best known (Caesar for Gaius Julius Caesar and Tiberius for Tiberius Julius Caesar Augustus).

Main Ancient Authors:

Cassius Dio (c. A.D. 164–230). Lucius Cassius Dio was a Greek senator from Asia Minor who composed an 80-book history of Rome, all of which survives, in full or summary (*epitome*) form. More useful for imperial than republican history, Dio is especially illuminating when addressing contemporary events under the Severans.

Cicero (3 January 106 B.C.–7 December 43 B.C.). Marcus Tullius Cicero, a "new man" from Arpinum, was a moderately successful politician but a master craftsman of Latin prose. His huge corpus of surviving writings includes letters, treatises, and speeches. All are historical sources of unparalleled usefulness.

Diodorus Siculus (fl. c. 60–30 B.C.). This Greek writer from Sicily wrote a universal history in 40 books, of which 15 survive intact. Diodorus focuses on Greek and Sicilian affairs down to the First Punic War (264–241 B.C.) and thereafter on Roman affairs. He is particularly useful for Philip II and the Hellenistic era.

Dionysius of Halicarnassus (fl. c. 30–10 B.C.). Dionysius was a teacher of rhetoric who arrived in Rome at the beginning of Augustus's reign and published his 20-book *Roman Antiquities* about 20 years later. The work covered Roman history from earliest times to the outbreak of the First Punic War, and the first 11 books have survived intact, taking the story down to 441 B.C., with fragments of the rest also known. As such, Dionysius's work is a valuable resource for the early history of Rome. Rather like Livy, however, Dionysius's work often reads like a eulogy of Roman virtues, as manifested among "the ancestors" (*maiores*).

Herodotus (fl. c. 450–400 B.C.). Herodotus is called the "Father of History" or the "Father of Lies," depending on one's viewpoint. He was the first writer to work out a theory of causality in human affairs. He wrote, in eight books, a history of Greece's wars with Persia in the early 5th century. His method was to interview (Greek) survivors personally. His presentation is conversational and discursive, with many digressions on matters he found interesting: ethnography, geography, topography, cultural history, and so on.

Homer (fl. c. 750 B.C.). Traditionally, Homer was a single blind poet who wrote the two epic poems that stand as the foundation stones of Greek civilization, the *Iliad* and the *Odyssey*. Modern scholars dispute almost everything about Homer, right down to whether he existed. The consensus today is that two Homers wrote each of the poems, perhaps 30–50 years apart in the late 8th century. Both poems take as their subject matter events surrounding the Trojan War (c. 1200 B.C.), but both clearly draw on and refer to a tradition about this conflict that stood independent of their composition.

Livy (59 B.C.–A.D. 17). Titus Livius hailed from Patavium in Cisalpine Gaul and benefited from the explosion of literary culture in Augustan Rome. He composed a 142-book history of Rome called *"From the City's Founding"* (*Ab Urbe Condita*), of which all but 2 books survive in full or summary form (the so-called *Periochae*). Taking Rome's history to 9 B.C., Livy's work is marred by overt moralization and patriotism.

Plutarch (c. A.D. 50–c. 120). L. Mestrius Plutarchus is an excellent example of the truly Greco-Roman culture that the Romans forged in the imperial period. Born and raised in Chaeronea in central Greece, he traveled widely in the empire, including to Egypt and Rome, but lived most of his life in Greece. Yet he considered himself "Roman." His voluminous writings include his very useful series of *Parallel Lives* of famous Greek and Roman historical figures. He also wrote rhetorical and philosophical treatises, dialogues, and antiquarian investigations ("Greek Questions" and "Roman Questions"), mostly of a religious bent. Plutarch spent his last 30 years as a priest at Delphi in Greece. His biographies constitute his most useful contributions to this course.

Polybius (c. 200–118 B.C.). Polybius, son of Lycortas, was a prominent Greek politician in the Achaean League; after Pydna in 168 B.C., he was denounced to the Romans and interned as a hostage in Italy. Here, he was befriended by the Scipiones and wrote 40 books of *Histories* to document and explain Rome's rapid rise to world dominion. Only 5 books survive intact; most others are known from excerpts, fragments, and summaries. Polybius, our earliest extant source for Roman history, provides a unique outsider's view on the Middle Republic and, as such, can be used with great profit.

Suetonius (c. A.D. 70–130). Gaius Suetonius Tranquillus hailed from an equestrian background, probably from North Africa. He was a friend of Pliny the Younger and became a secretary in the imperial service of Hadrian but was fired in c. 120. Among other things, he wrote the biographies of *The Twelve Caesars* (Julius Caesar–Domitian), which are racy and entertaining to read but not the most reliable as historical sources.

Tacitus (c. A.D. 56–120). So little is known of Cornelius Tacitus's life that his *praenomen* is not recoverable with any certainty (it may have been Publius or Gaius). He had a successful senatorial career under the tyrant Domitian and reached the governorship of Asia under Trajan. He wrote several monographs, but his masterpiece was the *Annals*, covering the reigns of the Julio-Claudian emperors; he also wrote the *Histories*, describing the civil wars of A.D. 69 and the Flavian dynasty. Neither work survives intact. Tacitus wrote in a clipped, acerbic style and, possessed of an acute intelligence and republican inclinations, presents a dark and gloomy picture of life under the emperors.

Thucydides (c. 455–400? B.C.). Thucydides was an Athenian statesman and general, exiled after failure to protect Amphipolis from Spartan assault in 424 B.C. He wrote a history of the Peloponnesian War between power blocs led by Athens and Sparta respectively (431–404 B.C.). Considered more "scientific" in his approach than his contemporary Herodotus, his presentation is coldly factual but no less biased in its own way. His research methods differed in no significant way from those of Herodotus.

Velleius Paterculus (c. 20 B.C.–A.D. 31 or later). This provincial of equestrian and, later, senatorial status served in the Roman army under the later emperor Tiberius in A.D. 4–12. His *Compendium of History* in two books was published in A.D. 30 or early in 31 and is widely excoriated for its sycophantic praise of Tiberius (emperor at the time of publication) and poor Latinity. The date of his death cannot be established with any certainty.

Xenophon (c. 430–352? B.C.). Xenophon was an Athenian aristocrat who took part in and wrote about the expedition of the Ten Thousand (401–399 B.C.) and was elected one of its new leaders when the generals were treacherously murdered by the Persians during a parley. He was exiled from Athens and spent the rest of his life as a guest of Sparta and then of Corinth. Xenophon wrote other philosophical, biographical, and historical works, including the *Hellenica*, which documents Greek troubles in the 4th century, prior to the emergence of Philip II of Macedon as the dominant force in Greek affairs. The date of his death cannot be established with any certainty.

Historical Figures:

Alcibiades (451–403 B.C.). An immensely energetic Athenian aristocrat, Alcibiades was raised by Pericles and befriended by Socrates. He was an open advocate of Athenian imperial power and an implacable enemy of Sparta. He was largely responsible for urging the disastrous expedition to Sicily in 415–413 B.C., which he initially commanded with Nicias and Lamachus. Recalled to face charges of sacrilege as the expedition arrived in Sicily, he jumped ship and became an exile at Sparta and, ultimately, Persia. He was murdered by the so-called Thirty Tyrants, sponsored by Sparta.

Alexander III of Macedon ("The Great") (356–323 B.C.). One of the towering giants of history, Alexander's life was as short as it was action packed. The son of Philip II's fourth wife, Olympias, he commanded the Macedonian cavalry at the Battle of Chaeronea in 338 B.C. After his father's assassination in 336 B.C.—in which he may have had a hand—he became king and turned his full attention to the anti-Persian crusade Philip had been planning when he was killed. He crossed into Asia in 334 B.C., never to return. After 11 years of almost relentless campaigning that saw him enthroned as pharaoh in Egypt and Great King over Persia, his armies revolted in the Punjab, and he was forced to return to Babylon, where he died of a fever on 10 June 323 B.C., aged 32.

Antiochus III of Syria ("The Great") (c. 242–187 B.C.): Antiochus came to the throne of the Seleucid Hellenistic Kingdom in Syria in 223 B.C. and reigned as an energetic military commander in nearly every corner of his vast realm. He earned Roman suspicion by hosting the exiled Hannibal from 195 B.C. onward, and in 192 B.C., he foolishly answered a call to "liberate the Greeks" from the Romans. He was soundly defeated in the Balkans, then chased by the legions into Asia Minor (the first time the Romans crossed into Asia). At Magnesia-ad-Sipylum in 190 B.C., his army was defeated by the Roman legions (his navy, shortly thereafter), and he was forced to sign a humiliating peace in 188 B.C. He died, suitably enough, on campaign the following year.

Arminius (c. 19 B.C.–A.D. 21). Arminius was a chief of the Cherusci tribe, based along the Weber River in north central Germany. As a young man, he served as a Roman auxiliary officer, earned Roman citizenship on discharge, and was promoted to equestrian status. He returned to his people, however, and organized their resistance to Roman incursions then ongoing under Augustus. He was the architect of the ambush in the Teutoburg Forest in A.D. 9 that saw three full Roman legions massacred—the most crushing defeat ever inflicted by native troops on a disciplined army. Arminius earned great renown for this feat. When the emperor Tiberius was offered a chance to have him poisoned in A.D. 19, he refused on grounds of honor, but fractious tribal politics claimed Arminius's life in A.D. 21.

Artaxerxes II (404–358 B.C.). Artaxerxes was the Great King of Persia, successor to his father, Darius II. In 401 B.C., his rule was challenged by his brother, Cyrus, then satrap of western Asia, at the Battle of Cunaxa, near Babylon. Cyrus was defeated and perished in the battle, but a corps of 13,000 Greek mercenaries he had hired remained undefeated. Artaxerxes, through representatives, threatened and negotiated with the mercenaries and finally chased them out of his realm. From this shaky beginning, the rule of Artaxerxes went to be one of the longest in Achaemenid history.

Augustus, Imperator Caesar (23 September 63 B.C.–19 August A.D. 14). Arguably the single most important and influential man in Roman history, he was born Gaius Octavius, of humble stock. His great-uncle, however, was Julius Caesar, in whose will he was adopted in 44 B.C. Despite being unknown and inexperienced, Octavius, now Gaius Julius Caesar Octavianus (Octavian), embarked on a bold and dangerous political career that showed daring and ruthlessness in equal measure. Along with Antony and Lepidus, he became of a member of the Second Triumvirate, a legally instituted board of military dictators, and competed with Mark Antony and the

Liberators for the leadership of the Roman world. By 31 B.C., he had secured this goal and, renamed Imperator Caesar Augustus in 27 B.C., he became Rome's first emperor, ushering in the Imperial Age and establishing the Principate, which remained the institutional and administrative basis for the Roman Empire for 300 years. He died peacefully at a villa in Nola on the 19th day of the month that bore his name.

Caesar, Gaius Julius (100 B.C.–15 March 44 B.C.). Gaius Julius Caesar was born into an ancient but eclipsed patrician family. Possessed of astonishing intellectual talents and great charisma, he rose through the ranks and became Rome's most powerful citizen. In 60 B.C., he joined former rivals Pompey and Crassus to form the so-called First Triumvirate, an informal agreement that the three work together. His consulship of 59 B.C. was marred by violence and intimidation. From 58–49 B.C., he conquered all of Gaul for Rome. During this time, the Triumvirate broke apart, and Pompey and Caesar were left to fight it out. An enormous civil war (49–45 B.C.), our main focus in this course, saw Caesar victorious on all fronts. Ensconced in the dictatorship and displaying no tact in the exercise of power, Caesar died at the hands of a conspiracy of noblemen calling themselves the Liberators.

Clearchus (c. 450–401 B.C.). This Spartan mercenary commander was contracted by Cyrus to command a huge force of hoplites to press his claim on the Persian throne. Xenophon, who knew Clearchus well, portrays him as rather dour but steadfast and courageous. Having led his men to victory at Cunaxa but then finding himself on the losing side, Clearchus was murdered by the Persians during a parley in 401 B.C.

Cyrus the Great (r. 559–530 B.C.). After the Persians overthrew their Media masters, Cyrus became king of Persia and Media. He established the Achaemenid dynasty, and he and his successors forged the largest land empire yet seen. He was killed in action while campaigning in the eastern part of his realm.

Cyrus (the Younger) (?–401 B.C.). Brother of Artaxerxes II and satrap at Sardis in Asia Minor, Cyrus resented his brother's accession to the throne and his near-execution on suspicion of plotting. He raised a large army, including some 13,000 Greek mercenaries, and invaded the Persian heartland in 401 B.C. to press his claim. He perished at the Battle of Cunaxa. The date of his birth cannot be firmly fixed, but he appears young and energetic in Xenophon's *Anabasis*.

Darius I (r. 521–486 B.C.). This Great King of Persia usurped the throne in 521 B.C. and, thus, became the successor to Cambyses (r. 530–522 B.C.). Aside from various acts of consolidation, he was an active military commander and launched major campaigns to the east and west of the Persian heartland. His Scythian campaign saw him conquer Thrace. The Greek cities of Ionia (on the western shores of Asia Minor) revolted in 499 B.C., calling on the mainland Greeks for help. Only Athens and Eretria responded by sending small forces. Once the revolt was crushed in 494 B.C., Darius launched a seaborne attack on the upstart Greek mainlanders, thus initiating the Persian Wars. His expeditionary force met with unexpected and crushing defeat at the hands of the Athenians at Marathon in 490 B.C. Darius died before being in a position to launch another expedition against the Greeks, but his son Xerxes attempted a general conquest of the peninsula in 480–479 B.C.

Darius III (r. 336–330 B.C.). Darius III was the last king of Achaemenid Persia. In the same year he came to the throne, his nemesis Alexander acceded in Macedon. Darius's reign, therefore, was dominated by his (unsuccessful) attempts to ward off his brilliant opponent. After failing to stop Alexander at the Issus in 333 B.C., he lost control of the Mediterranean regions of his realm. Retiring east, he raised a huge royal army and confronted Alexander again at Gaugamela in 331 B.C. on ground of his own choosing. He still lost. Fleeing east, he was treacherously murdered by members of his entourage the following year as the Macedonian pursuit closed in. Alexander is said to have wept over his body.

Demetrius I of Macedon ("Poliorketes") (336–283 B.C.). Son of one of Alexander's leading generals, Demetrius gained fame for his ability at sieges and, thus, was named "Taker of Cities" (*Poliorketes*). His most monumental efforts went into the unsuccessful siege of Rhodes in 305–304 B.C., which saw the construction of the most monstrous siege engine on record from the ancient world, the nine-story Helepolis ("City-Destroyer"), which stood 150 feet high and moved on eight massive wheels. The siege ended in negotiated settlement. Demetrius went on to rule Macedon for seven years (294–287 B.C.). After other failed military adventures, he ended his days as a captive of his rival Seleucus of Syria, where he died a drunk.

Eanatum I (c. 2450 B.C.). Ruler of Lagash in Sumer, Eanatum fought two battles with the neighboring city-state of Umma over disputed borderlands called the Gu'eden. In the second battle, he was wounded by an arrow. These battles, recorded on the Vulture Stela, which is now in the Louvre, constitute our earliest written records of organized warfare.

Eleazar ben Yair (died the night of 15–16 April A.D. 73). Eleazar ben Yair was the leader of a Jewish rebel group called *sicarii* ("knifemen") who occupied the stronghold of Masada during the Jewish revolt of A.D. 66–70. After resisting a determined Roman siege of several months' duration, ben Yair succeeded in persuading his command, which included women and children, to commit suicide rather than fall into Roman hands alive.

Epaminondas (died 362 B.C.). With the aid of his compatriot Pelopidas, this brilliant Theban general experimented with the way the hoplite phalanx was deployed to gain major victories over the Spartans at Leuctra in 371 B.C. and Mantinea in 362 B.C. At the latter battle, he was killed at the very moment of victory.

Fabius Maximus Verrecosus ("Cunctator"), Q. (c. 270–203 B.C.). This scion of a prominent Roman house was consul in 233 and 228 B.C. and censor in 230 B.C. After the defeat by Hannibal at Lake Trasimene in 217 B.C., he was made dictator and instituted a strategy of "delaying" (hence the name *Cunctator*, "the Delayer") by shadowing Hannibal's movements and avoiding direct engagement. The strategy was not popular and was abandoned in 216 B.C., with disastrous results at Cannae that year. Fabius's policy was rehabilitated, and as consul in 215, 214, and 209 B.C., he oversaw some successes in the field. He opposed the aggressive plan of Scipio to invade Africa but lost the argument. He did not live to see Hannibal's final defeat by Scipio in 202 B.C.

Flamininus, T. Quinctius (c. 229–174 B.C.): This Roman aristocrat, general, and diplomat was elected consul for 198 B.C. to prosecute the Second Macedonian War against Philip V, which had been dragging on since 200 B.C. Flamininus proved an energetic commander and successfully brought the war to a conclusion with a victory at the Battle of Cynoscephalae in 197 B.C. The following year, he proclaimed the freedom of the Greeks in Europe and thereby caused a misunderstanding that plagued Greco-Roman relations for the next 50 years. He remained active in Roman eastern diplomacy for the rest of the 190s and 180s, after which he faded into obscurity.

Flaminius, C. (c. 265–217 B.C.). Flaminius was a Roman politician and general whose early career is shrouded in uncertainty but was reportedly marked by a strikingly populist stance with regard to the wedge issue of land distribution. He was elected consul for 223 B.C. and fought a battle against the Gauls of the Po Valley but was then forced to abdicate amidst claims of unfavorable prodigies. Elected to the consulship a second time for 217 B.C., he led his forces into Hannibal's ambush at Lake Trasimene and perished with his army in the ensuing massacre.

Fritigern (died c. A.D. 380). Gothic leader of the Tervingi group, Fritigern orchestrated the migration into the Roman Empire in A.D. 376, as his people sought refuge from the oncoming Huns. Harsh treatment by local Roman commanders and a failed attempt to capture him led Fritigern to instigate a revolt, which led to the Gothic War of A.D. 376–382. His greatest achievement was the decisive victory at Adrianople, at which the eastern emperor Valens was killed. Fritigern was not heard from again after A.D. 380, suggesting either that he was eclipsed by political rivals or dead by that date.

Gratian (A.D. 359–383). Nominated co-emperor of the west by his father, Valentinian I, at the age of 8 in A.D. 367, Gratian became sole ruler of the west on the latter's death in A.D. 375. A Christian, he accelerated the proscription of pagan cults, removing the celebrated statue of Victory from the senate house, for instance. He was an able general and dealt effectively with barbarian threats along the Rhine-Danube frontier. He was summoned to aid his uncle Valens against Fritigern's Goths in A.D. 378, but the disaster at Adrianople took place before he could bring his forces to bear. He was overthrown and murdered in A.D. 383.

Hannibal (247–182 B.C.): Hannibal was a Carthaginian general who almost broke the back of Roman power in Italy during the Second Punic War. He hailed from a prominent and militant Carthaginian family, the Barcids. Having commanded Punic forces in Spain in 221–219 B.C., Hannibal invaded Italy in 218 and inflicted three crushing defeats on the Romans at Trebia, Trasimene, and Cannae.

Defeated at Zama in North Africa in 202 B.C., he was hounded by the Romans until he committed suicide in 182 B.C.

Hezekiah (r. 726–697 B.C.). The 13th king of Judah and son of Ahaz, Hezekiah rejected idolatry and mandated worship of Yahweh. He watched as his northern neighbor, the Kingdom of Israel, succumbed to Assyrian rule and sought to block further Assyrian expansion by an alliance with Egypt. This activity made his lands one of the targets of Sennacherib's third campaign in 701 B.C. Although successful at Lachish, Sennacherib's army failed to take Jerusalem. (It is possible the Assyrians were bought off.) Judah appears to have been a vassal state of Assyria thereafter.

Miltiades (c. 550–489 B.C.). An Athenian aristocrat, politician, and general, Miltiades was chief magistrate (*archon*) in Athens in 524 B.C. He engaged in military and political adventures in the Chersonese and on Lemnos but returned to Athens and the position of general (*strategos*) in 490/89 B.C. He was later credited, perhaps exaggeratedly, with orchestrating the Athenian victory at Marathon in 490 B.C. After leading a failed attack on Paros, he was put on trial and fined the huge sum of 50 talents. Shortly afterward, he died of gangrene from a wound received on Paros. His son, Cimon, was later an influential figure in Athenian politics, which might account for the inflation of Miltiades's role in the events at Marathon.

Muwattalis II (r. c. 1295–1271). King of the Hittites, Muwattalis presided over their empire during the height of its power. He led a large Hittite force to Kadesh in 1285/75 B.C. to confront the northward incursions of Ramesses II of Egypt. There, a great but inconclusive battle took place that paved the way for a lasting Hittite-Egyptian treaty.

Narmer (a.k.a. Menes) (c. 3000 B.C.). First king of the First Dynasty, Narmer united Egypt and initiated the Old Kingdom. Little can be said about Narmer in historical terms, and source material is scant. His most famous monument is the Narmer Palette, which depicts him subduing enemies, leading armies, and surveying the corpses of enemy soldiers.

Nicias (c. 470–413 B.C.). Nicias was an Athenian aristocrat, politician, and general. After the death of Pericles in 429 B.C., he opposed the more aggressively imperialistic and demagogic "new politicians" in Athens, such as Cleon and Alcibiades. He was a moderate who supported negotiating peace with Sparta, the Peloponnesian War being in full swing in these years. This he succeeded in bringing about in 421 B.C. with the Peace of Nicias. But both sides regarded it as a pause in their dispute rather than a definitive settlement of it. Nicias objected to the proposed expedition to Sicily but was appointed one of its three commanders. Through a series of unfortunate events, he found himself in sole command there and proved a vacillating and equivocating commander. When the expedition collapsed, Nicias was captured and executed by the Syracusans.

Paullus, L. Aemilius (1) (c. 260–216 B.C.). This Roman politician and general was consul in 219 B.C. He was elected consul again for 216 B.C., with M. Terentius Varro, on a platform of taking a more aggressive stance with regard to Hannibal than the strategy of delaying favored by Q. Fabius Maximus had thus far allowed. He perished at the resulting disaster at Cannae. Our main sources (Polybius and Livy) are clearly well-disposed toward Paullus and try to pin the blame for Cannae squarely on Varro, but a close reading of the pertinent texts shows that Paullus and Varro disagreed only on the issue of when to engage Hannibal. The outcome would probably have been the same, regardless of who was in command on the day of the catastrophe.

Paullus, L. Aemilius (2) (c. 229-160 B.C.). Son of L. Aemilius Paullus (1), he was a prominent politician and general of the 2nd century B.C. He served in a variety of official positions before rising to the consulship for 182 B.C. Elected to a second consulship for 168 B.C., he campaigned against King Perseus of Macedon Thessaly and brought the Third Macedonian War to a successful conclusion with a decisive victory at Pydna in that year. A keen philhellene, he kept nothing of the riches of Perseus for himself, except for the king's library.

Perseus of Macedon (c. 213–c. 165 B.C.). Son of Philip V of Macedon, Perseus succeeded to the throne on his father's death in 179 B.C. He started off on a good footing with the Romans, but his diplomatic efforts in extending his influence in Greece soon earned their suspicion. It did not help that Rome's ally, Eumenes II of Pergamum, was an injured party in Perseus's success. Against a backdrop of Eumenes's denunciations, war was declared in 171 B.C. Perseus's reign—and Macedonian independence—ended at the

Battle of Pydna in 168 B.C. Perseus was taken captive to Italy, where he died an exile.

Pharnaces II (r. 63–47 B.C.). Son of Rome's troublesome enemy Mithridates VI Eupator of Pontus, Pharnaces ruled initially as a client of Pompey. He appears to have done little until he made his move while Rome was distracted by the Caesar-Pompey civil wars of 49–45 B.C. He then attempted to expand his realm by conquest and enjoyed some initial success. But he soon found himself confronted by Caesar at Zela in 47 B.C. Soundly defeated in this battle, he returned discredited to his kingdom and was murdered by a political rival.

Philip II of Macedon (382–336 B.C.). This king of Macedon and reformer laid the foundations for his son Alexander's empire and the subsequent Hellenistic Age. As a prince, Philip witnessed firsthand the military innovations of Epaminondas at Thebes, which may have inspired him as king to reform the Macedonian army radically. He united the kingdom, created the fearsome Macedonian phalanx, and elevated the cavalry to the role of decisive strike force. He also brought siege warfare to new heights. He expanded Macedonian influence in all directions, including southward to Greece, control of which he finally achieved after the Battle of Chaeronea in 338 B.C. He then planned an invasion of Persia and sent an advance force over in 337 B.C. but was murdered at a festival in 336 B.C. His tomb may have been identified at Vergina in Greece.

Philip V of Macedon (238–179 B.C.). As a teenager, Phillip V succeeded to the throne of Macedon in 221 B.C. and embarked on a series of military campaigns. In the wake of Cannae, he made a pact with Hannibal (215 B.C.) but never acted on it in any concrete way, much to the Romans' fortune. He was also blocked by a Roman force sent across the Adriatic in 215 B.C., starting the so-called First Macedonian War (215–205 B.C.). Further military and diplomatic activity followed, leading to the Second Macedonian War (200–197 B.C.), which ended at Cynoscephalae. Until his death, Philip had to deal with constant Roman interference in his affairs, resulting in his having to execute his own son, Demetrius, in 180 B.C.

Pompey ("the Great") (106–48 B.C.). Gnaeus Pompeius Magnus, the political ally and then archrival of Julius Caesar, was born of a prominent Picene family and entered Roman politics as an upstart supporter of Sulla in 83 B.C. Successful in military matters, most spectacularly against the pirates in 66 B.C., he became a popular hero. He formed the First Triumvirate with Caesar and Crassus in 60 B.C., but thereafter relations with Caesar deteriorated until civil war erupted in 49 B.C. Now posing as the champion of the republic against Caesarian tyranny, Pompey met defeat at Pharsalus in 48 B.C. and, on fleeing to Egypt, was ignominiously decapitated by a claimant to the Ptolemaic throne in that year.

Pyrrhus of Epiros (318–272 B.C.). Pyrrhus was king of Epiros, a Hellenistic kingdom across the Adriatic from Italy. An ugly man with great military skills and personal courage, Pyrrhus acceded at the age of 17. Frustrated in his aspirations for expansion in the Balkans, he accepted an invitation from the Greek colony of Taras (Tarento) to help in the disputes with the encroaching Romans. He invaded Italy with almost 25,000 infantry, 3,000 horses, and 20 war elephants. His first two encounters with the Romans—at Heraclea (280 B.C.) and Asculum (279 B.C.)—were victorious but costly. These encounters were the first time the Roman legions had faced a Macedonian phalanx. After an unsuccessful sojourn in Sicily, Pyrrhus returned to southern Italy in 275 B.C. and fought the Romans again at Beneventum. Having lost this battle, he withdrew back across the Adriatic. He was killed trying to invade Greece, when a woman threw a roof tile at him from her perch above.

Ramesses II ("the Great") (r. c. 1279–1213 B.C.). One of Egypt's most famous pharaohs and a prolific builder, Ramesses had one of the longest reigns on record, lasting some 66 years. Not long after his accession, he fought the Battle of Kadesh against the Hittites, which he clearly regarded as a moment of signal importance in his rule because scenes of it grace the walls of so many of his monuments.

Sargon (r. c. 2330–2280 B.C.). Sargon was the historical founder of the Akkadian Empire in Mesopotamia whose life later became quasi-legendary. His polity was the first to unite Babylonia and Sumer under a single ruler; it seems also to have stretched north toward Syria. Sargon's grandson Naram-Sin seems to have acquired divine status, as reflected in his inscriptions and monuments (for example, the Victory Stela of Naram-Sin in the Louvre).

Scipio Africanus (c. 236–183 B.C.). Publius Cornelius Scipio Africanus was an eminent figure in the Scipionic family. He rose to prominence leading Roman armies to victory over the Carthaginians in Spain and defeated Hannibal at Zama in 202 B.C. He was involved in subsequent Roman campaigns in Spain and the eastern Mediterranean.

Sennacherib (r. 704–681 B.C.). Assyrian king and son of his predecessor, Sargon II, Sennacherib faced difficult times in the Assyrian Empire and spent much of his reign campaigning to put down revolts. He waged ferocious wars in Babylonia and, in his third campaign (701 B.C.), struck into Palestine and Judea to challenge an Egyptian-Judean alliance against him. It was during this campaign that he besieged both Lachish and Jerusalem. He was murdered in a palace coup by two of his sons.

Themistocles (c. 524–459 B.C.). An Athenian statesman, general, and admiral, Themistocles was instrumental in turning Athens into the supreme naval power in Greece in the decade 490–480 B.C. He fought at Marathon and convinced his fellow citizens to use funds from state silver mines to build a fleet. As commander of the Athenian contingent resisting Xerxes's invasion in 480 B.C., he orchestrated, by trickery, the Battle of Salamis that crushed the invading Persian fleet and sent Xerxes back to Susa. Following the Persian Wars, he helped Athens build its walls. In the late 470s, he was exiled from Athens and, after many travels, ended up at the Persian court. There, he was honored by the Great King, and he ended his life as a Persian governor of the city of Magnesia.

Thutmose III (r. c. 1504–1452 B.C.). One of the longest reigning kings of New Kingdom Egypt, Thutmose came to power as a boy, but his position was usurped for 22 years by his stepmother and regent, Hatshepsut. Whether or not Thutmose collaborated with Hatshepsut's rule is disputed. In c. 1479 B.C., he emerged as sole ruler and launched his campaign into Palestine within three months of accession, culminating in the Battle of Megiddo. Sixteen more campaigns north were to follow, so that Thutmose is sometimes dubbed the Napoleon of ancient Egypt.

Valens (r. A.D. 364–378). Valens was the younger brother of Valentinian I (r. A.D. 364–375), who proclaimed him emperor of the eastern empire. Very much the junior partner in this relationship, Valens faced difficult challenges in the form of external threats from Goths and Persians and internal dissension over doctrinal matters— he was a Christian of the Arian sect. When the scale of Fritigern's

Gothic-led revolt in Thrace became clear, he marched to put it down and summoned aid from his nephew Gratian in the western empire. But before Gratian arrived, Valens confronted the Goths at Adrianople; his army was crushed and he himself killed.

Varro, C. Terentius (consul 216 B.C.). Varro was a Roman politician and general of obscure and perhaps lowly origins. As consul with L. Aemilius Paullus, he commanded the army that Hannibal annihilated at Cannae in August of that year. While Paullus perished, Varro escaped with the cavalry, and on his return to Rome, he was thanked for not despairing of the state. Our sources' attempts to scapegoat him for the disaster do not meet with general acceptance, not least because he continued in public life down to 200 B.C. and, thus, was clearly not a pariah to his contemporaries.

Varus, Publius Quinctilius (c. 45 B.C.–A.D. 9). A Roman aristocrat, bureaucrat, and general, Varus had important connections with the house of Augustus, as his consulship with Tiberius in 13 B.C. and subsequent marriage to Augustus's grandniece demonstrate. He had administrative and (limited) military experience in Africa and Syria when, in A.D. 6, he was appointed to the command of Germany. His charge seems to have been to consolidate what many considered a completed conquest. While returning to winter quarters in the autumn of A.D. 9, his army was led into an ambush by Arminius the Cheruscan and slaughtered in a three-day massacre in the Teutoburg Forest. Varus did the honorable thing and committed suicide on the field. Ever afterward, he had the dubious pleasure of having this catastrophe named after him: the *clades Variana*, "the Varan Disaster."

Vercingetorix (?–46 B.C.). Chieftain of the Arverni tribe of Gauls, Vercingetorix led a great revolt against Caesar in Gaul in 52 B.C., the last attempt by the Gauls to throw off the tightening yoke of Roman dominance. He enjoyed some initial successes, notably at Gergovia, and attempted to implement a scorched-earth policy to starve the Romans out of his homeland. But after defeat in an engagement in the field, he retreated to the stronghold of Alesia, where Caesar initiated astonishing siege operations to defeat him. Captured after Caesar's efforts proved successful, he was held captive until 46 B.C., when he walked in Caesar's triumph in Rome and then, following custom, was executed.

Xerxes (r. 486–465 B.C.). Son of Darius I, Xerxes was the Great King of Achaemenid Persia who invaded Greece in 480–479 B.C. and met with crushing and astonishing defeat. Herodotus portrays him as one would expect a Greek to: weak, vain, despotic, and capricious. But he was not entirely unreasonable, nor unintelligent. He fell to a murderer in 465 B.C.

Bibliography

Important note: This bibliography is perforce restricted to particularly pertinent and/or influential works. The notes and bibliographics of the titles below can readily lead the curious and the diligent to further landscapes of interest.

The centrality of warfare to Classical civilization lends the output of ancient historical writers an overwhelmingly military character. Most can, therefore, be consulted with profit. In particular, consult those listed below for the Greco-Roman battles discussed in this course.

*Denotes essential reading.

Ancient Works

(All references are to any editions of English translations in the Penguin Classics series, unless otherwise indicated.)

Sumer, Egypt, and the Near East:

Cooper, J. S. *Reconstructing History from Ancient Inscriptions: The Lagash-Umma Border Conflict.* Malibu, CA: Undena Publications, 1983. A short and technical but remarkably readable treatise that includes translations of all pertinent materials (the Vulture Stela included).

Lichtheim, M. *Ancient Egyptian Literature: A Book of Readings*, 3 vols. Berkeley: University of California Press, 1973–1980. An assemblage of papyri and inscriptional texts in translation, including many pertaining to warfare.

Luckenbill, D. D. *Ancient Records of Assyria and Babylon*, 2 vols. Chicago: University of Chicago Press, 1926–1927. Still a standard collection of Near Eastern inscriptions and tablets in translation. Volume 2 is especially useful for the Neo-Assyrian Empire.

Pritchard, J. B. *Ancient Near Eastern Texts Relating to the Old Testament.* Princeton: Princeton University Press, 1969, 3rd ed. Classic collection of Near Eastern and Egyptian texts in translation, including those pertaining to the battles of Megiddo and Kadesh.

Greece:

*Sage, M. M. *Warfare in Ancient Greece: A Sourcebook.* London: Routledge, 1996. A handy collection of some ancient sources, in translation, covering the "Homeric" to the Hellenistic periods.

*Aeschylus. D. R. Slavitt and P. Bovie, eds. *Aeschylus 2: The Persians, Seven Against Thebes, The Suppliants, Prometheus Bound.* Philadelphia: University of Pennsylvania Press, 1999.

*Arrian. *Anabasis,* a.k.a. *Campaigns of Alexander the Great.*

*Diodorus Siculus. *Library of History,* 11 vols. Cambridge, MA: Loeb Classical Library series, Harvard University Press, 1933–1967.

*Herodotus. *The Histories.*

*Homer. *The Iliad.*

*Nepos. *Illustrious Lives.*

*Pausanias. *Guide to Greece.*

*Quintus Curtius. *History of Alexander.*

*Thucydides. *The Peloponnesian War.*

*Xenophon. *Anabasis,* a.k.a. *The Persian Expedition.*

Rome:

Campbell, B. *The Roman Army, 31 BC–AD 337: A Sourcebook.* London: Routledge, 1994. A collection of pertinent sources in translation.

*Ammianus Marcellinus. *The Later Roman Empire.*

*Appian, *Roman History.*

*Caesar. *The Civil War.*

———. *The Conquest of Gaul.*

*———. *The Gallic War.*

*Dio. *Roman History.* The Penguin Classics feature *The Reign of Augustus* (Books 50–56 of the original work).

*Dionysius of Halicarnassus. *Roman Antiquities.* Cambridge, MA: Loeb Classical Library series, Harvard University Press, 1974.

*Florus. *Epitome of Roman History.* Cambridge, MA: Loeb Classical Library series, Harvard University Press, 1929.

The *Historia Augusta,* a.k.a. *Scriptores Historiae Augustae.* Available in three volumes in the Loeb Classical Library series. Cambridge: Harvard University Press, 1921-32.

*Josephus. *The Jewish War.*

*Livy. *The History of Rome from Its Foundation,* featuring *The Early History of Rome* (Books 1–5), *Rome and Italy* (Books 6–10),

The War with Hannibal (Books 21–30), and *Rome and the Mediterranean* (Books 31–55).

*Plutarch. *Parallel Lives*, featuring *Makers of Rome* and *The Fall of the Roman Republic.*

*Polybius. *The Rise of the Roman Empire.*

*Sallust. *Jugurthine War and Conspiracy of Catiline.*

*Suetonius. *The Twelve Caesars* (Caesar–Domitian).

*Tacitus. *The Annals of Imperial Rome.*

———. *Germania.*

———. *The Histories.*

*Velleius Paterculus. *Compendium of Roman History*. Cambridge, MA: Loeb Classical Library series, Harvard University Press, 1924.

Note also the curious corpus of the so-called tacticians, military handbooks of little literary merit and dubious historical value that usually collate de-contextualized anecdotes or offer overly systematized analyses. That said, they can be plumbed for useful tidbits. The chief tacticians are as follows:

Aelian. *Tactica.*

Frontinus. *Stratagems.*

Polyaenus. *Stratagems of War.*

Vegetius. *Epitome of Military Science.*

Modern Works

General:

Ancient World at War. Oxford: Blackwell Publishing. A series of books by credited scholars, either published or in production, on various aspects of ancient warfare.

Anglim, S., P. G. Jestice, R. S. Rice, S. M. Rusch, and J. Serrati. *Fighting Techniques of the Ancient World, 3000 BC–AD 500: Equipment, Combat Skills and Tactics*. New York: Thomas Dunne, 2002. A useful and well-illustrated overview of the subject by unit type.

*Connolly, P. *Greece and Rome at War*. London: Greenhill Books, 1998, rev. ed. An accessible survey of the subject, with excellent illustrations and reconstructions.

Cowley, R., ed. *What If? The World's Foremost Military Historians Imagine What Might Have Been*. New York: Putnam, 1999.

Interesting assemblage of battle counterfactuals, including Jerusalem, Salamis, Alexander the Great, and the Teutoburg Forest.

Creasy, Edward S. *Fifteen Decisive Battles of the World: From Marathon to Waterloo.* New York: Da Capo, 1994. Pioneering 19th-century work establishing the "great battle" genre.

*Dawson, D. *The Origins of Western Warfare: Militarism and Morality in the Ancient World.* Boulder, CO: Westview, 1996. An erudite contemplation that does much to establish the centrality of warfare in the ancient Mediterranean, especially in the Classical world.

Delbrück, H. *History of the Art of War.* London: Greenwood, 1975. A seminal work, originally published in four volumes between 1900 and 1920. The first volume and the opening of the second concern antiquity.

Diamond, J. *Germs, Guns and Steel: The Fates of Human Societies.* New York: Norton, 1989. Brilliantly argued case that geographic and biological circumstances have shaped the broad geopolitical demographics of the planet.

Du Picq, A. *Battle Studies: Ancient and Modern Battle*, trans. J. N. Greely and R. C. Cotton. New York: Macmillan, 1921. A 19th-century French colonel offers tremendous insights into the rigors of combat.

*Ferrill, A. *The Origins of War: From the Stone Age to Alexander the Great.* Boulder, CO: Westview Press, 1997, rev. ed. The title is slightly misleading given that the book is less about the origins of warfare than it is a concise survey of military history from the Stone Age to Alexander.

Fuller, J. F. C. *A Military History of the Western World*, 3 vols. New York: Da Capo, 1954–1956. A classic treatment of the topic. The first volume concerns antiquity and discusses many of the battles treated in this course.

*Gabriel, R. A., and D. W. Boose. *The Great Battles of Antiquity: A Strategic and Tactical Guide to Great Battles That Shaped the Development of War.* Westport, CT: Greenwood Press, 1994. Useful and detailed study that incorporates many of the battles covered in this course but is marred by a somewhat uncritical reading of sources. It tends, however, to impute uncritically some modern practices to ancient armies.

*Hackett, J. *Warfare in the Ancient World.* New York: Facts on File, 1989. Excellent text by recognized experts; complemented by fine illustrations.

*Hanson, V. D. *Carnage and Culture: Landmark Battles in the Rise of Western Power.* New York: Anchor Books, 2001. Extends the thesis of the Western way of war over an analysis of key battles from Salamis (480 B.C.) to the Tet Offensive (1968).

*Keegan, J. *The Face of Battle: A Study of Agincourt, Waterloo and the Somme.* London: Cape, 1976. Although it does not address any of our featured battles, the book is essential reading for its methodology, which has influenced many succeeding studies of warfare.

―――. *A History of Warfare.* New York: Knopf, 1993. A sweeping survey of the whole scope of warfare, from prehistoric origins to the modern age. Takes an anthropological long view of the subject.

*Kern, P. B. *Ancient Siege Warfare.* Bloomington, IN: Indiana University Press, 1999. This is the fullest and most systematic study of the topic in print thus far, although it is stronger on description than analysis.

Lendon, J. E. *Soldiers and Ghosts: A History of Battle in Classical Antiquity.* New Haven: Yale University Press, 2005. Argues a provocative and thought-provoking thesis that ancient military affairs were molded by a reverence for a heroic and legendary past. While this central contention is unconvincing, the book is well worth reading.

Lloyd, A. B., and C. Gilliver, eds. *Battle in Antiquity.* London: Duckworth in association with the Classical Press of Wales, 1996. Collection of essays by scholars on various aspects of the topic. Excellent reading and well documented.

McGrail, S. *Boats of the World: From the Stone Age to Medieval Times.* Oxford: Oxford University Press, 2001. Comprehensive and technical survey of maritime technology, including consideration of Egyptian, Assyrian, Phoenician, and Greek warships.

Montagu, J. D. *Battles of the Greek and Roman Worlds: A Chronological Compendium of 667 Battles to 31 B.C., from the Historians of the Ancient World.* Mechanicsburg, PA: Stackpole Books, 2000. The title is self-explanatory, and the book is very useful as a reference work, particularly as a guide to the relevant passages in ancient sources.

Neiberg, M. S. *Warfare in World History*. London: Routledge, 2001. A brief introduction to the topic.

Osprey Warrior Series and *Osprey Military Elite Series*. Oxford: Osprey, Warrior Series: 1994–2003; Elite Series: 1986–2005. Useful surveys of various ancient armies are included in these two series of short books, usually well illustrated and written by respectable scholars.

Parker, G., ed. *The Cambridge Illustrated History of Warfare*. Cambridge: Cambridge University Press, 1995. A standard reference work with contributions by many scholars; only the first three chapters, all composed by V. D. Hanson, deal with Greek and Roman warfare.

Von Clausewitz, C. *On War*, trans. M. Howard and P. Paret. Princeton: Princeton University Press, 1989. In his classic 19th-century treatise, the Prussian officer lays out what might be called a "philosophy of war."

Warry, J. *Warfare in the Classical World*. Norman, OK: University of Oklahoma Press, 1980. A well-illustrated and readable general survey of the subject.

Prehistory and the Origins of War:

Carman, J., and A. Harding, eds. *Ancient Warfare: Archaeological Perspectives*. Stroud, UK: Sutton, 1999. An excellent example of how theoretical modeling is applied to archaeological evidence in an anthropological paradigm.

*Dawson, D. *The First Armies*. London: Cassell, 2001. A volume in the *Cassell History of Warfare* series. The chapters on the origins of war are thought provoking, but the subsequent text advocates an unconvincing and radical thesis. Excellent illustrations.

*Guilaine, J., and J. Zammit. *The Origins of War: Violence in Prehistory*, trans. M. Hersey. Oxford: Blackwell, 2005. An archaeologist and a medical doctor offer a comprehensive survey of the prehistoric evidence for organized violence.

*Keeley, L. H. *War Before Civilization*. Oxford: Oxford University Press, 1996. Pioneering work that assembles and discusses all the material evidence for prehistoric warfare.

*Kelly, R. C. *Warless Societies and the Origins of War*. Ann Arbor, MI: University of Michigan Press, 2000. A thorough, if rather technical, example of ethnographic modeling to investigate early warfare.

*LeBlanc, S. *Constant Battles: The Myth of the Peaceful, Noble Savage.* New York: St. Martin's Press, 2003. An archaeologist lays out the case for widespread warfare throughout human history, with roots in simian behavior.

Turney-High, H. H. *Primitive War: Its Practice and Concepts,* 2nd ed. Columbia, SC: University of South Carolina Press, 1971. Groundbreaking anthropological study that has exerted great influence over the subsequent study of early warfare.

Wrangham, R., and D. Peterson. *Demonic Males: Apes and the Origins of Human Violence.* Boston: Houghton Mifflin, 1996. The most thorough sociobiological argument for the genetic origins of warfare in print. Unfortunately, it is almost wholly unconvincing.

Sumer, Egypt, and the Near East:

Cline, E. H. *The Battles of Armageddon: Megiddo and the Jezreel Valley from the Bronze Age to the Nuclear Age.* Ann Arbor, MI: University of Michigan Press, 2000. A stimulating transhistorical survey of a frequently contested battleground.

Faulkner, R. O. "Egyptian Military Organization," *Journal of Egyptian Archaeology* 39 (1953): 32–47. Seminal article interpreting textual terms pertaining to warfare from the Old to New Kingdoms.

Gelb, F. "Prisoners of War in Early Mesopotamia," *Journal of Near Eastern Studies* 32 (1973): 70–98. Somewhat technical article that illustrates how cuneiform texts can be mined for military information. Disregard the Sumerian philology and trace the mode of argument.

*Gnirs, A. "Ancient Egypt," in Raaflaub and Rosenstein, eds., *War and Society in the Ancient and Medieval Worlds,* pp. 71–104. Cambridge, MA: Harvard University Press, 1999. Excellent overview with ample reference to prior work.

*Goedicke, H. *The Battle of Megiddo.* Baltimore: Halgo, 2000. Comprehensive account by an expert on Egyptian military matters; somewhat technical in parts but very useful in its overview of the engagement.

*———. *Perspectives on the Battle of Kadesh.* Baltimore: Halgo, 1985. A collection of essays that offer excellent and thoughtful analyses on various issues.

Hackett, J. W. *Warfare in the Ancient World*, pp. 15–35. New York: Facts on File, 1989. Combined survey of military developments in the ancient Near East and Egypt. Good illustrations.

*Kuhrt, A. *The Ancient Near East, c. 3000–330 BC*, 2 vols. London: Routledge, 1995. Excellent survey and summary of current understanding about the period covered. Rich bibliography points to more specific studies.

Lawrence, A. W. "Ancient Egyptian Fortifications," *Journal of Egyptian Archaeology* 51 (1965): 69–94. Surveys a series of forts and fortresses, notably the Middle Kingdom fort Buhen in Upper Egypt.

Oded, B., *Mass Deportations and Deportees in the Neo-Assyrian Empire*. Wiesbaden, Germany: Dr. Ludwig Reichert Verlag, 1979. Essential reading for those interested in the consequences of Near Eastern siege warfare. Elucidation of a core element in Assyrian policy.

———. *War, Peace, and Empire: Justifications for War in Assyrian Royal Inscriptions*. Wiesbaden, Germany: Dr. Ludwig Reichert Verlag, 1992. Thorough study of the Assyrian texts documenting and analyzing the topic covered in the title.

Schulman, A. R. *Military Rank, Title and Organization in the Egyptian New Kingdom*. Berlin: Hessling, 1964. Major study of the officer class of the New Kingdom army.

Shaw, I. "Battle in Ancient Egypt: The Triumph of Horus or the Cutting Edge of the Temple Economy," in Lloyd and Gilliver, eds., *Battle in Antiquity*, pp. 239–269. London: Duckworth in association with the Classical Press of Wales, 1996. Excellent survey of Egyptian battle scenes in art; stresses the role of materialism in motivating Egyptian warfare.

*Spalinger, A. J. *War in Ancient Egypt: The New Kingdom*. Oxford: Blackwell, 2005. One in the Blackwell series *War in the Ancient World*. A readable and well-documented overview of the subject.

*Ussishkin, D. *The Conquest of Lachish by Sennacherib*. Tel Aviv: Tel Aviv University, Institute of Archaeology, 1982. Excellently illustrated survey and discussion of all the ancient evidence—archaeological, textual, and iconographic—for the siege of Lachish.

Van De Mieroop, M. *A History of the Ancient Near East, ca. 3000–323 BC*. Oxford: Blackwell, 2004. An up-to-date and very readable overview of the subject, with plenty of citations from primary materials.

Winter, I. J. "After the Battle Is Over: The Stele of the Vultures and the Beginning of Pictorial Narrative in the Art of the Ancient Near East," in H. L. Kessler and M. S. Simpson, eds., *Pictorial Narrative in Antiquity and the Middle Ages*, pp. 11–32. Washington, DC: National Gallery of Art, 1985. Detailed but concise study of an essential piece of evidence for early Mesopotamian warfare, the Vulture Stela, with some consideration also of the Royal Standard of Ur.

*Wiseman, D.J. "The Assyrians," in J. Hackett, *Warfare in the Ancient World*, pp. 36–53. New York: Facts on File, 1989. A readable overview complemented by fine illustrations.

*Yadin, Y. *The Art of Warfare in Biblical Lands in the Light of Archaeological Study*, 2 vols. London: McGraw-Hill, 1963. Although out of print and in need of updating, this remains a standard source, especially for finds of weapons. Excellent illustrations.

Greece:

Anderson, J. K. *Military Theory and Practice in the Age of Xenophon*. Berkeley: University of California Press, 1970. The title is self-explanatory.

Burgess, J. S. *The Tradition of the Trojan War in Homer and the Epic Cycle*. Baltimore: Johns Hopkins University Press, 2001. A literary study that sets the story of the Trojan War against a wider context than Homer.

Cartledge, P. *The Spartans: The World of the Warrior-Heroes of Ancient Greece.* Woodstock: Overlook Press, 2003. Comprehensive and readable survey of Spartan history by their leading modern historian.

Clough, E. "Loyalty and Liberty: Thermopylae in the Western Imagination," in T. J. Figuera, ed., *Spartan Society*, pp. 363–384. London: Classical Press of Wales, 2004. Enlightening look at how the events at Thermopylae perform as cultural capital.

Ducrey, P. *Warfare in Ancient Greece*, New York: Schocken Books, 1986. A concise overview and useful introduction to the subject.

Goldsworthy, A. K. "The *Othismos*, Myths and Heresies: The Nature of Hoplite Battle," *War in Society* 4 (1997): 1–26. Sane and sensible discussion of a hotly disputed issue.

*Green, P. *The Greco-Persian Wars*. Berkeley: University of California Press, 1996. Readable and up-to-date narrative and analysis by an eminent historian of Greece.

Hammond, N. G. L. "The Campaign and Battle of Marathon," *Journal of Hellenic Studies* 88 (1968): 13–57. Detailed analysis of the ancient sources and topography of this pivotal battle.

*Hanson, V. D. *The Western Way of War: Infantry Battle in Classical Greece*. 2nd ed. Berkeley: University of California Press, 2000. An influential work, modeled in part on Keegan's *Face of Battle*, arguing that the Greeks of the Archaic Age invented the "Western" military ethic: massed confrontation in decisive pitched battle.

How, W. W., and J. Wells. *A Commentary on Herodotus*, 2 vols. Oxford: Clarendon Press, 1928, corrected version. An older but excellent source for the Battles of Marathon, Thermopylae, Salamis, and Plataea.

Kagan, D. *The Peloponnesian War*. New York: Penguin, 2003. A leading historian of ancient Greece offers a readable, if debatable, survey of this great conflict.

*Lane Fox, R., ed. *The Long March: Xenophon and the Ten Thousand*. New Haven: Yale University Press, 2004. Collection of papers exploring various aspects of this extraordinary event.

*Latacz, J. *Troy and Homer: Towards a Resolution of an Old Mystery*, trans. K. Windle and R. Ireland. Oxford: Oxford University Press, 2004. Brilliantly argued case for the essential historicity of the Homeric poems and the Trojan War.

*Lazenby, J. *The Defence of Greece, 490–79 BC*. Warminster, UK: Aris & Phillips, 1993. Detailed military and political analysis of the Persian Wars with meticulous documentation, ancient and modern.

Lloyd, A. *Marathon: The Crucial Battle That Created Western Democracy*. London: Souvenir Press, 1973; reprint 2004. An engagingly written, if undocumented, popular account of this vital battle.

Powell, B. B. *Blackwell Introductions to the Classical World: Homer*. Malden, MA: Blackwell, 2004. A recent, readable, and comprehensive introduction to Homer, including analysis of his usefulness as a historical source.

Pressfield, S. *Gates of Fire*. New York: Doubleday, 1998. A novel of the Battle of Thermopylae that, while adhering strictly to the "orthodox" view of hoplite warfare, effectively conveys the horrors of edged-weaponed combat.

Pritchett, W. K. *Studies in Greek Topography*, vol. 2, *Battlefields*. Berkeley: University of California Press, 1969. Useful guide to the battlefields of Greece, if now a little dated.

———. *The Greek State at War*, 5 vols. Berkeley: University of California Press, 1971–1991. A standard treatment of the topic. Particularly useful for its exhaustive collection of relevant ancient sources.

*Strauss, B. *The Battle of Salamis: The Naval Encounter That Saved Greece—and Western Civilization*. New York: Simon and Schuster, 2004. Despite the title, the book is a readable overview of the Persian invasion of 480 B.C.

Trundle, M. *Greek Mercenaries*. London: Routledge, 2004. An up-to-date social, political, and cultural history of this institution.

*Van Wees, H. *Greek Warfare: Myths and Realities*. London: Duckworth, 2004. Provocative reassessment of the nature of Greek warfare based on a critical evaluation of ancient sources.

. ———. "Homeric Warfare," in I. Morris and B. Powell, eds., *A New Companion to Homer*, pp. 668–693. Leiden, The Netherlands: Brill, 1997. Excellent survey of various views on Homeric warfare by the leading scholar of Greek warfare, including his own sensible solution.

*———, ed. *War and Violence in Ancient Greece*. London: Duckworth, 2000. Superb collection of essays on all aspects of Greek warfare, from the causes of Greek wars to the role of war in religious life.

The Macedonians, Philip, and Alexander:

Ashley, J. R. *The Macedonian Empire: The Era of Warfare under Philip II and Alexander the Great, 359–323 BC*. London: McFarland, 1998. A wargamer's nuts-and-bolts exploration of the Macedonian army, battle techniques, and campaigns. A very useful resource, but Greek terminology is often misused.

Bosworth, A. B. *Conquest and Empire: The Reign of Alexander the Great*. Cambridge: Cambridge University Press, 1988. In a welter of Alexander biographies, this stands out for its concision, meticulous documentation, and clarity of exposition.

*Briant, P. "Ancient Egypt," in Raaflaub and Rosenstein, eds., *War and Society in the Ancient and Medieval Worlds,* pp. 105-128. Cambridge, MA: Harvard University Press, 1999. Survey of the Achaemenid Persian army and the role of the military in Persian life by the world's leading expert on the era.

Cartledge, P. *Alexander the Great: The Hunt for a New Past*. Woodstock, NY: Overlook Press, 2004. A recent thematic life by one of the world's leading Greek historians.

Cawkwell, G. *Philip of Macedon*. London: Faber, 1978. Concise and readable account of Philip's life, with a strong focus on military matters.

Green, P. *Alexander the Great: A Historical Biography*. Berkeley: University of California Press, 1991. A leading historian of the Hellenistic world surveys the essential life of this era.

Hammond, N. G. L. *Philip of Macedon*. Baltimore: Johns Hopkins University Press, 1994. A thorough survey of Philip's life, replete with perceptive insight.

Lane Fox, R. *Alexander the Great*. New York: Dial Press, 1974. An eminently readable account by an insightful scholar.

Rome:

Ben-Yehuda, N. *Sacrificing Truth: Archaeology and the Myth of Masada.* Amherst, MA: Humanity Books, 2002. A sociologist challenges the archaeological "verification" of the events at Masada, alleging nationalist bias and even deception among the archaeologists who excavated the site.

Cornell, T. J. *The Beginnings of Rome*. London: Routledge, 1995. Superb discussion of Rome's early history down to the eve of the Punic Wars. Includes useful discussions of military matters, especially the Servian reforms.

*Daly, G. *Cannae: The Experience of Battle in the Second Punic War*. London: Routledge, 2002. Comprehensive study of the battle, written following Keegan's "battle mechanics" approach; includes useful surveys of the Roman and Carthaginian military systems.

Goldsworthy, A. *Cannae*. London: Cassell Military, 2001. Well-illustrated and readable account of the battle and its context.

———. *The Complete Roman Army*. London: Thames and Hudson, 2003. A useful and well-illustrated survey of most aspects of its subject; the book is hampered by a lack of precise references to its source material.

———. *The Roman Army at War, 100 BC–AD 200*. Oxford: Oxford University Press, 1993. An application of Keegan's *Face of Battle* approach to the ancient evidence leads to mixed results. Evocative in parts, but major changes in the Roman army during the period covered by the book make aggregate citation of ancient evidence in support of particular points hazardous.

Hammond, N. G. L. "The Battle of Pydna," *Journal of Hellenic Studies* 104 (1984): 31–47. Thorough analysis of this crucial confrontation.

———. "The Campaign and Battle of Cynoscephalae in 197 BC," *Journal of Hellenic Studies* 108 (1988): 60–82. As with the preceding entry, a thorough analysis of a crucial confrontation.

Harris, W. V. *War and Imperialism in Republican Rome, 327–70 BC*. Oxford: Clarendon Press, 1979. Ingeniously argued reassessment of Roman imperial aggression that features an extensive discussion of militarism in Roman culture.

Heather, P. J. *The Goths*. Oxford: Blackwell, 1996. Overview of Gothic history and identity.

———. *Goths and Romans*, pp. 332–489. Oxford: Clarendon Press, 1991. Careful analysis of Gotho-Roman relations that includes the background to Adrianople.

*Keppie, L. *The Making of the Roman Army from Republic to Empire*, rev. ed. Norman, OK: University of Oklahoma Press, 1998. Succinct and lucid account of the development of the Roman army to the principate of Augustus.

Lapham, L. "Furor Tuetonicus," in Cowley, R. ed., *What If? The World's Foremost Military Historians Imagine What Might Have Been*, pp. 59–69. New York: Putnam, 1999. Entertaining counterfactual speculation about how different European history may have been, had Arminius been defeated in the Teutoburg Forest in AD 9.

*Lazenby, J. F. *Hannibal's War*, rev. ed. Norman, OK: University of Oklahoma Press, 1998. As with the same author's *The Defence of Greece*, a thorough and well-documented survey of this pivotal conflict.

*Lenski, N. *Failure of Empire: Valens and the Roman State in the Fourth Century AD.* Berkeley: University of California Press, 2002. Thorough study of the period; includes an excellent chapter on Adrianople that challenges some of Heather's arguments.

Marsden, E. W. *Greek and Roman Artillery*, 2 vols. Oxford: Clarendon Press, 1969–1971. The most comprehensive study of the subject available; includes text and translation of pertinent ancient treatises, as well as commentary.

Rawson, E. "The Literary Sources for the pre-Marian Army," *Papers of the British School in Rome* 39 (1971): 13–31 (= Rawson, E. *Roman Culture and Society*. Oxford: Oxford University Press, 1991, pp. 34–57). Excellent discussion of the topic.

Sabin, P. "The Face of Roman Battle," *Journal of Roman Studies* 90 (2000): 1–17. Extends the arguments of the previous entry into a model of Roman-era combat as a whole.

———. "The Mechanics of Battle in the Second Punic War," in T. J. Cornell, N.B. Rankov, and P. Sabin, eds., *The Second Punic War: A Re-Appraisal*, pp. 59–79. London: School of Advanced Studies, 1996. Investigates the nature of Roman legionary combat.

Schlüter, W. "The Battle of the Teutoburg Forest: Archaeological Research at Kalkriese near Osnabrück," in J. D. Creighton and R. J. A. Wilson, eds., *Roman Germany: Studies in Cultural Interaction*, pp. 125–159. Portsmouth, RI: Journal of Roman Studies Supplementary Series 32, 1999. The main excavator lays out the case for locating the battle at Kalkriese. One of the few presentations of the case available in English.

Stephenson, I. P. *Roman Infantry Equipment: The Later Empire*. Stroud, UK: Tempus, 1999. A good study of the topic with plenty of illustrations; focuses especially on the transitional 3rd century.

*Wells, P. S. *The Battle That Stopped Rome: Emperor Augustus, Arminius, and the Slaughter of the Legions in the Teutoburg Forest.* New York: Norton, 2003. An up-to-date account by a leading scholar of the Central European Iron Age that includes consideration of the recent archaeological finds at Kalkriese.

Yadin, Y. *Masada: Herod's Fortress and the Zealots' Last Stand.* London: Weidenfeld and Nicholson, 1966. Comprehensive and lively account of the excavations at the site and how they illuminate the written accounts.

War and Ancient Society:

Garlan, Y. *War in the Ancient World: A Social History.* London: Chatto and Windus, 1975. As the title suggests, a social-historical approach to the role of warfare in ancient societies.

*Raaflaub, K., and N. Rosenstein, eds. *War and Society in the Ancient and Medieval Worlds.* Cambridge, MA: Harvard University Press, 1999. The book ranges widely over world cultures, including the Maya and medieval Japanese, for instance, and there are excellent essays by respected scholars on Egypt, Greece, and Rome. Also useful for its comparative approach.

Rich, J., and G. Shipley, eds. *War and Society in the Greek World* and *War and Society in the Roman World.* New York: Routledge, 1993. A collection of essays exploring various ways that war shaped the contours of Greek and Roman life.

Internet Resources

The Ancient History Sourcebook. http://www.fordham.edu/halsall/ancient/ asbook.html. A good website with many original texts online.

Ancient Warfare. http://www.dean.usma.edu/history/web03/atlases/ ancient%20warfare/ancient%20warfare%20index.htm. This site is most useful for maps and plans.

De Imperatoribus Romanis: An Online Encyclopedia of Roman Emperors. http://www.roman-emperors.org/startup.htm. A comprehensive website that includes links to battle descriptions, battle maps, catalogues of Roman coins, and information about Roman emperors.

The Perseus Digital Library. http://www.perseus.tufts.edu. This is an excellent resource for all sorts of classics-related material.

A Visual Compendium of Roman Emperors. www.roman-emperors.com. An illustrated list of Roman emperors, along with links to other sites with information about individual emperors.